2011

The UN and the Middle East Crisis, 1967

The UN and the
Middle East Crisis, 1967

ARTHUR LALL

Columbia University Press

New York & London   1968

Arthur Lall, formerly Ambassador to the United Nations from India, is Adjunct Professor of International Affairs at Columbia University.

Preface

THE YEAR 1967 saw both the most cataclysmic Arab-Israeli hostilities and the most intensive and the most successful United Nations efforts to negotiate the basis of a settlement of the Middle East situation. The war was brief—a six-day affair; but the processes of negotiation ground on for six months before they reached a climax in the adoption by the Security Council of Resolution 242 on November 22, 1967. And that completed only the first phase of the negotiations. Since then the attempt to implement Resolution 242 has gone on, and at the time of writing this preface it has been in progress for some seven months.

Not only will more time be required to translate the very real diplomatic gains incorporated in Resolution 242 into tangible results in the Middle East. A sustaining effort by the Security Council will be even more necessary. Indeed, by now the Security Council should have taken one or other of the opportunities offered by events in the Middle East—the incidents on the cease-fire line, or the Jerusalem parade—to reaffirm its resolution of November 22, 1967, and to insist on compliance.

Modalities are always a problem, and in this case especially so. But there are possibilities of surmounting the enormous obstacles that exist. One such possibility is suggested in Chapter XV of this book. Undoubtedly those that are intimately connected with working out a settlement—the great powers, the Secretary-General's representative, and others—will diligently examine all possible modalities. It has very rarely been possible in a delicate and complex international situation to insist on one and only one method of settlement. There has to be in operation a constant sensitivity to the factors involved and a continuing process of trial and adjustment of modalities to the varying needs and nuances of the situation. In this particular case, behind this process and spurring it on is fortunately the agreement on the principles on which a settlement is to be reached—Resolution 242 of the Security Council.

I should like especially to thank Dean Andrew W. Cordier of the School of International Affairs, Columbia University, for his encouragement and for many kinds of assistance without which this book would not have been written. To my former colleagues and my friends at the United Nations I remain indebted and grateful.

ARTHUR LALL

June, 1968

Contents

  I. The Security Council Fails 1
  II. UNEF and Its Withdrawal 11
  III. The State of Belligerency and the Gulf of Aqaba:
     The Security Council Again Falters 22
  IV. The Security Council and the War 46
  V. A Firm Cease-Fire 77
  VI. Observations on the First Phase of the Security
     Council's Effort 107
  VII. The Convening of the Fifth Emergency Special
     Session of the General Assembly 116
  VIII. The Statement of Positions in the Assembly 123
  IX. The Latin American Position 153
  X. The Emergency Assembly Fails to Act 169
  XI. The Security Council Helps Out 194
  XII. The Emergency Assembly's Last Chance 204
  XIII. The Elusive Solution 220
  XIV. The Security Council in High Gear 230
  XV. The Task Ahead 271

Appendixes

  1. Joint Draft Resolution of Canada and Denmark,
    May 24, 1967 281
  2. Draft Resolution of the United States, June 1, 1967 282
  3. Resolution 233, June 6, 1967 283
  4. Resolution 234, June 7, 1967 284
  5. Draft Resolution of the United States, June 9, 1967 285
  6. Resolution 235, June 9, 1967 286
  7. Draft Resolution of the United States, June 10, 1967 287

8. Resolution 236, June 12, 1967 288
9. Revised Draft Resolution of the Union of Soviet
Socialist Republics, June 13, 1967 289
10. Resolution 237, June 14, 1967 290
11. Draft Resolution of the Union of Soviet Socialist
Republics, June 19, 1967 291
12. Draft Resolution of the United States, June 20, 1967 293
13. Draft Resolution of Argentina, Bolivia, Brazil, Chile,
Colombia, Costa Rica, Ecuador, El Salvador,
Guatemala, Guyana, Honduras, Jamaica, Mexico,
Nicaragua, Panama, Paraguay, Trinidad and Tobago,
and Venezuela, June 30, 1967 294
14. Revised Draft Resolution of Afghanistan, Burundi,
Cambodia, Ceylon, Congo (Brazzaville), Cyprus,
Guinea, India, Indonesia, Kenya, Malaysia, Mali,
Pakistan, Senegal, Somalia, United Republic of
Tanzania, Yugoslavia, and Zambia, July 3, 1967 296
15. Resolution 2253 (ES-V), July 4, 1967 298
16. Consensus Expressed by the President and Approved
by the Security Council at the 1366th Meeting on
July 9–10, 1967 299
17. Draft Resolution of the Union of Soviet Socialist
Republics, October 24, 1967 300
18. Draft Resolution of the United States, October 24, 1967 301
19. Resolution 240, October 25, 1967 302
20. Joint Draft Resolution of India, Mali, Nigeria,
November 7, 1967 303
21. Draft Resolution of the United States, November 7,
1967 305
22. Draft Resolution of the Union of Soviet Socialist
Republics, November 20, 1967 307
23. Resolution 242, November 22, 1967 309
24. Statement by the President of the Security Council,
December 8, 1967 311
25. Operative Paragraphs of the Tentative U.S.–Soviet
Draft Resolution, July 19, 1967 312

Index 313

The UN and the Middle East Crisis, 1967

CHAPTER I

The Security Council Fails

LOOKING BACK TO the menacing developments in the early part of 1967 in the relations between Israel and the Arab states on its frontiers, United Nations Secretary-General U Thant wrote on May 19 of that year: "There has been a steady deterioration along the line between Israel and Syria, particularly with regard to disputes over cultivation rights in the Demilitarized Zone, since the first of the year." [1]

When the disputes over cultivation came to a head their dangerous potential was not immediately evident. Moreover, it was perhaps wise policy to make little of them, hoping that the disputants would thereby be encouraged to keep their differences within manageable limits. U Thant himself appeared to choose this course when at his press conference on January 10, 1967, in reply to a question, he stated: "On the question of cultivation in the Demilitarized Zone, you will remember that this is a time of the year when the rains begin to fall in the area, the grass grows and cultivation starts. At this time of the year, whenever cultivation starts, there are sporadic shootings and incidents. So I would say that *the present phase, in certain sections of the Demilitarized Zone between Israel and Syria, is more seasonal than anything else.*" [2]

That U Thant had been using the diplomacy of understatement became clear a short five days later when he appealed to

[1] Security Council Doc. S/7896, May 19, 1967, p. 1. In subsequent footnote references, Security Council documents are designated by the prefix "S."
[2] UN Press Release SG/SM/637, January 10, 1967, p. 8. Italics added.

both Israel and Syria to agree to revive the Israeli-Syrian Mixed Armistice Commission (ISMAC) as a vehicle of efforts to settle the cultivation issue.[3] The states concerned agreed and ISMAC was reconvened on January 25, 1967, after a lapse of seven years, the immediately preceding meeting having taken place on February 16, 1960.[4] This limited success of United Nations diplomacy did not stem, much less resolve, the border problems. Israel and Syria were unable to agree to discuss the agenda item on cultivation difficulties even though they had approved this item in advance of their meetings. ISMAC remained convened on paper but in fact stalemated.[5]

That the explosiveness of the situation was related to wider issues than cultivation rights in the narrow Demilitarized Zone became evident on April 7, 1967, when a serious clash occurred between Israeli and Syrian armed units resulting in loss of life on both sides. The armed forces of Israel and Syria quickly disengaged but the tension between the two states continued to rise. As a result, on May 4, General Odd Bull, the Chief of Staff of the United Nations Truce Supervision Organization (UNTSO), appealed to the two governments to exercise the utmost restraint, to observe the cease-fire, and to use ISMAC machinery in resolving differences which might arise between them.[6] Four days later U Thant endorsed General Bull's efforts and approved and supported his "intention to continue, in the light of the responsibilities entrusted to UNTSO by the Israel-Syria General Armistice Agreement and by the relevant Security Council resolutions, to exert every possible effort to help maintain an atmosphere of quiet by averting incidents between the parties."[7]

Since the situation had reached danger point, U Thant cir-

[3] S/7683, January 15, 1967.
[4] *UN Monthly Chronicle*, IV, No. 2 (February, 1967), 10.
[5] S/7877, May 8, 1967.   [6] *Ibid.*   [7] *Ibid.*

culated as a Security Council document his message to General
Bull of May 8. This did not amount to use by the Secretary-
General of his powers under Article 99 of the Charter, but it
nevertheless put all members of the Security Council on notice
about the Israeli-Syrian situation; inasmuch as Security Council
documents are as a matter of course available to the full membership of the United Nations, the Secretary-General was making the international community as a whole aware of the
situation.

Three days later he faced the United Nations Press Corps
with the obvious purpose of subjecting himself to questions on
the dangerous potentials of the Middle East. At this press conference on May 11 he was asked to assess the situation and to
comment specifically on what the Israeli Ambassador to the
United Nations had called the "rapidly deteriorating situation"
on the Israel-Syria border. U Thant's reply was critical of the
"El Fateh type of incidents" which had for some months been
launched against Israel.

By their nature they seem to indicate that the individuals who
committed them have had more specialized training than has usually
been evidenced in El Fateh incidents in the past. That type of
activity is insidious, is contrary to the letter and spirit of the Armistice Agreements and menaces the peace of the area. All Governments concerned have an obligation . . . to take every measure
within their means to put an end to such activities.[8]

This strong and clear statement, based on UNTSO reports to
U Thant, was recorded in a paper which, though not bearing
the official United Nations insignia, was virtually a United Nations document. Unfortunately the Secretary-General's statement of May 11, taken together with Security Council Document S/7877 circulated only three days previously, did not lead
to consultations among the members of the Security Council

8 UN Press Release SG/SM/708, May 11, 1967, p. 13.

with a view to convening a meeting that would at least warn
the parties that breaches of the Armistice Agreement could not
be countenanced. Such action would have been all the more
appropriate considering that the Security Council had slipped in
failing to react to the armed clash between Israel and Syria on
April 7. Even as late as mid-May it could have expressed its
disapproval of that incident. However, there is no evidence
whatsoever that the Security Council membership informally
discussed the situation immediately following U Thant's press
conference of May 11. This omission, which was hardly in conformity with the terms of Articles 24 and 28 of the United
Nations Charter, may be explained, though not justified, by the
following circumstances.

First, neither the parties to the dispute, Israel and Syria, nor
the other Arab states made a request for a meeting of the Security Council. A general assumption regarding a dispute tends
to be that if the parties directly concerned do not seek the
assistance of the United Nations the situation probably has not
reached the danger point: the parties appear confident that they
can deal with it either themselves or with the assistance (in this
case) of the already existing United Nations machinery. A
second factor which inhibits consultations among those states
that have been entrusted by the Charter with major responsibilities for the maintenance of international peace and security
is the reserve which for several years has strongly inhibited the
Soviet Union from entering into discussions with the United
States with a view to planning joint action on international
issues. The Soviets have been reluctant to give the Chinese Communists, and perhaps even Hanoi at certain times, cause for
thinking that United States–Soviet collusion exists, in a wide
sense, on the international plane. Without some degree of cooperation between the United States and the Soviet Union,
Security Council meetings are of little value. A third inhibitory
factor is the absence of a lively habit of continuing consultation

among the members of the Security Council. This amounts to an absence of a full recognition by the Council members that they are required by the Charter to be ever-vigilant watchmen of the peace. The Charter so organizes the Council that it is able to function continuously; it is, moreover, the only organ of the United Nations which is directed to meet periodically at a high level. Both the spirit and the letter of Article 28.2 of the Charter have been ignored to the detriment of the Organization. In 1955 Dag Hammarskjöld suggested to the permanent members of the Security Council that it would be in conformity with Article 28.2 of the Charter if the Council were to meet from time to time at the level of foreign minister. The great powers, however, were unresponsive.[9] U Thant has raised the question more officially by devoting to it four paragraphs in his "Introduction to the Annual Report of the Secretary-General on the Work of the Organization" for 1966–67.[10]

These successive efforts by two Secretaries-General have been directed toward stimulating the Council to a greater awareness of its Charter responsibilities. In addition to periodic meetings at the level of foreign minister, it would seem appropriate that at least the permanent members of the Security Council should engage in private consultations once every week so as to keep in constant review developments in sensitive regions of the world. The absence of such conventions as these conduces to the frequent deterioration of situations to a much greater degree than should take place before the Council becomes active.

A fourth factor which inhibited early consultation on the worsening Middle East situation was the inability of the President of the Council for the month of May to initiate private discussion. Active presidents of the Security Council have played

---

[9] Dag Hammarskjöld told the author of these efforts in August, 1955.

[10] General Assembly Doc. A/6701/Add. 1, September 15, 1967, pp. 58–59. In subsequent footnote references, General Assembly documents are designated by the prefix "A."

a major role in promoting discussion among Council members. This role presupposes not only tact and good sense on the part of the President but his acceptability to the generality of Member States. The President for the month of May, 1967, suffered from the disability that the government he represents (the Republic of China) was recognized by a small minority of the membership of the Security Council. Of the fourteen members (other than the Republic of China itself), three of the four permanent members (France, the Soviet Union, and the United Kingdom) and six of the ten nonpermanent members recognized the government of Peking as being the government of China. Thus only five of the fourteen members of the Council (other than Taiwan China)—about one third—recognized the Taiwan government. This situation seriously inhibited the Representative of China, in his capacity as President of the Council, in the initiation of consultations with and among his colleagues. Indeed, Ambassador Chieh Liu of the Republic of China was aware of this factor and stated it with some diplomatic skill when he opened the first meeting of the Security Council on the Middle East crisis on May 24. He said: "I should like to say how much I regret that circumstances did not permit me to have fuller consultations with my colleagues personally and individually, as I should have liked to do." [11] He went on to suggest that it was the urgency of the situation that had prevented consultations from taking place, but this formulation too was a style of "diplomacy." However, the handicaps afflicting the Representative of Taiwan do not fully explain his quiescence as Security Council President. The President for a particular month performs his duties within the framework of the tension of forces that exists on the international scene. We have seen how this overriding factor is an inhibitory one, and it tends to hold in check most Presidents of the Security Council.

The remissness of the Security Council, particularly in April,

[11] S/PV.1341, May 24, 1967, p. 2.

1967, contributed to the building up of explosive tensions in the Middle East. Had the Council met after the "serious armed clash" [12] of April 7, it would have had before it five accusatory communications from Israel and Syria which were circulated as Security Council documents following that clash.[13] As it was, even this spate of communications did not push the Council into activity. Had the Council met and adopted a firm resolution, including in its terms the withdrawal of Israeli and Syrian forces from the immediate vicinity of the border, great service would have been done to the maintenance of peace in the Middle East. This is all the more so since a few weeks later the Arab states directly involved, as well as other states, pointed to the Israeli-Syrian situation as the main reason for such ominous developments as the demand for the withdrawal of the United Nations Emergency Force (UNEF) and the movement of United Arab Republic forces across the Sinai to the Israeli border.

On May 22, 1967, President Nasser in his address to the United Arab Republic Air Force, which was broadcast nationally from Cairo, said:

On May 12 a very impertinent statement was made. . . . The statement said that the Israeli commanders have announced that they would carry out military operations against Syria in order to occupy Damascus and overthrow the Syrian Government. On the same day, Israeli Premier Eshkol made a strongly threatening statement against Syria.[14]

Nasser added that Israel apparently believed that Egypt could not move because it was bogged down in Yemen. To this he said: "We are capable of bearing our duties in Yemen . . . and in attacking if Israel attacks Arab Country. . . . The decision

---

[12] S/7896. This was the description used by the Secretary-General in his report to the Security Council.

[13] These documents were: S/7843, Israel's letter of April 7; S/7845 and S/7849, Syria's letters of April 9 and 12; S/7853, Israel's letter of April 14; and S/7863, Syria's letter of April 28, 1967.

[14] New York *Times*, May 26, 1967.

made by Israel at this time was to carry out an aggression against Syria as of May 17." [15]

Nasser asserted that it was the information regarding an allegedly impending attack on Syria that precipitated Egyptian moves. "On May 16 we requested the withdrawal of the UNEF," he said.[16]

It was widely known at the United Nations that the Soviet Union had warned the Egyptian authorities that moves by Israel against Syria were likely. Whether this information was correct or not—and it was *not* supported by UNTSO reports—the point remains that Nasser was able to cite the antagonistic relationship between Syria and Israel as the reason for the military preparations which precipitated the Arab-Israeli war of 1967.

The unfolding of these portentous events made the absence of any serious effort to convene a Security Council meeting in April, 1967, or even in the first half of May all the more regrettable and in some degree inexplicable. The inexplicability was perhaps unintentionally attested on the opening day of the Security Council's meetings on the crisis—May 24—when Ambassador George Ignatieff of Canada, who had been the Council President for April, stated: "I was only too keenly aware of this [the signs of the increasingly dangerous deterioration of the situation], Mr. President, when last month I had the responsibility which you now have. Steady reports of deterioration along the frontier lines between Syria and Israel were reported in correspondence which I received and forwarded to my colleagues as President. . . . Tension also grew as a result of sabotage and terroristic activities on the borders of Syria and Israel." [17] That so dedicated and concerned a representative as the Ambassador of Canada should not have thought it feasible to press for a Security Council meeting in April when, on his own admission, reports of increasingly dangerous deterioration were coming in is an indication of how strong have become the

[15] *Ibid.*   [16] *Ibid.*   [17] S/PV.1341, p. 11.

inhibitory factors which arrest timely and peaceful remedial action by the organ of the United Nations specifically designed to fulfill just this function. Without exception, all of the Security Council members are against war and for peace, but when it comes to preventive action to preserve the peace, then such elements intervene as national interests and the calculations— and often enough the miscalculations—of the states directly concerned, as well as those of the great powers. At times, as in the present case, these intervening elements thwart the process of pacification with disastrous results.

It has been suggested that some members of the Council were awaiting a comprehensive report on the Middle East situation by the Secretary-General before deciding whether to call for a meeting. In support of this position was the fact that as far back as 1949 the Chief of Staff of the United Nations Truce Supervision Organization had been charged with the responsibility of reporting "to the Security Council on the observance of the cease-fire in Palestine"; [18] over the years numerous such reports, as well as reports of the Secretary-General, had been furnished to the Council.

However, in the present instance there were two circumstances that mitigated the absence of a report by the Secretary-General in April and in the early part of May. First, on May 8 the Secretary-General had circulated to the members of the Security Council the text of his message of that date to General Odd Bull (Document S/7877). This message, in a broad way, indicated the seriousness of the dispute between Israel and Syria. Second, at his press conference of May 11 the Secretary-General had clearly stated the gravity of the situation. To these two overt circumstances should be added the consideration that there are ways in which individual members of the Security Council, or groups of them acting jointly, may without any difficulty informally suggest to the Secretary-General that a

[18] Security Council resolution of August 11, 1949.

report on a particular situation would be timely and helpful. There is no indication that such a suggestion or request was addressed to U Thant in April or the early part of May. The fact also remains that there is no indication that the Chief of Staff of UNTSO sent any special report during this period apart from his reports on the specific issue of disputes relating to cultivation in the Demilitarized Zone between Israel and Syria.

However, there was disquieting evidence in plenty which renders it impossible to acquit the Security Council of the charge that in April and much of May, 1967, it failed to read the writing on the wall and did not discharge its Charter functions and responsibilities in regard to the maintenance of international peace and security. Timing is important in any situation and never more so than when it comes to arresting the build-up of an eruptive crisis. The Security Council failed to respond to the clear needs of the hour. By so failing it contributed to the rapid development of militant actions which took place in the Middle East during the second half of May and the first half of June, 1967.

CHAPTER II

UNEF and Its Withdrawal

IN THE LIGHT OF the events of 1967, four points relating to the creation of UNEF ten years earlier acquire special significance.

First, UNEF was conceived as a temporary instrument but the duration of its use was neither determined nor laid down.

Second, its acceptance by Egypt—a vital element in the creation of the Force—was governed by a declaration of the government of that country to the effect that it would "be guided, in good faith, by its acceptance of General Assembly Resolution 1000 (ES-I) of 5 November 1956." [1] This meant that Egypt bound itself to observe strictly the provisions of the Egyptian-Israeli General Armistice Agreement of 1949, including desisting from raids across the armistice lines. It also undertook to refrain from introducing military goods into the area of hostilities. To a significant degree both Egypt and Israel were under a similar obligation of disengagement through Article VII of the Armistice Agreement, which limited "to defense forces only" both the Egyptian army in the forward areas of the Sinai and the Israeli forces in the areas bordering on the Sinai.

The original proposal made by Lester Pearson, then Foreign Minister of Canada, on November 1, 1956, was for a United Nations force "large enough to keep these borders at peace while a political settlement is being worked out." [2] Immediately after Pearson's speech, John Foster Dulles, U.S. Secretary of State,

[1] Annex to General Assembly Doc. A/3375, November 20, 1956.
[2] General Assembly Official Records, 562d plenary meeting, November 1, 1956, p. 36.

expressed his "complete agreement with what he said, and not only my personal agreement, but the feeling of President Eisenhower, with whom I talked a few hours ago about this aspect of the matter." [3] However, the draft resolution introduced by Pearson on November 3 did not mention the large problem of political settlement. It referred only to Resolution 997 (ES-I), the very first resolution of the First Emergency Special Session of the General Assembly, which confined its attention to a cease-fire, the withdrawal of forces, desistance from armed raids, scrupulous observance of the provisions of the Armistice Agreement, desistance from introducing military goods into the area, and the reopening of the Suez Canal. The General Assembly returned, somewhat obliquely, to the matter of the political settlement in its Resolution 1125 (XI) of February 2, 1957, which stated that the "scrupulous maintenance of the Armistice Agreement requires the placing of the UNEF on the Egyptian-Israeli armistice demarcation line and the implementation of other measures as proposed in the Secretary-General's report . . . with a view to assisting in achieving situations conducive to the maintenance of peaceful conditions in the area." In other words, side by side with the deployment of UNEF the United Nations was to proceed to the development of measures which would contribute to the stabilization of peaceful conditions between Israel and the Arab states. It should be noted that the Arab states and Israel abstained in the vote on this resolution although it was adopted by a large majority. For the United Nations as a whole, however, the continuing validity of this part of Resolution 1125 (XI) was emphasized by Secretary-General U Thant in his report of May 18, 1967. In paragraph 5 of that report he quotes the part of the resolution to which attention has just been drawn. [4] In February, 1957, the United Nations had taken upon itself the obligation to try to move toward a stable peace

---

[3] *Ibid.*   [4] A/6669, May 18, 1967.

in the Middle East and it had recognized that, as a practical matter, UNEF should continue till the attainment of this objective, or at any rate until it was in sight. This is the third point of significance.

Fourth, UNEF was created by the General Assembly in a series of resolutions adopted at its First Emergency Special Session and the Eleventh Regular Session. The Secretary-General's powers in regard to the Force were set out mainly in Resolution 1001 (ES-I) of November 7, which authorized him "to issue all regulations and instructions which may be essential to the effective functioning of the Force, following consultation with the Committee aforementioned, and to take all other necessary administrative and executive action." The committee referred to was the Advisory Committee, composed of one representative each from Brazil, Canada, Ceylon, Colombia, India, Norway, and Pakistan, with the Secretary-General as Chairman. This committee was to "undertake the development of those aspects of the planning for the Force and its operation not already dealt with by the General Assembly and which do not fall within the area of the direct responsibility of the Chief of the Command." The Secretary-General was to consult with it in all matters relating to the functioning of the Force, and provision was made that the Advisory Committee, "in the performance of its duties, shall be empowered to request, through the usual procedures, the convening of the General Assembly and to report to the Assembly whenever matters arise which, in its opinion, are of such urgency and importance as to require consideration by the General Assembly itself." [5]

The General Assembly made considerable delegations of

[5] The quotations on the powers of the Secretary-General and of the Advisory Committee are all from General Assembly Resolution 1001 (ES-I) of November 7, 1956. The author served on the Advisory Committee throughout the formative period of UNEF and for two years thereafter as the representative of India.

functions to the Secretary-General and the Advisory Committee, but it made no specific delegation of its power, such as it was, in regard to the extinguishing of the functioning of UNEF. It is, of course, a principle of jurisprudence that an authority which creates an institution retains the power to abolish its own creation unless it makes a specific delegation of that power. In this case, however, there was the complicating factor of the rights of Egypt as the state that had agreed to accept UNEF.

As noted above, it was envisaged that important matters concerning UNEF might arise which would warrant calling into session the General Assembly and that the Advisory Committee was given a delegation of power to this effect. Indeed, the first draft of the resolution did not contain the words "through the usual procedures" in regard to the convening of the Assembly. The Assembly's first thought was that the Advisory Committee should be given an extraordinary power, distinct from and in addition to all existing procedures, of convening the Assembly. However, this thought could not be implemented through a resolution of the Assembly, for it required an amendment of the Charter itself. Nevertheless, the essence of the idea remained in that the Assembly stood ready to convene to deal with important issues that might arise in the course of the life of the Force.

On the very day of the adoption of Resolution 1001 (ES-I) Dag Hammarskjöld, in one of his most important statements on UNEF, said:

I have been asked for an interpretation of what I have said about the length of the assignment of the Force being determined by the need arising out of the present conflict. I am sure the Members will appreciate that, in the still unclear situation, it would be premature for me to say how the needs might develop after the end of the immediate crisis. *However, the Force being under the ultimate authority of the General Assembly, I think that the point need not give rise to worries.*[6]

[6] General Assembly Official Records, 11th Session, 567th plenary meeting, November 7, 1956, p. 115. Italics added.

On February 25, 1957, Dag Hammarskjöld and the representative of Israel, Abba Eban, had a discussion on certain points relating to UNEF. On that occasion the Israeli representative raised the important question of the deployment of the Force in the Sharm el Sheikh area that commands the entrance to the Gulf of Aqaba. In raising this question what was at issue was not the total withdrawal of the Force but modification of deployment in a specific area which was not on the Egyptian-Israeli border. Therefore, the stationing of the Force in the Sharm el Sheikh area could perhaps, at some future date, be regarded as an action over and above what was originally contemplated in the General Assembly resolutions. Israel was especially anxious to seek clarification regarding this particular deployment of the Force. Its representative asked whether the Secretary-General would give notice to the General Assembly before UNEF would be withdrawn from this one area. Hammarskjöld's reply was interesting and correct:

On the question of notification to the General Assembly, the Secretary-General wanted to state his view at a later meeting. An indicated procedure would be for the Secretary-General to inform the Advisory Committee on the UNEF, which would determine whether the matter should be brought to the attention of the Assembly.[7]

In short, Hammarskjöld was referring to the mandate in Resolution 1001 (ES-I) and he was doing so on a matter of deployment as distinct from the question of the extinguishing or total withdrawal of UNEF.

To return to the birth of UNEF, the General Assembly's act of creation of the Force could not be completed unless it was followed by reciprocal action on the part of the parties to the conflict. One of them—Israel—refused to take such action and the Force remained stillborn on its side of the border. On the Egyptian side it came to life with the decision of the government

---

[7] General Assembly Official Records, Agenda Item 66, Annexes, 11th Session, Doc. A/3563, February 26, 1957, p. 71.

of Egypt to give its consent to the stationing of the Force along its border and at other points within its territory. In practice there was, then, a duality in the act of creation which could, in fact, be undone by either party—the General Assembly or Egypt.

Two other points regarding the creation of UNEF must be borne in mind. First, although Egypt abstained in the vote on the first of the resolutions creating the Force, it telegraphed the Secretary-General on November 5, 1956, accepting Resolution 1000 (ES-I), the substantive resolution creating the Force and its Command. This resolution is integrally linked with "*all* the terms of General Assembly Resolution 997 (ES-I)." The significance of the word *all* calls for a brief explanation. When Lester Pearson introduced his draft resolution asking the Secretary-General to submit a plan for the setting up of an international force (Resolution 998 [ES-I]), he referred to the terms of Resolution 997 (ES-I). However, there seemed to be some possibility in this formulation that a selective process might come about whereby only some of the terms of Resolution 997 would be taken into account in the drawing up of the terms of reference of the Force. To make it quite clear that all the terms of that resolution should be engaged, I requested Lester Pearson, in my capacity as the representative of India at the 563d plenary meeting of the General Assembly, to "introduce the word 'all' into that phrase between the word 'with' and the words 'the terms' " [8] in his draft resolution.

Pearson made this amendment, which enabled India and a number of other countries to vote in favor of his proposal. One effect of the amendment was to bring within the terms of Egypt's acceptance of Resolution 1000 (ES-I) such matters as scrupulous observance of the provisions of the Armistice Agreement and refraining from introducing military goods into the

[8] General Assembly Official Records, 563d plenary meeting, November 4, 1956, p. 70.

area of hostilities. There is no time limit on these obligations, and their strict meaning would entail restraint by Egypt from deploying concentrations of forces close to the Israeli border in the Sinai and elsewhere. A corresponding obligation rests on Israel.[9] Egypt's obligation may be regarded as somewhat greater because it voted for Resolution 997 and signified its acceptance of Resolution 1000 (ES-I).

The second point to be taken into account concerns the position of the Soviet Union and by implication that of the other Communist members of the United Nations. These countries abstained on the resolutions creating UNEF. V. V. Kuznetsov, First Deputy Foreign Minister of the Soviet Union, on November 7, 1956, explained that his government regarded it to be the prerogative of the Security Council to create UN forces, but that taking into account that the "victim of aggression has been compelled to agree to the introduction of the international force, in the hope that this may prevent any further extension of the aggression, the Soviet delegation did not vote against the draft resolution, but abstained." [10] The words "has been compelled" did not, of course, relate to any action taken in the Assembly, but rather to the nature of the circumstances in which Egypt was placed at that time. However, and more importantly, Kuznetsov went on to state the following:

The Soviet Union is prepared to make its own contribution towards putting an end to the aggression against Egypt in the briefest possible space of time, towards a settlement of the Suez problem based on due regard for the interests of Egypt, a sovereign and independent State, and towards ensuring *freedom of navigation for all prospective users of the Canal.* Such a settlement of the Suez question would also serve the cause of world peace.[11]

[9] Article VII, pars. 4 and 5, of the Egyptian-Israeli General Armistice Agreement of February 24, 1949.

[10] General Assembly Official Records, 567th meeting, November 7, 1956, p. 128.

[11] *Ibid.* Italics added.

Here, then, the Soviet government states through one of its senior diplomats that it envisages navigation in the Suez Canal as being open to all users—a concept which obviously includes Israel—and that it would assist toward the attainment of this objective. The Soviet position is significant for the chances of success of future efforts in the United Nations to achieve a long-term settlement in the Middle East.

The withdrawal of UNEF, for which orders were issued on May 18, 1967, has to be viewed in the light of the foregoing remarks on the creation of the Force, the legal position regarding its continuance involving both the UN and Egypt, and Hammarskjöld's statement on the ultimate authority of the General Assembly. Among the significant factors relevant to the withdrawal, primacy of place rests with the general situation in the Middle East, to which attention has been drawn in Chapter I. The circumstances were such that U Thant characterized them as being "extremely menacing." [12] In such a situation the United Arab Republic's demand for withdrawal of the Force was, on the face of it, inconsistent with the terms and conditions of its own acceptance of the Force.

The Force had been created for the express purpose of assisting in the pacification of the Middle East. Even on a narrow interpretation of its functions the government of Egypt (as it then was) had bound itself "to be guided, in good faith, by its acceptance of General Assembly Resolution 1000 (ES-I) of 5 November 1956," to which Resolution 997 stands in an integral relationship. The obligations which Egypt accepted included strict observance of the Armistice Agreement, which, in its terms, included observance of "the injunction of the Security Council against resort to military force in the settlement of the Palestine question." [13] In spite of this injunction, on May

[12] Report by the Secretary-General, S/7896, May 19, 1967.

[13] Article I, par. 1, of the Egyptian-Israeli General Armistice Agreement, February 24, 1949: Security Council Official Records (4th Year), Special Supplement No. 3. Also published in United Nations, *Treaty Series*, Vol. 42, p. 251.

16 General I. J. Rikhye, the Commander of UNEF, was handed a letter signed by General M. Fawzy, Chief of Staff of the UAR armed forces, which stated: "I have my instructions to all United Arab Republic armed forces to be ready for action against Israel the moment it might carry out any aggressive action against any Arab country. Due to these instructions our troops are already concentrated in Sinai on our Eastern borders." [14] Here, the Egyptian Chief of Staff reveals concentration of forces on the borders of Israel. True, the claim is that military action was to be taken only in the event of aggression by Israel, but, Article 51 of the Charter notwithstanding, the Armistice Agreement, to which Egypt had again given its adherence in the context of the creation of UNEF, reiterates the Charter injunction against resort to military force in resolving the Palestine question. Egypt's action was an admission of default in its obligations under the Armistice Agreement. If it felt that Israel was about to attack any Arab country, then Egypt's obligations required it to ask for remedial action through the United Nations, such as an urgent convening of the Security Council with a view to obtaining measures to ensure the maintenance of peace. To ask instead for the withdrawal of UNEF in order to adopt an effective military posture in a situation that was already explosive was to negate the United Nations efforts to maintain peace in the area. It is true that UNEF could function only so long as Egyptian consent to the continuance of the Force was operative, but a demand for withdrawal of the Force in order to battle effectively with the adversary was in direct opposition to the whole series of actions comprising the creation of the Force and its deployment in the area. Situations in which the Force could and should have been withdrawn would have possessed characteristics directly opposite to those that had come to exist in the middle of May, 1967.

The failure of the Advisory Committee for UNEF to ask for

[14] A/6669, May 18, 1967, p. 4.

an immediate session of the General Assembly to deal with the situation is totally inexplicable in the light of the terms of its mandate contained in Resolution 1001 (ES-I).[15] That mandate clearly envisaged the calling of the Assembly in circumstances *falling short of* such a dramatic crisis as that engendered on May 16–18 by the United Arab Republic's demand. There was no question but that the UAR's demand for the extinguishing of the Force, in terms both of the principles of jurisprudence and of Hammarskjöld's statement to the Assembly on November 7, 1956, warranted the convoking of the General Assembly. But the Secretary-General reported that, when he met with the UNEF Advisory Committee on May 18, "no proposal was made that the Advisory Committee should exercise the right vested in it by General Assembly Resolution 1001 (ES-I) to request the convening of the General Assembly to take up the situation arising from the United Arab Republic communication." [16] U Thant went on to state:

At the conclusion of the meeting it was understood that the Secretary-General had no alternative other than to comply with the UAR's demand although some representatives felt the Secretary-General should previously clarify with that Government the meaning of its request that withdrawal should take place "as soon as possible." [17]

As a result of the failure of the Advisory Committee to act in accordance with its responsibilities, U Thant naturally felt that he had no alternative but to issue instructions for the withdrawal of the Force. In notifying the Foreign Minister of the United Arab Republic of his instructions, U Thant rightly cautioned Cairo as follows:

Irrespective of the reasons for the action you have taken, in all frankness, may I advise you that I have serious misgivings for, as I have said every year in my annual reports to the General Assembly

15 See page 13 above.
16 General Assembly Doc. A/6730/Add. 3, June 26, 1967, Report of the Secretary-General on the Withdrawal of the UNEF, p. 8.
17 *Ibid.*

on UNEF, I believe that this Force has been an important factor in maintaining relative quiet in the area of its deployment during the past ten years and that its withdrawal may have grave implications for peace.[18]

It is evident that, since UNEF had been deployed on Egyptian territory with the consent of the UAR, the withdrawal of consent by the sovereign power would in fact extinguish an essential part of the basis for the continued deployment of the Force. However, if the full range of procedure implied and assumed at the time of the creation of the Force had been put into operation, either by some of the parties concerned or by the Advisory Committee, an opportunity would have been given to exert significant diplomatic pressures on the UAR to reconsider its request for withdrawal. At the same time, pressures could have been developed urging Israel to accept deployment of the Force on its side of the line, and it is not inconceivable that the crisis would have led to the strengthening of this United Nations activity rather than to its cessation. It was also open to the Advisory Committee to urge an immediate convening of the Security Council so as to impose restrictions on the conduct of all the parties at a time of dangerously mounting crisis. It is even conceivable that the Security Council would, at some stage, have considered altering the nature of UNEF into a Force with functions to maintain the peace in accordance with Chapter VII of the Charter. The point is that the failure to apply the full range of United Nations procedures curtailed gravely the diplomatic flexibilities upon which the peaceful resolution of dangerous situations must depend.

[18] *Ibid.,* p. 9.

CHAPTER III

The State of Belligerency
and the Gulf of Aqaba:
The Security Council Again Falters

ADHERENCE TO the classical concept that a state of belligerency continues when a conflict terminates in an armistice or truce, as distinct from a peace settlement, has done much to keep alive the flames of war in the Middle East.

It is of course true that there is a distinction between a state of armistice and a fully fledged peace. Moreover, in the particular case of Israel and the Arab states their relations are in part governed by the series of Armistice Agreements concluded in early 1949 after the Arab states had attacked Israel. There is, for example, the Egyptian-Israeli General Armistice Agreement of February 24, 1949, which might be interpreted to contain provisions supporting the view that a state of war continues between Israel and the United Arab Republic. Thus, Article IV, paragraph 1, affirms: "1. The principle that no military or political advantage should be gained under the truce ordered by the Security Council is recognized."

Though both sides have at various times quoted the immediately succeeding paragraph of Article IV to their own advantage, it has the general sense of tending to stabilize the situation at the armistice lines. This paragraph reads:

It is also recognized that the basic purposes and spirit of the Armistice would not be served by the restoration of previously held military positions, changes from those now held other than as specifically provided for in this Agreement, or by the advance of the military forces of either side beyond positions held at the time this Armistice Agreement is signed.[1]

Again, there is Article XI of the Egyptian-Israeli Armistice Agreement: "No provision of this Agreement shall in any way prejudice the rights, claims and positions of either Party hereto in the ultimate peaceful settlement of the Palestine question."

While the precise meanings of any concept related to a state of war have fluctuated in some degree, particularly with the dramatic changes which have occurred in recent decades in the nature of armed conflict, it remains generally agreed that "an armistice effects nothing but a suspension of hostilities; the war still continues." [2] This, in its turn, is consistent with the Hague Regulations on the Laws and Customs of War on Land, annexed to Hague Convention IV of 1907. Article 36 of the Hague Regulations stipulates that it is only if the duration of the armistice is "not defined" that "the belligerent parties may resume operations at any time, provided always that the enemy is warned within the time agreed upon, in accordance with the terms of the Armistice." The Middle East Armistice Agreements do not leave the duration undefined. They state clearly that they "shall remain in force until a peaceful settlement between the parties is achieved." [3] Though this is so, the parties have repeatedly acted as if the duration of the armistice were undefined. The raids across frontiers and the punitive expeditions of which both sides have been guilty are breaches of this

[1] During the debate in the Security Council on May 29, 1967, Ambassador M. A. El-Kony quoted this paragraph in support of his view that the state of war between Israel and the UAR still continued.

[2] Commercial Cable Co. v. Burleson, U.S. District Court, Southern District of N.Y., 1919, 255 F. 99.

[3] Article XII, par. 2, of the Egyptian-Israeli General Armistice Agreement, February 24, 1949.

clause of the Agreement, as are the oft proclaimed readiness to use force and the threat to use it, which again have become almost normal instruments of policy.

The classical writers and texts have not been unanimous as to what is and what is not permissible during an armistice or truce. Grotius[4] was somewhat more restrictive than Vattel.[5] The United States Rules of Land Warfare "follow the view that anything may be done during the armistice which is not in express terms prohibited by the agreement."[6] Though these concepts of the residual military potentials of a state of armistice are mentioned as part of the explanation of the warlike events which have erupted in the Middle East,[7] permissible practice in the area is theoretically subject to a double set of restrictions: first, there are the provisions of the Armistice Agreements themselves, which should not be overstepped; and second, there is the Charter of the United Nations, which is the governing document. Any inconsistency or ambiguity between the Armistice Agreements and the Charter must be resolved in favor of the provisions of the latter more severely restrictive document.

Since, in accordance with the law of previous eras, armistice has meant the continuance of a state of war, the parties in the Middle East have been at some pains to explore their rights as belligerents. This exploration has been so thorough that it has not always taken into account the provisions of Article 22 of the Hague Regulations.[8] Furthermore, Article 23 of the Regulations forbids the destruction or seizure of the enemy's property, unless such destruction or seizure is imperatively demanded by the necessities of war. In the Middle East the exception to this provision has become the rule.

---

[4] *De jure belli ac pacis*, Book III, Chapter XXI, par. 7.

[5] *Droit des Gens*, Book III, par. 245.

[6] Charles G. Fenwick, *International Law*, 2d ed. (New York, 1934), p. 494.

[7] The terms of Article XL of the Hague Regulations notwithstanding; see Charles C. Hyde, *International Law*, 2d rev. ed. (Boston, 1945), III, 1785.

[8] Article 22: "The right of belligerents to adopt means of injuring the enemy is not unlimited."

Since maritime considerations are especially important in the Middle East, much stress has been laid on belligerent rights in regard to shipping and cargo. The right to capture, and in some circumstances to destroy, an enemy merchant ship is embodied in all rules of warfare. In World War I, when the German U-boats became active, the governments of the United States and Germany discussed the issue at length. As a result the German government reformulated its position and notified the United States government as follows:

In accordance with the general principles of visit and search and destruction of merchant vessels recognized by international law, such vessels both within and without the area declared as naval war zone, shall not be sunk without warning and without saving human lives, unless these ships attempt to escape or offer resistance.[9]

Cargoes have generally been looked upon as liable to confiscation or plunder. Dana's Note to Wheaton (8th edition, 1866) sets out the position which has continued to find general approval: "Merchandise sent to sea is sent voluntarily, embarked by merchants or an enterprise of profit taking the risks of war; its value is usually capable of compensation in money, and may be protected by insurance; it is in the custody of men trained and paid for the purpose; and the sea, upon which it is sent, is *res omnium*, the common field of war as well as of commerce." [10] When it comes to neutral shipping carrying cargoes to an "enemy port," the question whether steamship or cargo is lawful prize must therefore depend on whether the steamship has a concealed or ulterior destination in an enemy country.[11] It is in the shelter of this doctrine that the UAR has taken the view that cargoes destined for Israeli ports are subject to confiscation if they attempt passage through the Suez Canal or the Strait of

[9] See Official Communication by German Foreign Office to Ambassador Gerard, May 4, 1916 (White Book No. 3 of Department of State, p. 305).

[10] Quoted by Herbert W. Briggs, *The Law of Nations* (New York, 1946), p. 945.

[11] The Zamora, Gt. Britain Judicial Committee of the Privy Council 1916 (1916) 2 A.C. 77.

Tiran. In regard to the Canal, the UAR has contended that there is the additional consideration that the protection of this vital international waterway necessitates the exclusion of Israeli ships which might seek to use the Canal with intent to damage it.

On May 22, 1967, the government of the United Arab Republic announced that ships flying the Israeli flag or carrying strategic materials to Israel would be excluded from the Gulf of Aqaba. On that date President Nasser made the following remarks in his speech to the UAR Air Force Advance Command: "What is the meaning of the armed forces' occupation of Sharm el Sheikh? It is an affirmation of our rights and our sovereignty over the Aqaba Gulf." [12] In these remarks President Nasser appeared to base the exclusion of Israeli ships and strategic goods bound for Israel on the view that the Gulf constitutes the territorial water of his country. Perhaps he meant that the entrance to the Gulf, the Strait of Tiran, came within this definition. The Gulf itself is bounded by four states, of which Egypt is one, and even if it is to be considered a *mare clausum*, its waters cannot be subjected to the rule of only one of the four states. However, the salient point here is that Nasser is not saying that non-strategic cargoes will be excluded from the Gulf if they are bound for Jordan. It follows that he is basically cognizant of the face that the Gulf does constitute a waterway for international navigation and that there is a basic right in international law of peaceful navigation to the ports of nations on its littoral. It follows that in regard to Israel he based his position on a concept of belligerency. He was adamant about the flag of the enemy, and he firmly debarred it from passing through the Gulf. So far as the Suez Canal is concerned, the Constantinople Convention notwithstanding, Egypt and subsequently the United Arab Republic have been unyielding in their exclusion of all

[12] For text of Nasser's speech, as broadcast by Radio Cairo, see New York *Times*, May 26, 1967.

Israeli shipping and all ships carrying cargoes to Israeli ports. This is so in spite of the fact that Resolution 95 (1951) of the Security Council "calls upon Egypt to terminate the restrictions on the passage of international commercial shipping and goods through the Suez Canal wherever bound and to cease all interference with such shipping beyond that essential to the safety of shipping in the Canal itself and to the observance of the international conventions in force." [13] Perhaps this formulation of the Security Council does not clear the way for *all* Israeli shipping, but it certainly does so for goods carried by other ("neutral") ships. In short, it does not permit the application to the Suez Canal of the regulations of warfare governing the seizure of cargoes in neutral ships destined for an enemy port.

This analysis indicates that the classical concept related to a state of belligerency have continued to determine the attitudes of states, particularly of the Arab states, in the Middle East. The net effect is the prevailing tendency to regard belligerency as a right and to be ready for the recrudescence of hostilities as and when circumstances appear favorable. There has thus been no renunciation of resort to force. The right to use force is widely regarded by the states concerned as a residuary right not extinguished by the Armistice Agreements. Take, for instance, the situation in regard to Syria in May, 1967, as the Arabs saw it. President Nasser stated on May 22 that "on May 12 a very impertinent statement was made. . . . The statement said that the Israeli commanders have announced that they would carry out military operations against Syria in order to occupy Damascus and overthrow the Syrian Government. On the same day, Israeli Premier Eshkol made a strongly threatening statement against Syria." [14] Assuming that Syria too felt that the facts were as stated by President Nasser, one is faced with the ex-

---

[13] Security Council Official Records (6th Year), Resolutions, p. 11.
[14] New York *Times*, May 26, 1967.

traordinary situation that the government of Syria, on being subjected to such a direct threat to its integrity and independence, did not report the threat to the United Nations Security Council, and much less did it ask for an urgent (or even routine) meeting of the Council. This is all the more extraordinary if one takes into account the fact that in April, on matters less vital to its security, though bearing on it, Syria addressed the Council thrice.[15] A possible explanation is that Syria decided to make its own arrangements to meet the threat of force, that it regarded the status of armistice as one that was moving inexorably to a recrudescence of hostilities as a logical outcome of the asserted state of belligerency in the area.

An alternative explanation may be based on the following statement by Ambassador Gideon Rafael of Israel in the Security Council on June 3, 1967:

> Various Arab spokesmen have now enlightened us by attributing to responsible leaders of Israel statements to the effect that Israel was ready to march on Damascus and overthrow the Syrian Government. I am grateful to the Arab representatives for giving us this clarification. However, I am sorry that I cannot oblige them and confirm their allegations. I can state quite categorically that no such statements have been made. . . . Israel has no interest in the nature of the regime in Syria or in its activities so long as they are confined to Syria.[16]

The Security Council's effort from May 24 to June 3, 1967, was largely directed toward containing the dangers emanating from the concept of belligerency to which the parties, more particularly the Arabs, seemed to be wedded. The basis of the Council's approach was to be found primarily in the report of Secretary-General U Thant after his dramatic mission to Cairo on May 23–25. U Thant, finding that the general plea for restraint in his report of May 19, 1967 (S/7896), had not had any tangible effect and that the situation was further deteriorat-

---

15 Security Council Docs. S/7845, S/7849, and S/7863.
16 Security Council provisional record S/PV.1346, June 3, 1967, p. 21.

ing because of the massive movement of forces—his report stated that "troop movements on both sides have been observed" —decided to make a personal attempt to obtain a more peaceful situation in the area.

During his absence the Security Council held its first meeting of the year, on May 24, 1967. The membership was strongly divided as to the need for the meeting and some members took umbrage that the traditional consultations on calling the Council into session had not preceded the meeting.[17] Several members also felt that they could not really help the situation by discussion in the Council while U Thant was personally in Cairo trying to obtain results through quiet diplomacy. Others, including the United States, felt that the Secretary-General's hands could be strengthened by a resolution enjoining restraint on the parties. The Soviet Union, on the other hand, insisted that the situation was being dramatized and that there was not "sufficient ground for such a hasty convening of the Security Council." [18] It was Ambassador Hans Tabor of Denmark who showed the greatest acuteness in assessing the essentials of the situation. He said: "There has been a military build-up along the borders of Israel and the United Arab Republic, and there is no way of denying that the stage is set for a major military clash . . . . the slightest miscalculation, the slightest misunderstanding of one or the other side of the opponent's intentions, could lead to large-scale hostilities." [19] Though two meetings were held on May 24, the proceedings of the Council were largely infructuous; a Canadian-Danish draft resolution expressing full support for the efforts of the Secretary-General and requesting all Member States to refrain from steps which might worsen the situation was not put to the vote,[20] the USSR to the end maintaining that there had been no need for a Council

[17] See statements of India and Ethiopia, S/PV.1341, May 24, 1967, pp. 26 and 31.
[18] *Ibid.*, p. 6.   [19] *Ibid.*, pp. 38–40.   [20] S/7905. See Appendix 1.

meeting. This view was supported by Ambassador M. A. El-Kony of the United Arab Republic, who also insisted that the situation was being dramatized.[21]

The objections of the UAR and the USSR to convening the Security Council on May 24 have to be viewed from two levels. First, one might say that traditionally the personal efforts of the United Nations Secretary-General have come to acquire a special significance in the Middle East. There is no doubt that Arab delegates in particular felt that the Council could not contribute anything when a topmost leader (President Nasser) was engaged in quiet exchanges with U Thant. However, another level in understanding the attitude of these states is revealed by the general tone of confidence in their own military power which was expressed at the time by Arab leaders. On May 22 President Nasser said: "We are ready for war. Our armed forces and all our people are ready for war . . . . we have built a strong national army and achieved our objectives." [22] Other Arab leaders had been even more forthright in their statements regarding the anticipated outcome of a trial of strength between their countries and Israel.

While Soviet diplomats admitted that their government had warned the Egyptians that Israel was plotting against Syria and while it was clear that the USSR felt it had a special interest in bolstering the Al-Atassi government in Syria—not to mention the Nasser government in the United Arab Republic—the Soviet Union did not encourage these states to test their armaments against Israel. It is known authoritatively that, in fact, the UAR did not consult with the Soviet Union about the withdrawal of UNEF. Moscow was taken by surprise by Cairo's demand for withdrawal and Soviet diplomats assiduously inquired from all who might have some special knowledge of Arab intentions why Nasser had taken this step and how far he was prepared to go.

[21] S/PV.1342, pp. 37-40.   [22] New York *Times*, May 26, 1967.

Similarly, the action of the UAR in regard to the Gulf of Aqaba, which Nasser recognized would take the Middle East to the brink of war, was taken without prior information to the Soviet Union. Though the Soviet Union was confronted with these unexpected events, its position in the Middle East remained one of yielding to none in the level of support that it would give to its allies and friends. On May 23 the Soviet government issued a statement on the Middle East situation which Ambassador Nikolai Fedorenko read into the Security Council records on May 24. This statement contained the following sentence: "But let no one have any doubts about the fact that, should anyone try to unleash aggression in the Near East, he would be met not only with the united strength of Arab countries but also with strong opposition to aggression from the Soviet Union and all peace-loving States." [23] Here, then, was an apparently clear statement of one element in the Soviet position. But no government can afford to be simplistic about matters of war and peace, and wise Arab statesmen would have done well to understand clearly the final paragraph of the Soviet government's statement, which contained the following sentences:

The Soviet Government . . . proceeds from the fact that the maintenance of peace and security in the area directly adjacent to the Soviet borders touches upon the vital interests of the Soviet peoples. Taking due account of the situation, the Soviet Union is doing and will continue to do everything in its power to prevent a violation of peace and security in the Near East.

In other words, peace in the area was a vital necessity and the Soviet Union would strive to preserve it. It became widely known that the Soviet Union at the highest level had sought, after the UAR forces moved to their positions on the brink, to obtain assurances from Cairo that the UAR would not launch an offensive against Israel. It is said that these assurances were, in fact, given to Moscow. In short, Soviet support for the Arab

[23] S/PV.1342, May 24, 1967, p. 27.

cause on May 24, 1967, was subordinate to adherence by the Arabs to a containment of their postures of belligerence within limits that would remain short of actual hostilities.

If the meetings of the Security Council on May 24 did not resolve the issues that were menacing the peace of the Middle East, they did show, for those who would study carefully the situation on the record and behind the scenes, that armed strife might perhaps be averted. In these circumstances what became of supreme importance was the assessment which U Thant would bring back from his visit to Cairo.

The Secretary-General presented his report on May 26, 1967, and it was so consequential a document that the Security Council did not meet again until May 29. Of prime importance was the section of the report in regard to the situation in the Gulf of Aqaba. U Thant had expressed to the Egyptian leaders his "deep concern" about "the dangerous consequences which would ensue from restricting innocent passage of ships in the Straits of Tiran" and his "hope that no precipitate action would be taken." [24] In addition to attempting in this manner to arrest the exercise of claimed rights of belligerency, U Thant's report urged "all the parties concerned to exercise special restraint, to *forgo belligerence* and to avoid all other actions which could increase tension, to allow the Council to deal with the underlying causes of the present crisis and to seek solutions." [25]

In view of the Secretary-General's suggestions, the restraining of belligerence became the keynote of the Council's deliberations from May 29 to June 4.

United States Ambassador Arthur Goldberg opened the Security Council's substantive proceedings on May 29 by asking the Council to support the appeal of the Secretary-General to the parties to forgo belligerence. At the same time he stressed the possibilities of conciliation by concentrating his attention on

[24] S/7906, May 26, 1967, p. 4.   [25] *Ibid.*, p. 5. Italics added.

evidence that both Israel and the UAR, at the highest level, would prefer peaceful solutions to conflict. He drew attention to Prime Minister Eshkol's statement of May 28 to the effect "that his Government had decided to rely on 'the continuance of political action in the world arena' to stimulate 'international factors to take effective measures to ensure free international passage' in the Strait of Tiran." Goldberg added, "That statement is very much to be welcomed." [26]

Goldberg asked for the same spirit to be matched by the other parties and governments concerned; and in this connection he took note of the following sentence in U Thant's report: "President Nasser and Foreign Minister Riad assured me that the United Arab Republic would not initiate offensive action against Israel." [27] Recognizing that diplomacy was operating within very narrow limits and on a short-term schedule, Goldberg was right in directing the attention of both the Council and the parties to trends toward mutual restraint. Furthermore, to have suggested that the Council should unanimously attach its own great authority to the Secretary-General's appeal for a state of nonbelligerency was a sound negotiating effort to multiply the effect of that appeal, which had been made in the best traditions of conciliatory diplomacy developed particularly by Hammarskjöld and U Thant himself. We have already noted that the Secretary-General has come to acquire a special relationship to Middle East problems. It was therefore all the more appropriate at this juncture to underline his appeal.

Goldberg then took up the specific issue of Aqaba and expressed his belief that "forgoing belligerence must mean forgoing any blockade of Aqaba during the breathing spell requested by the Secretary-General." [28] In support of this view he marshaled three lines of argument: first, U Thant's report had foreseen dangerous consequences from any restrictions of

[26] S/PV.1343, May 29, 1967, p. 12.   [27] *Ibid.*   [28] *Ibid.*, p. 16.

innocent passage through the Strait of Tiran.[29] Second, he cited
the basic view of the United States as set out by President
Johnson on May 23: "The United States considers the Gulf to
be an international waterway. . . . The right of free, innocent
passage of the international waterway is a vital interest of the
international community." [30] Third, Arthur Goldberg stated that
the law in the matter was contained in the 1958 Geneva Convention on the Territorial Sea and the Contiguous Zone. He quoted
Article 16, paragraph 4, of the Convention, which states as
follows: "There shall be no suspension of the innocent passage of foreign ships through straits which are used for international navigation between one part of the high seas and
another part of the high seas or the territorial sea of a foreign
state." [31]

Dwelling on the other manifestations of belligerence, particularly sabotage and terrorist activity, Goldberg suggested
the remedy of taking "effective steps . . . to reaffirm the General Armistice Agreements and revitalize the Armistice machinery." [32] It is significant, from the point of view of the effort to
achieve a successful negotiation of the situation, that, apart from
the regulation of the Aqaba situation by the Geneva Convention
of 1958, all that Goldberg asked specifically was a return to a
revitalized Armistice regime. He did not suggest any long-term
measures to resolve Middle East problems. When a situation is
dangerous but not critical, is explosive but has not yet exploded,
the tendency of negotiators, even among those who normally
try to achieve lasting settlements, is rather to seek to adjust positions on the basis of already agreed arrangements, even if provisional, to keep the peace. The philosophy of this approach is
that the maintenance of such arrangements helps to instill among
the parties the habit of peace, which may stabilize the situation

[29] S/7906, par. 10.
[30] For text of President Johnson's statement, see New York *Times,* May
24, 1967.
[31] United Nations, *Treaty Series,* Vol. 516, p. 216.
[32] S/PV.1343, pp. 18–20.

either on the basis of the provisional arrangements or, through later negotiations, on the basis of other acceptable terms.

Arthur Goldberg was immediately followed by El-Kony, the main protagonist of the Arab case. El-Kony's tactic was to present the Security Council with instances of serious violations by Israel of the Armistice Agreement and thereby to put his government, and that of the other Arab states, in the position of being parties in search of legitimate redress. He went on to accuse Prime Minister Eshkol of having talked of possibilities of all-out war to topple Syria's army regime.[33] He contended that the Gulf of Aqaba was an inland waterway "subject to absolute Arab sovereignty." [34] He asserted that Israel was at Elath in violation of the Armistice Agreement and therefore had no standing as a littoral state. This, he said, established exclusive rights for the Arabs in the Gulf of Aqaba under international law.

So far, Ambassador El-Kony had put his argument on the basis of facts as he saw them and on international law pertaining to specific issues. He now chose to advance his case by seeking to stand on the international status of a belligerent, and in so doing he placed himself in a position of rejecting U Thant's appeal which Goldberg had strongly supported. El-Kony stated that "it is a general, incontestable rule of international law that the conclusion of a partial or general armistice agreement does not end the state of war." He called in the reputable name of Oppenheim in support of the rights of belligerency which flow from this concept of an armistice: "In spite of such cessation [of hostilities], the rights of visit and search over neutral merchantmen therefore remains intact, as do likewise the right to capture neutral vessels attempting to break a blockade, and the right to seize contraband of war." [35] Ambassador El-Kony went on to say:

---

[33] *Ibid.*, p. 28.   [34] *Ibid.*, p. 31.
[35] L. Oppenheim, *International Law*, ed. H. Lauterpacht, 7th ed. (New York, 1952), II, 547.

There is no shade of a doubt as to the continued existence of the state of war between the Israelis and both the Arabs of Palestine and their brethren in the Arab countries. . . . My Government has the legitimate right, in accordance with international law, to impose restrictions on navigation in the Strait of Tiran with respect to shipping to an enemy. After this rather lengthy elaboration, it is quite evident and unequivocal that according to international law a state of belligerency exists between the Arab States whose territories circumscribe the entirety of the Gulf of Aquaba, and Israel.[36]

The upshot of Ambassador El-Kony's lengthy presentation was that apart from Aqaba, where his and the U.S. point of view were diametrically opposed, he asked for the same remedy as did Ambassador Arthur Goldberg. Specifically he asked that "this Council should, in its endeavor to deal with the present situation, recognize the continuing validity of the Egyptian-Israeli General Armistice Agreement and that the United Nations machinery emanating therefrom should be fully operative."[37] He asked the Council to call on the Israeli government to respect and abide by its responsibilities under that agreement.

In a sense, then, while rejecting the appeal for nonbelligerency made by the Secretary-General, the United Arab Republic was suggesting that the way to achieve desirable results in that phase of negotiation lay in revitalizing and hardening the Armistice Agreements. Was this a course worth pursuing? Ambassador Goldberg had seen in the reinforcement of the Armistice Agreements a resolution of one of the principal problems of the situation: the terrorist raids—El Fateh activities—which were menacing the peace of the area. The Secretary-General, too, had pointed out that the revitalization of the full range of machinery established by the Armistice Agreements would help to maintain quiet in the area.[38]

On the other hand, though such a move would certainly have beneficial results, including perhaps security for Israel from ter-

[36] S/PV.1343, pp. 36–37.   [37] *Ibid.*, p. 46.
[38] S/7896, May 19, 1967, pars. 16 and 17.

rorism, it would leave unresolved the question of shipping through the Strait of Tiran and, of course, the question of the use of the Suez Canal by Israeli ships and by other ships bound for Israeli ports. Moreover, such a solution would have left intact the theory of belligerency and the alleged rights accruing therefrom. In these circumstances it was, to put it mildly, most doubtful that Israel would see its way to acceptance.

However, even such a solution, as a step toward pacification and eventual improvement of the Middle East situation, was perhaps one which the Council might have accepted as a last resort while continuing to battle separately with the problem of Aqaba. The Council might have been prompted to accept this step-by-step approach by the fact that, in the ten-year period in which the Gulf of Aqaba had been open to Israeli ships, only five such ships had used the Strait of Tiran. The last Israeli ship to do so entered the Strait about eighteen months before President Nasser reestablished the blockade on May 22, 1967. In short, as a practical matter, it was more important to keep the Gulf of Aqaba open to non-Israeli shipping bound for Elath. This might have been more readily acceptable to the United Arab Republic and would have meant that oil from Iran and other important cargoes could have been discharged at Elath from ships flying flags other than those of Israel. Though such an arrangement would have been unpalatable to Israel, that state might conceivably have decided, reluctantly, to put up with it while efforts continued to be made to reach more satisfactory arrangements. These views are expressed in the context that existed before the armed clash of early June, 1967, in which the Israelis gained a decisive victory. What would have been acceptable before the victory was, of course, different from the demands and expectations after the war.

After the statements of Ambassador Goldberg and El-Kony, on the whole the Council continued to address itself to the task of getting the parties to forgo belligerence or, at any rate, of appealing to them to exercise restraint and caution, which would, in the circumstances, have amounted to some mitigation of the alleged rights of belligerence. The delegates of Brazil and Canada specifically endorsed the Secretary-General's appeal in paragraph 14 of his report, which included the forgoing of belligerence, while the representatives of Argentina, Ethiopia, and India endorsed the Secretary-General's appeal for special restraint by the parties so as to create a breathing spell for further work in the direction of pacification.

The Soviet Union, however, condemned Israel for its warlike preparations, particularly those against Syria. And as late as the evening of May 29 Ambassador Fedorenko still seemed doubtful that the Council need address itself to the situation in the Middle East: "My delegation expresses its conviction that if there is now any need for the Security Council to discuss the situation in the Near East with all due seriousness, this must be done within the framework of the well-founded complaint addressed to the Council by the United Arab Republic." [39] Fedorenko was referring to Document S/7907 presented by the UAR, which contained charges against Israel's policy toward its Arab neighbors. Thus, at the end of the day while the preponderance of Council membership was in favor of restraint and there was a considerable degree of feeling that there should be specific endorsement of the Secretary-General's appeal, which would include a forgoing of belligerence, the Council was by no means unified. However, the proceedings tended to show that, if a draft resolution calling for restraint had been presented on that evening, it would have been adopted with perhaps the Soviet Union and Bulgaria abstaining.

The absence of the introduction of a draft resolution calling for restraint is not easily explained except in terms of evidence of miscalculation on the part of the members of the Council in

[39] *Ibid.*, p. 102.

believing that there was still time to discuss matters and to arrive at some degree of pacification. The only delegate who had given expression to a real sense of nearness of conflict was Ambassador Tabor of Denmark.

This explains why, when the Council met again on the next afternoon, May 30, it allowed the session to be taken up almost entirely by the parties to the dispute instead of by the Council members themselves, who should have been formulating proposals to forestall the clash of the massed armed forces. Of the Council's members, only the representatives of Nigeria, Denmark, and China expressed positions on behalf of their governments. All of them endorsed U Thant's appeal for restraint and indicated their willingness to go along with a resolution which would make such an appeal to the parties.[40] These brief statements did something to add to the mounting pressure on the Council in this direction, but on the whole the Council displayed no sense of real urgency. The only permanent member of the Council to make a statement was Arthur Goldberg, but his purpose was mainly to deal with a new legal point advanced by Ambassador El-Kony in regard to Aqaba, based again on the idea of belligerence. In this context the United States representative drew attention to Security Council Resolution 95 of 1951, which contained the following relevant clause: "Considering that since the Armistice regime, which has been in existence for nearly two and one half years, is of a permanent character, neither party can reasonably assert that it is actively a belligerent." [41]

In sum, the Council let another day pass, though the actions and statements of the disputants in the Middle East, and their speeches around the Council table itself, showed how menacing the situation had become. It was not until the following afternoon, May 31, that the Council made a specific move toward an appeal to the parties. After listening to Ambassador Akira Mat-

[40] S/PV.1344, pp. 7, 51, 61.
[41] Security Council Official Records (6th Year), Resolutions, p. 11.

sui of Japan, who supported the Secretary-General's appeal for restraint and the forgoing of belligerence, Arthur Goldberg submitted a draft resolution which would call on the parties to comply with the Secretary-General's appeal and to encourage international diplomacy in the interests of pacifying the situation and seeking peaceful and just solutions, while keeping the door open to the Security Council to take further steps in the exercise of its responsibilities.[42]

After the Jordanian representative had made a speech on behalf of his country, Ambassador El-Kony presented a draft resolution which would have the Council decide that the Egyptian-Israeli Armistice Agreement was still valid, call upon Israel to respect it, and take other steps to enforce it.[43]

On the question of belligerency Ambassador El-Kony reiterated the stand of the Arab states that they were entitled to act as belligerents. Referring to Ambassador Goldberg, he said: "Justice Goldberg went further; he denied us the state of belligerency, basing himself on the fact that we signed an Armistice Agreement. In his view that should terminate the state of war. This we contest." [44]

The Indian delegate gave cautious endorsement to the United States resolution. He stated that he had already endorsed the idea of an appeal but that the terms of the Council's appeal would have to be carefully drafted so as to command the approval of the overwhelming majority of the Security Council. Furthermore, at the appropriate time and after due consideration by the Council, India would ask for a vote on the draft resolution introduced by the representative of the United Arab Republic (this procedure was required because the UAR was not a member of the Security Council). The representative of Ethiopia did not comment on the draft resolutions, and the only other representative to raise the matter was Ambassador Roger

[42] S/7916. See Appendix 2.   [43] S/PV.1345, pp. 51–52.   [44] *Ibid.*, p. 56.

Seydoux of France, who said that the "United States proposal calls for very careful study on the parts of their Governments. . . . All I have said applies equally to the text that was read out by the representative of the United Arab Republic." Indeed, in order that the text should be so studied, Ambassador Seydoux asked for a two-day adjournment of the Council.[45]

The Soviet representative made three statements on May 31, all after Ambassador Goldberg had introduced his draft resolution, but none of these statements contained reference to the American proposals. The Council accepted the suggestion of the representative of France and adjourned its session for two days!

In view of the wide support in the Council for the idea of restraint—and it is to be noted that even the Soviet Union had not attacked the U.S. proposal—the Council at this stage was unnecessarily and unwisely delaying action. Even assuming that the representatives of some of the governments needed instructions before they could vote on or even make specific suggestions to amend the U.S. text, these instructions could and should have been obtained overnight and the Council should have reconvened on the morning of Thursday, June 1, to formulate the final text of a restraining resolution. Had it so acted it would have demonstrated to the parties in the Middle East and to the world in general that it was fully cognizant of the extreme gravity of the situation and was determined to do everything possible to avoid an explosion. As it was, however, the Council, by choosing to work with a degree of dilatoriness, was both undermining its own position and failing to respond adequately to just that kind of situation for which the United Nations Charter had provided: "The Security Council shall be so organized as to be able to function continuously" (Article 28).

To make matters worse, instead of meeting as planned on

45 *Ibid.*, p. 77.

Friday, June 2, the Council gave itself the luxury of another postponement and in fact did not meet until Saturday, June 3, at 10 A.M. The reason for this delay was said to be that consultations had been taking place between the members with a view to ascertaining whether a consensus could be reached in regard to a possible resolution of the Council.

However, when the Council did reconvene few members spoke directly about the possibilities of a resolution. Ambassador Milko Tarabanov of Bulgaria commended the moderation of the Council and asked for a formal promise from Israel that it would not attack its neighbors and would join them in observance of the Armistice Agreements. Ambassador Moussa Léon Keita of Mali implied dissatisfaction with the draft resolutions presented by the United States and the United Arab Republic and expressed the belief that it would be wise to explore new avenues.[46] Roger Seydoux of France then took the floor. Three days previously he had asked for a two-day reprieve in order to obtain instructions on the draft resolutions before the Council. He now spoke with diplomatic skill which did not directly pronounce itself on those drafts but indicated that the important point was to obtain a consensus on the terms of an appeal: "The most urgent task which the Security Council must perform today is to agree on the terms of an appeal to the parties to abstain, during this breathing spell, from supporting their claims by a resort to force of whatever nature." [47] In addition he suggested that the permanent members of the Council should join together in efforts "in order to steer this grievous crisis, now engulfing the Near East on the road which . . . is likely to lead to peace." This was a revival of General de Gaulle's earlier suggestion that the great powers should meet together to help resolve the issue. It should be noted that, simultaneously with Ambassador Seydoux's statement, President de Gaulle made a declaration on the Middle East question affirming

[46] S/PV.1346, pp. 87–90.   [47] *Ibid.*, p. 92.

the neutrality of France; he expressed his view that all the states in the area had the right to live but that the worst of all eventualities would be an outbreak of hostilities and that consequently that state in the region which would be the first to employ its forces would not have the approval and much less the support of France. He also repeated the proposal for a meeting of minds between the four permanent members of the Security Council for the resolving of such questions as the use of the Gulf of Aqaba.[48]

The remarks made by Ambassador Seydoux were supported specifically by Ambassador Lij Endalkachew Makonnen of Ethiopia.[49] Ambassador Arthur Goldberg said a few words in support of his own draft resolution: "Our objective today is a very simple one. It is to support an appeal made by the impartial agency of the United Nations, the Secretary-General. Our draft resolution was cast in those plain terms. It did not seek to go beyond them." [50] However, in using the past tense Ambassador Goldberg appeared to recognize that perhaps the Council should find a new formulation for the proposed appeal. Ambassador Fedorenko made two or three brief interventions but, again, none of them referred to the draft resolutions before the Council. Lord Caradon of the United Kingdom remained silent. It was clear that the Council, though generally in favor of an

48 The text of General de Gaulle's brief statement is as follows:

"La France n'est engagée à aucun titre ni sur aucun des Etats en cause. De son propre chef, elle considère que chacun de ces Etats a le droit de vivre. Mais elle estime que le pire serait l'ouverture des hostilités. En conséquence, l'Etat qui le premier et où que se soit emploierait les armes n'aurait ni son approbation ni, à plus forte raison, son appui.

"Au cas où la situation actuelle d'expectative pourrait être maintenue et ou une detente de fait se produirait en conséquence, les problèmes posés par la navigation dans le golfe d'Akaba, la situation des réfugiés palestiniens et les conditions de voisinage des Etats intéressés devraient être réglés au fond par décisions internationales, de telles décisions devant donner lieu au préalable à une entente des quatre puissances qui sont membres permanents du Conseil de sécurité. La France maintient la proposition qu'elle a faite à cet égard."

From *Le Monde*, June 3, 1967.

49 S/PV.1346, pp. 103–5.　　　　50 *Ibid.*, p. 101.

appeal to the parties, had allowed three more valuable days to pass without reaching agreement on the precise terms of the appeal.

At that same meeting of the Council, statements were made which showed conclusively that the situation in the Middle East had further deteriorated and was now extremely dangerous. The following citations made seriatim as delivered before the Council illustrate the point. Ambassador Rafael presented the following quotation to the Council:

On 25 May, Radio Cairo in its broadcast at 2 pm proclaimed: "The Arab people is determined to wipe Israel off the map. . . ." On the Egyptian television on 1 June, at 6:30 pm, the Commander of the Egyptian Air Force told his audience that "the Egyptian forces spread from Rafah to Sharm el Sheik are ready for the order to begin the struggle to which they have looked forward for so long." [51]

Mr. G. Al-Rachach of Saudi Arabia said:

If war breaks out . . . the Arab world will meet this challenge with courage and fortitude and will resolve once and for all Zionist aggression in Palestine; I repeat, once and for all, Zionist aggression in Palestine.[52]

Another element in the warlike situation was indicated by Ambassador Tarabanov of Bulgaria. He said that General Rabin, the Israeli Chief of Staff, had, according to *Newsweek*, "publicly observed that the time might have come to seize Damascus and topple the Syrian Government." The same magazine added: "And Prime Minister Levi Eshkol warned that if the terrorism continues, Israel would choose the time, the place and the means to counter the aggressor." [53]

The evidence before the Council of explosive elements in the Middle East situation now was overwhelming. Instead of staying at its task on Saturday, June 3, the Council rose at 2:20 P.M., having decided to reconvene on the afternoon of Monday, June 5. As the events proved, this was in fact the last opportunity

[51] *Ibid.*, pp. 8–10, 11.   [52] *Ibid.*, p. 66.   [53] *Ibid.*, p. 26.

that the Council was to have to make a clear and urgent appeal for restraint by the parties. It is difficult to take the view that the Council had had insufficient time to discharge this responsibility. A week had passed since it had reconvened on May 29. Indeed, the Council had had more than a week, inasmuch as the Secretary-General issued his report on his return from Cairo on May 26. The Council therefore had had eight days in which to formulate a position. In view of the extreme gravity and urgency of the situation, it was not time that the Council lacked but, unfortunately, a clear perspective of the dangers involved and a determination to grasp the full nature of its own responsibility. With this failure on the part of the Council, the chance to restrain belligerence was, for the time being, lost and the task before the United Nations was to become even more complex than it had hitherto been. It is also to be noted that though the parties to the dispute, Israel and the Arab states, spoke frequently and at length during this period, none of them demanded urgent action by the Security Council. The UAR had, it is true, introduced a draft resolution, but it had not pressed for a vote on it. The emphasis of each side was on the threats of the other side, and on its own determination to fight and to destroy. This lack of will among the parties to find a truly peaceful solution was an important contributory factor to the failure of the Council to act as it should have done.

CHAPTER IV

The Security Council and the War

ON SATURDAY, June 3, the Council had chosen to give itself a vacation until 3 P.M. on Monday, June 5. Events, however, cut this period short. The Council reconvened at 9:30 A.M. on June 5, to be told by its President, Ambassador (later Foreign Minister) Hans Tabor of Denmark, that at 3:10 that morning he had been informed by the representative of Israel that Egyptian land and air forces were moving against Israel and that Israeli forces were engaged in repelling the enemy. Twenty minutes later, at 3:30 A.M., the permanent representative of the United Arab Republic informed Ambassador Tabor that Israel had committed aggression against the UAR and was launching attacks against various parts of the country. Confronted with these definitive reports of hostilities, Ambassador Tabor had "felt it my duty, in the exercise of my responsibilities as President of the Security Council, to convene the Council for this urgent meeting." [1] The Security Council's rules of procedure empower the President to call a meeting at any time he deems necessary.[2]

The Council members seemed too dazed to respond immediately to the new situation of war. They listened to a statement by U Thant, who had received some information on the sudden outburst of war from both General Rikhye, the Commander of UNEF, and General Odd Bull, the Chief of Staff of UNTSO.

---

[1] S/PV.1347, pp. 4–5. We take note of this initiative of Hans Tabor since it was characteristic of his month as President of the Council that he conducted its affairs with firmness and drive.

[2] Security Council Provisional Rules of Procedure, Doc. S/96/Rev. 4.

After the delegate of India had referred briefly to the death of a few members of the Indian contingent to UNEF, the Council proceeded to hear statements by the representatives of Israel and the UAR. The Israeli representative, Ambassador Rafael, claimed that from the reports he had received "it is evident that in the early hours of this morning Egyptian armored columns moved in an offensive thrust against Israel's borders. At the same time Egyptian planes took off from airfields in Sinai and struck out towards Israel." [3]

Ambassador El-Kony, on the other hand, stated that "for several hours now the Israeli armed forces and the Israeli Air Force have again committed a cowardly and treacherous aggression against my country." [4]

Both the Israeli and the Egyptian representative asserted that the forces of his country were repelling the enemy. Again, neither of them asked for Security Council action to stem the tide of war. Both sides seemed possessed with an implacable spirit of conflict that brooked no obstacle to the attainment of their own ends. The UAR delegate asked that "this aggression . . . be vigorously condemned by the Security Council." [5] This request, however, called for a move by the Council which was not within the terms of its functions as defined in the Charter of the United Nations. Among the various steps which the Security Council is to take under the Charter, condemnation is not included. Ambassador El-Kony's reference to action, as in the case of his Israeli counterpart, was to action which his own country was taking: "In view of this treacherous aggression, my country has no other choice than to defend itself by all means at its disposal, in accordance with Article 51 of the Charter of the United Nations." [6]

It soon became clear that, apart from sporadic shooting across the frontier, the massive military strike on the morning of June

[3] *Ibid.*, pp. 17–20.   [4] *Ibid.*, p. 22.   [5] *Ibid.*, pp. 27–30.   [6] *Ibid.*

5 was in fact commenced by Israel. Indeed, privately, Israeli diplomats admitted this to be the case. An act of aggression has a special significance under the Charter and may be the basis of severe responsive action by the Security Council. At the same time, the Charter equally outlaws among the members of the United Nations not only the use of force or aggression but the threat to use force; such threats may also call forth severe responsive action by the Security Council. On this plane both sides were already deeply culpable, even before the actual commencement of massive hostilities. A vast range of material exists to show how the parties were moving toward conflict and doing so without asking for restraining action by the United Nations. On the one side, there is, for example, the step-by-step account in the New York *Times* of moves in Israel before the war.[7] This account records that, with the news of the blockade of the Strait of Tiran, the situation plummeted toward conflict: "Israeli leaders agree now that war, from that moment, seemed inevitable." Coming to June 5 the account records flatly: "Two days later, on June 5, Israeli planes blasted the Arab air forces on their runways. At the same time, Israeli armored units charged into Sinai."

On the other hand, it was reported that on June 3 the Egyptian commander of the UAR's large armies in the Sinai stated: "The eyes of the whole world are on you in your glorious war against the Israelis' aggressiveness on the soil of your homeland, hoping to see the outcome of your holy war in victory for the rights of the Arab people. . . . Reconquer the stolen land with God's help and the power of justice and with the strength of your arms and your united faith."[8] The above rendition of General Murtagi's statement was contained in the Israeli representative's speech of June 5, and it has never been contradicted by the other side.

[7] New York *Times*, July 10, 1967.   [8] S/PV.1347, p. 21.

On the morning of June 5 the President of the Security Council urged that the best course to follow would be "to hear the two parties and then to have a *short* recess for *urgent* consultations . . . as to the course of action to be taken by the Council in this *emergency* situation." [9] In this one brief sentence Ambassador Tabor used three adjectives to stress the immediacy of the situation. The Council accepted his suggestion and a short recess was called at 11:15 A.M. after the Israeli-UAR statements were heard. Since only a short recess had been called, the Council members remained in and around the Council chamber while the President took to his room groups of delegates for consultation. In these consultations some countries, notably France and India, suggested formulations for a draft resolution which would have linked cessation of hostilities with withdrawal of forces. But to which positions were the forces of the two sides to be withdrawn? According to the Indian answer, to the positions they held on June 4. To some of the members and to the Israelis this was no solution, since it would reestablish 80,000 or more heavily armed Egyptian forces on Israel's borders in the Sinai. What was perhaps even worse from the Israeli point of view, it would leave the Egyptians in control of Sharm el Sheikh, blockading the Strait of Tiran. The French suggestion on the matter of withdrawal was that the two sides should return to their positions "before hostilities broke out." The problem would then be to determine when precisely hostilities did break out. How was this to be resolved? The Israelis would certainly contend that the blockading of the Gulf was a hostile act. The Egyptians would retort that it was impossible for a country to commit a hostile act on its own territory. With these questions unanswered, the French formula did not seem able to resolve the situation. Meanwhile events were moving fast in the Middle East. Information was coming in of rapid Israeli advances.

[9] *Ibid.*, pp. 16–17. Italics added.

Other formulas were talked about, such as disengagement. Again the problem was how to define this concept. A further complication in the negotiations on June 5 was the Soviet Union's demand that the Security Council should condemn Israel's aggression, and the Soviets showed no disposition to withdraw their demand. Though they were supported in this attitude only by Bulgaria and less forcefully by Mali, the insistence on condemnation trammeled the movement of negotiation toward a consensus, since the Soviet Union could veto a resolution which did not meet its mimimum requirements. However, from 6 P.M. onwards on June 5, every now and again some members of the Council would resume their seats around the table and it looked as if the Council were about to meet and pronounce itself on the situation. It was not until 10:20 P.M. that the Council did resume its session, but then the President announced briefly: "I had hoped indeed that the recess would be considerably shorter. However, consultations are still going on . . . and will continue tomorrow morning." [10] The Council decided to adjourn until 11:30 A.M. on June 6.

Events were eroding diplomatic positions. The French no longer pushed for their formula, particularly since its definition was becoming increasingly difficult. The Indian delegation still stood for complete withdrawal, and on the morning of June 6 the Soviet position still seemed to demand condemnation of Israel. Informally the Council members decided that no purpose would be served by meeting as planned at 11:30 that morning. They continued their consultations around the Council chamber while it became increasingly clear that the United Arab Republic's forces were unable to stem Israeli advances and that the efforts in the east by Jordan were no more successful. The fighting was fierce along the borders of northern Israel and Syria but the Arabs were achieving no successes. On the Jorda-

[10] *Ibid.*, p. 31.

nian frontier, the letter which Secretary-General U Thant [11] had issued on the morning of June 5 to King Hussein requesting that the Jordanian troops vacate Government House in Jerusalem had become out of date: the Israelis had driven out the Jordanians and had taken possession of the property for themselves.

The United States delegate now worked even harder than before for a Council resolution calling simply for an immediate cease-fire. On June 5 other delegations had thought that there seemed to be some flexibility in this U.S. position—that the U.S. would have agreed to couple with cessation of hostilities a formula which would have returned the Israeli and Arab forces to positions held on May 18, i.e., before the massive movements into the Sinai and Aqaba. However, the Arab delegations were unwilling to countenance deep withdrawals within Arab territory. By the early afternoon of June 6 it became clear that if the Council wished to stop the war it would have to concentrate its attention solely on a cease-fire. Late that afternoon the Egyptians informed the Soviet Union that they would accept a cease-fire unless they received immediate military assistance. It was clear, however, that such assistance could not be given. The Arab states had received well over a billion dollars worth of armaments from the Soviet Union and its allies. More armaments for Egypt would not turn the tide, and to bring in other ground forces was unrealistic. The European Communist states could hardly go to the aid of their Arab friends when they had not yet gone to the aid of a Communist state (North Vietnam) engaged in fighting against an infinitely more powerful enemy than Israel.

In the light of these compulsions the Council finally convened at 6:30 P.M. on June 6. Ambassador Tabor, the President, announced that consultations had resulted in unanimous agreement on a draft resolution, which he read out. It called simply for a

[11] *Ibid.*, pp. 11–15.

cease-fire and cessation of all military activity. The only suggestion that there were other matters involved was the phrase "as
a first step" used in connection with the cease-fire. The whole
resolution read as follows:

> *The Security Council,*
> *Noting* the oral report of the Secretary-General in this situation,
> *Having heard* the statements made in the Council,
> *Concerned* at the outbreak of fighting and with the menacing
> situation in the Near East,
>   1. *Calls upon* the Governments concerned as a first step to take
> forthwith all measures for an immediate cease-fire and for a cessa-
> tion of all military activities in the area,
>   2. *Requests* the Secretary-General to keep the Council promptly
> and currently informed on the situation.[12]

Solemnly, all fifteen members of the Security Council raised
their hands to adopt the resolution unanimously.

The Council proceeded to hear about what had gone on in
the negotiations. Ambassador Arthur Goldberg was the first
speaker. He said that for the past thirty-six hours the United
States had "vigorously urged as a first step the adoption of a resolution calling for an immediate cease-fire." [13] While this was
true, we have also noted that there had been in the earlier stages
of the consultations some flexibility in the United States position toward certain formulations relating to the withdrawal of
Israeli forces. The United Kingdom delegate, Lord Caradon,
expressed his government's "warm welcome for the resolution
which we have just adopted." [14] The Argentine delegate stated
that "it was imperative that the Security Council make an appeal
to the parties for an immediate cease-fire. This is our first duty
so that the conflict will not be extended." [15] However, Ambassador José Maria Ruda was uneasy about the delays which had
bogged down the Council. He saw the prestige of the Organization at stake. "Let us not tomorrow have to rue the fact that we

---

[12] Security Council Resolution 233 (1967).   [13] S/PV.1348, p. 7.
[14] *Ibid.*, pp. 18–20.   [15] *Ibid.*, p. 31.

did not act today." He wanted the Council to proceed expeditiously and energetically to take further action. Canada, Brazil, Taiwan China, and Denmark were the remainder of the component of seven of the fifteen members of the Council who welcomed the resolution and thought it was the right step to take.

Close to the position of the aforementioned delegates was that of Ethiopian Ambassador Makonnen. But he added that the Council must "make up for the lost time and opportunity by following up" its decision on the cease-fire.[16] The position of India was near to that of the seven powers that had welcomed the resolution, inasmuch as Ambassador G. Parthasarathi also approved the unanimous decision ordering a cease-fire in the Middle East. He, however, stated unambiguously that it was "well known that my delegation, among others, would have preferred a resolution which called upon the Governments concerned for a withdrawal of armed forces to positions held by them prior to the outbreak of hostilities, that is as on 4 June 1967, along with the cease-fire." [17] This part of Ambassador Parthasarathi's statement was not unlike Ambassador Fedorenko's remark that "the Soviet delegation was always of the opinion that the Security Council should also have taken a decision concerning the immediate withdrawal of the forces of the aggressor behind the Armistice line." [18] It is interesting that the Indian position was able to embrace the positions of both the United States and the Soviet Union. On the one hand, India welcomed the Security Council's resolution, as had done the United States and six other countries, while on the other hand it took a firm stand on withdrawal, which had also been preferred by the Soviet Union. Bulgaria and Mali held positions analogous to that of the USSR.

As to the next step to be taken by the Council, eight states—the United States, Ethiopia, the United Kingdom, Argentina, Canada, Japan, Mali, and Taiwan China—identified the need to

[16] *Ibid.*, p. 13.   [17] *Ibid.*, p. 46.   [18] *Ibid.*, p. 27.

establish a lasting and just peace. The United States stand in favor of such a move was known. It was, however, of special significance that two African states on the Council also thought that a long-term solution must be found. Ambassador Makonnen said: "Let us . . . follow up our decision of today with concerted action which can lead to the creation of fair and equitable conditions for a just and lasting settlement." [19] Ambassador Moussa Léon Keita of Mali said that his delegation wanted to believe that the cease-fire resolution "will be followed by a serious study of the whole problem which has remained on our agenda for twenty years. If it were otherwise, we would again, alas, have added a few lines on a sheet of paper and we would have again thought that we had solved the problem which we shall soon meet again at the next crossroads." [20]

Equally interesting was the fact that Ambassador Seydoux of France was unspecific about the future. He stated simply that "once the fighting has stopped . . . we shall have to embark upon a lengthy process." [21] He did add that the stability of the Near East, as well as the prospect for peace, was at stake, but there was no indication of any precise step or goal. The Brazilian delegate spoke in general terms of the hope of his delegation that the cease-fire resolution would "be an effective and constructive step toward restoring peace to all nations involved in the fighting." [22] This was vague because there had in fact been very little stable peace in the Middle East for twenty years.

Ambassador Fedorenko stated that "the Soviet delegation decisively condemns the aggression of Israel, considers it to be the bounden duty of the Security Council to adopt *without any further delay* a decision concerning the immediate and unconditional withdrawal of the forces of the aggressor beyond the Armistice Lines." [23] It is interesting that the USSR did not

---

[19] *Ibid.*, p. 13.   [20] *Ibid.*, p. 42.   [21] *Ibid.*, p. 16.   [22] *Ibid.*, p. 36.
[23] *Ibid.*, p. 27. Italics added.

at this stage seek specifically for Council condemnation of Israel, as previously requested. Now, the Soviet delegate brought to the question of withdrawal a concentrated sense of great urgency.

The Indian delegate said that his delegation was "of the opinion that the Council should take up on an urgent basis the question of withdrawal." [24] India, therefore, while not ruling out specifically attention to the basic problems of the area, identified a return to the status quo as being the next step for the Council's agenda.

The position, then, on the next step to be taken was that as many as eight delegations, a majority of the Council, were in favor of a lasting peace being worked out. This in itself was of some significance. In the debates before the adoption of the first cease-fire resolution, during sessions from May 24 to June 3, Council members had not talked of long-term settlements. Their emphasis had been on a call for restraint. Even the United States had not emphasized the need for a basic settlement. At that time, then, the maximum expectancy was the avoidance of conflict. It is a seeming paradox, but nevertheless a recurring one in international affairs, that the worse the situation becomes, the more drastic are the remedies that commend themselves to the international community. The paradox is only superficial. Clearly, conflict in itself shows that the situation has deteriorated seriously and therefore demands a basic solution. Before the outbreak of conflict there is always the possibility that one side or another, or both of them, are engaged in brinkmanship and that there is a degree of artificiality in the confrontation of words and forces. This possibility is dispelled once conflict erupts. It is for this reason that in the short space of time from June 3 to June 6 the Security Council shifted its position drastically from a call for restraint to urging that a lasting peace be firmly es-

24 *Ibid.*, p. 46.

tablished. It is noteworthy that only three Member States identified a short-term goal (withdrawal) as the appropriate next
step for the Council.

Another point to note is that in the interventions on June 6
as many as six members of the Council—the United States, the
United Kingdom, Argentina, Canada, Brazil, and India—paid
tribute to the work of the President of the Council, Ambassador
Tabor, in the negotiations which led to unanimous acceptance
of the cease-fire resolution. This tribute indicated how important
it is for the member of the Council serving as President to pos-
sess personal qualities which can win the confidence of his
colleagues and to represent a government which is widely acceptable in the international community. We have observed in
Chapter I how the President for May was handicapped by the
fact that only five states on the Council recognized his government. On the other hand, Denmark is generally acceptable to
most governments, and fortunately its representative on the
Council was vigorous, politically sensitive, and highly person-
able. These characteristics sustained him in his grueling task of
stimulating and conducting negotiations at all times of the day
and night with his colleagues.

The long meeting of June 6 ended at about 11:30 at night
with a statement of the President to the effect that he would
take the necessary steps to see that everything possible was done
to ensure that the parties would comply with the Council's
decision on a cease-fire. Thus, he conceived his own task as not
having been completed, though the other members of the Council could now retire for the night. Ambassador Tabor announced
that he would consult with his colleagues concerning the date of
the next meeting of the Council.

That date was to be only a few hours off. In response to an
urgent request from Ambassador Fedorenko of the Soviet Union,
the Council reassembled at 1 P.M. on the very next day, June 7.

The expectation was that Ambassador Fedorenko, who, as

we have seen, had stressed the need for the Council to take urgent steps to secure a withdrawal of Israeli forces, would now demand such withdrawal. This would undoubtedly result in a confrontation of widely differing views—more than half of the Council having expressed itself in favor of basic measures rather than the reestablishment of the status quo. However, Ambassador Fedorenko did not raise the issue of withdrawal. He took the floor to reiterate his country's condemnation of Israel's aggression, but his main concern was that the war had not ceased and that Arab forces were being thrown farther and farther back with great loss of equipment and life. Belying expectations of a demand for the withdrawal of Israeli forces, he introduced a draft resolution calling for the cessation of conflict—along the lines of the one adopted a few hours earlier—with the addition of a time limit for the compliance of the warring states: June 7, 1967, at 2000 hours GMT.[25] After introducing his brief draft resolution Ambassador Fedorenko insisted on an immediate vote. Clearly his government was being pressed by its friends in the Middle East to ensure that the cease-fire should become effective immediately. Further delay could have political consequences. A government in defeat is an insecure government; and the USSR was striving to save the political foundations of certain governments in the Middle East. This task brooked no delay in the face of continuing Israeli military successes.

However, before asking the Council to vote, President Tabor called on the Secretary-General to inform the members of the contents of replies to the cease-fire resolution which had been transmitted to the parties late on the previous night. The Secretary-General reported that one Arab state—Jordan—had accepted the cease-fire. After the Secretary-General's remarks, the representative of Brazil suggested that, though the matter was extremely urgent, his delegation felt that there should be a

25 S/PV.1349, pp. 7–10.

short time "to reflect and meditate" on the Soviet text before a vote was taken. He said it was necessary at least to become acquainted with the wording of the text. For this purpose he asked for a twenty-minute recess.

Since the Soviet Union was now pressing for exactly what the United States had urged for two days—a cease-fire—at this stage Goldberg made a further revelation of some of the intricacies of the negotiation on June 6 which culminated that evening in the adoption of Resolution 233 on a cease-fire, and he referred also to the failure of the Council to act before the conflict erupted. He reminded his colleagues that for weeks his government had called for restraint in the area, while "certain Powers" had objected to statements about the gravity of the situation. This remark of Ambassador Goldberg was specifically aimed at the position of both the Soviet Union and the United Arab Republic. Both had objected to the Council's being convened and had expressed the view that no real emergency existed. The facts had so clearly belied this view that Goldberg could not resist drawing attention to the miscalculation of these powers. What was the purpose in raising the issue at this stage? First, to point to the lack of seriousness about a very grave situation on the part of some of the other states concerned and thereby to underline the greater awareness and sense of responsibility of the United States and like-minded delegations. Second, Ambassador Goldberg's purpose was to draw the attention of the Council to the need to exercise its responsibilities in due time. Certainly this was a relevant consideration in regard to the Middle East. By failing to adopt a resolution in the ten days at its disposal from the time of the Secretary-General's report on his visit to Cairo to the outbreak of hostilities, the Council had showed a lamentable lack of grasp of the essential nature of the situation with which it was supposed to be dealing.

Ambassador Goldberg went on to read out an abortive draft resolution which Ambassador Tabor of Denmark had submitted to his colleagues on the morning of Monday, June 5, immediately on receipt of the information that hostilities had broken out. That abortive draft resolution had been very much along the lines of the resolution which the Council proceeded to adopt some thirty-two hours later (Resolution 233). He revealed that from the outset the United States delegation had strongly urged the immediate adoption of Ambassador Tabor's text. However, the Soviets and others had opposed it and Goldberg was pinning on them the responsibility for the loss of thirty-two valuable hours and in a sense saying that, if the Soviets and the Arabs had been wiser two days earlier, the urgency for another resolution on the cease-fire, which the Soviets were now introducing, would not have existed.

Ambassador Fedorenko did not make any substantial rebuttal of Goldberg's remarks, contenting himself with a little sarcasm about the untimeliness of debate, reminiscence, and the quotation of one's own speeches whatever pleasure they might afford the author.[26] However, the Brazilian move for suspension was approved, and the Council adjourned for a half-hour or so.

When the Council reconvened, it immediately adopted the Soviet text unanimously without further debate.

Was this to be construed as a victory for the Soviet point of view? The answer is that, on the plane on which the Soviet delegation had been pressing for action by the Council, the resolution now adopted, Resolution 234 of June 7, 1967, was not directly relevant. It confined itself to the subject of the cease-fire, as is clear from the text:

The Security Council,
Noting that, in spite of its appeal to the Governments concerned to take forthwith as a first step all measures for an immediate cease-fire and for a cessation of all military activities in the Near East (resolution 233 [1967]), military activities in the area are continuing,

[26] *Ibid.,* pp. 21–25.

Concerned that the continuation of military activities may create an even more menacing situation in the area,

1. *Demands* that the Governments concerned should as a first step cease fire and discontinue all military activities at 2000 hours GMT on 7 June 1967;

2. *Requests* the Secretary-General to keep the Council promptly and currently informed on the situation.

At the same time the Soviet initiative, late though it was, had brought greater urgency to the Security Council's plea for an immediate cease-fire. The "call" to the governments made in Resolution 233 had now become a "demand," and a deadline only a few hours hence was given them for compliance. Finally, this was the first resolution on the conflict to be adopted on the initiative of an individual Council member, and tactically the Soviets could claim that they were meeting their responsibilities toward their Arab friends. Where the resolution was inexplicably weak and where it failed to meet an obvious need was that it contained no reference to United Nations measures to obtain compliance.

The Canadian delegate spotted this lacuna in the resolution and on June 7, indeed immediately preceding the vote on the Soviet text, he introduced a brief draft resolution which requested the President of the Security Council, with the assistance of the Secretary-General, "to take the necessary measures to bring about full and effective compliance with these resolutions." [27] Interestingly, the first speaker to support the Canadian text—and he did so almost immediately—was Ambassador Tarabanov of Bulgaria. "We are awaiting the adoption of another draft resolution submitted by the representative of Canada," he said.[28] But the Council's attention took a turn in another direction. Ambassador El-Kony made a statement on behalf of the United Arab Republic attacking both the United States and the United Kingdom for their alleged assistance to

[27] S/PV.1350, p. 6.   [28] *Ibid.*, pp. 7–10.

Israel. Having done this, he went on to state that the understanding of his delegation of the resolutions on the cease-fire—and by this time there were two—was that Israel should not only cease fire but withdraw behind the armistice demarcation lines. Though both the Soviet and Bulgarian delegates spoke shortly after him, neither of them supported this interpretation of the cease-fire resolutions.

Foreign Minister Abba Eban made his second intervention at the Council immediately after Ambassador El-Kony, and he drew a sharp distinction between the attitude of Israel and that of the Arab states on the call for a cease-fire. "The first Government to pronounce its attitude was that of Israel. I said that we welcomed the cease-fire resolution. . . . We welcome, we favor, we support, we accept the resolution calling for immediate measures to institute a cease-fire." [29] Turning to the attitude of the Arab states, he said that he had listened to every word spoken after the adoption of the first cease-fire resolution by the representatives of the UAR, Syria, and Iraq and he could not find in any of their speeches one single sentence saying that " 'we Syria; we Iraq; we UAR, welcome and accept the cease-fire resolution.' " [30] On the contrary, he referred to broadcasts and press reports from Cairo which indicated that the government of the United Arab Republic had rejected the cease-fire resolution. He pointed out that fortunately there had been one element of progress: the acceptance of the resolution by the government of Jordan. This was all to the good, but he contended that, since the Egyptian command now controlled the armed forces of Jordan, acceptance of a cease-fire by the latter alone could not be effective.

The only member of the Council to attempt to challenge Eban's reading of the situation was Ambassador Milko Tara-

---

[29] *Ibid.*, pp. 16–17. Eban's first intervention had been on the evening of June 6 after the adoption of Resolution 233.

[30] *Ibid.*, p. 17.

banov of Bulgaria, who argued that Israel was the aggressor and that it was for Israel to cease its aggression. If Israel did not do so, the Arabs could not cease their military activities of self-defense.[31]

This was a plausible view and no immediate rejoinder was forthcoming. On the other hand, upon analysis, it was clear that the necessary steps to achieve a cease-fire on any battlefront would include, first, acceptance of the cease-fire by both sides, an indication from each to the other of this acceptance, and then a silencing of the guns. It was to this point precisely that the Canadian draft resolution had been sensibly directed. Ambassador George Ignatieff returned briefly to his proposal, but after a short procedural debate, and somewhat unaccountably, the Council adjourned its session without taking any action on the Canadian proposal, though Ambassador Tarabanov said: "I am in favor of its adoption today if possible."[32] This was a case in which a sensible proposal was sidetracked and then put in cold storage when it would have served to revitalize necessary United Nations machinery in the area, for it could only be UN personnel who could make arrangements along the battlefront to see that acceptances of the Council's cease-fire resolutions were given prompt effect.

Though the original intention had been that on June 7 the Council should adjourn for no more than a half-hour or so, in fact it remained adjourned from 3:50 P.M. that day for exactly twenty-three hours and reconvened on June 8 at 2:50 P.M. The reconvening took place at the instance of both the United States and the Soviet Union, who separately and independently requested a Council session. The United States request was made specifically because, in spite of the calls and demands of the Security Council, fighting was still continuing. The meeting which followed at once showed the persisting basic divergences

---

[31] *Ibid.,* p. 26.   [32] *Ibid.,* p. 38.

of position between the United States and the Soviet Union. Arthur Goldberg stated that it was clearly necessary to bring a stable and just peace to the Middle East for all concerned. He presented a draft resolution which on the cease-fire side incorporated the Canadian proposal, thus making the latter redundant. Then, looking far ahead, the U.S. proposal called for "discussions promptly thereafter among the parties concerned, using such third party or UN assistance as they may wish, looking toward the establishment of viable arrangements encompassing the withdrawal and disengagement of armed personnel, the renunciation of force regardless of its nature, the maintenance of vital international rights and the establishment of a stable and durable peace in the Middle East." [33]

This United States proposal was significant in many ways. First, although it mentioned withdrawal and disengagement of armed personnel, it did not make it clear that the intention would be to obtain withdrawal beyond the armistice demarcation lines. Apparently it would be a matter for negotiation as to where the final lines should be drawn. Second, the United States proposal packed into one operative paragraph a number of separate though, in the last analysis, mutually supportive elements. There were to be direct negotiation, withdrawal and disengagement, renunciation of force, maintenance of international rights, and, finally, a stable and durable peace. The question arises whether it was tactically advisable to make so comprehensive a proposal when the military conflict was still in progress. Certainly all these objectives were commendable and even necessary, but were they not to be brought up after the cessation of warfare rather than at this stage? Did they not demand too strong a stomach of the parties directly involved, particularly of the losers in the conflict? Would it not have been wiser to stress in this draft resolution withdrawal, disengagement,

[33] S/PV.1351, p. 12. For full text of the U.S. proposal, see also Security Council Doc. S/7952 in Appendix 5.

and the renunciation of belligerency, making it clear that consequential steps would have to be worked out in appropriate
international forums? The immediate and informal response of
not only the Arab states but of some others at the UN was
that the draft resolution sought to do too much and was, at the
same time, somewhat imprecise on what should be the very
next step.

The call in the United States proposal for prompt discussions
among the Israelis and the Arabs after the cease-fire was widely
regarded as unimplementable, taking into account the current
factors of Middle East relationships. On the other hand, no
matter how serious a conflict, there is, in the last analysis, no
good substitute for direct negotiations between the parties to a
dispute or situation, by which means fundamental differences can
best be effectively resolved. Mediation may leave abrasive
issues not fully resolved because the triangularity of discussion
leaves room for misunderstanding so far as the disputants themselves are concerned. These considerations notwithstanding, it
might have been wiser for the proposed resolution to call for
negotiations without specifying the processes and methods of
negotiation which would be chosen by the parties. In brief, the
United States resolution was so full and far-reaching that it
overshot its mark.

But the Soviet delegate too had asked for an urgent meeting
of the Council. Nikolai Fedorenko had his own proposals to
make and was not much interested in the U.S. proposal. Indeed,
in his statement, extraordinarily enough, he did not even mention it. The Soviet approach seemed difficult to relate to Council action in which the Soviet Union itself had been a consenting
and even initiating party. Fedorenko stated that "the Arab
countries . . . must at present take defensive action against
Israel . . . as long as Israel refuses to end its military activities
. . . and as long as Israel has not withdrawn its forces from the
conquered areas." [34]

[34] S/PV.1351, pp. 22–25.

As was well known, the question of withdrawal was distinct from that of the cease-fire. This approach of the Soviet Union was confusing and it could have greatly complicated the situation but for two important facts. First, it picked up no wide support; second, immediately before Fedorenko's statement, the Secretary-General announced that he had received a letter dated June 8, 1967, from Ambassador El-Kony in which the latter informed him that his government had "decided to accept the cease-fire call, as it has been prescribed by the resolutions of the Council on 6 and 7 June 1967, on the condition that the other party ceases fire." [35] What the Arab governments had decided to do could obviously not be undone by Ambassador Fedorenko's view of what they should do.

Leading into his proposal, Ambassador Fedorenko made the following statement: "It is essential to condemn the aggressor—this is our principal task." [36] We have had occasion to observe that, in the full delineation of the tasks of the Security Council contained in the Charter, condemnation finds no place. Unfortunately it has become a tendency of certain organs of the United Nations to overlook the Charter injunctions relating to conciliation and the harmonizing of the actions of nations, and to substitute for these approaches that of condemnation. It may, of course, be a matter of opinion as to whether condemnation is a more effective approach toward achieving settlements than the approach of skillful urgings, even demands, and quiet pressures. However, the essential point is that the Charter rejects the former approach in favor of the latter, and whatever individual governments may say or do in their bilateral dealings, in the organs of the United Nations they should adhere to the Charter's approaches. This is particularly so of the great powers that played the initiatory and major role in the formulation of the Charter and of the United Nations itself.

Basing himself on the approach which we have noted,

[35] *Ibid.*, pp. 18–20.   [36] *Ibid.*, pp. 22–25.

Fedorenko introduced a draft resolution which would have had the Council note that Israel (and no other state) was disregarding the cease-fire resolutions and that it alone was continuing military activities and seizing additional territory. The resolution would then contain the following operative paragraphs:

1. *Vigorously condemns* Israel's aggressive activities and its violations of the aforementioned Security Council resolutions, of the United Nations Charter and of United Nations principles;
2. *Demands* that Israel should immediately halt its military activities against neighboring Arab States and should remove all its troops from the territory of those States and withdraw them beyond the armistice lines.[37]

The strongest debating point against Israel was that, after the Council had adopted its first resolution (Resolution 233) on a cease-fire, Israeli forces had continued to advance. Indeed, they had continued to advance after Eban himself had reiterated solemnly in the Council his government's acceptance of the cease-fire. True, he had indicated that the implementation of Israel's acceptance was dependent upon acceptance by the opposing forces. However, it remained a fact that at a certain stage in the military operations Israel had voluntarily acquiesced in the cessation of those operations. It would follow that Israel was able to accept the military situation as it then stood. In this view the Council could reasonably have demanded that Israel should withdraw to the positions it held at the time when it first announced acceptance of the cease-fire. Perhaps another approach would have been to demand withdrawal to the military positions that obtained at 2000 GMT on June 7, the deadline contained in the second resolution (Resolution 234) adopted by the Council. There would have been differences of view as to the exact positions of forces at that time, but pragmatic solutions based on UNTSO's information could have been arrived at.

Apart from the remarks already made, if the United States

[37] *Ibid.*, p. 26. For text of Soviet draft, see also Security Council Doc. S/7951 in Appendix 9.

draft resolution had overshot its mark in one direction, the Soviet text asking for vigorous condemnation had at least equally overshot its mark in another direction. Indeed, since it adopted an approach which was not strictly in consonance with the Charter, it was not really within range at all.

That afternoon (June 8), then, the Council faced three elements in the situation. First, there was the cease-fire, still unachieved *in toto*. But there had been progress, three of the four major participants having signified acceptance: Israel, Jordan, and the United Arab Republic. On the other hand, the Secretary-General on that afternoon had read to the Council a message from the Foreign Minister of Kuwait which contained the following sentences: "I am sorry to inform you that the Government of Kuwait will not observe nor adhere to these resolutions which do not condemn Israeli aggression. The resolutions also ignore the just rights of the Palestinians in their homeland." [38] This reply from Kuwait was not of great significance in the context of the actual facts of the situation. Kuwaiti soldiers were probably in Jordan, but they had not, according to any reports available to the Council, been very much in evidence in the fighting. Perhaps it was because of this practical factor that the Council seemed to pay no attention to the reply of the Foreign Minister of Kuwait. That reply, however, was not only a defiance of the Security Council, but, more seriously, it was a direct violation of Article 25 of the Charter. At some stage the Council should return to a consideration of this Kuwaiti communication. It is detrimental to the interests of the Organization and to the effort of the international community to advance toward international order and amity within the framework of the United Nations Charter, for a Member State to disregard its Charter obligations. Clearly the matter should not be allowed to rest there.

The other two elements in the situation were the two sets of

[38] S/PV.1351, p. 6.

widely diverging proposals presented by the United States and
the Soviet Union. Unless a considerable degree of flexibility
developed in the approaches of these two most important members, the Council would find it difficult to make further progress
in its work. Without modifying their basic positions, the United
States and the Soviets might pick out individual elements from
their proposals and make them the basis of less comprehensive
proposals to the Security Council. Both sets of proposals were
too drastic for the existing circumstances. They had brought the
Council to a crossroads but they did not render completely impossible the less spectacular path of compromise.

Sometimes the timing of Security Council interventions is
disastrous. At other times an intervention may more than rise to
the occasion. After the U.S. and Soviet proposals, the Council
heard a statement by Lord Caradon which happily fell within
the latter category. First, he regretted the sidetracking of the
reasonable draft resolution which Canada had brought to the
table on the preceding day. As we have noted, by being engulfed
in the unattainable prescriptions of the United States draft proposal, the sensible, modest step proposed by Canada had, in
fact, been missed, at least for the present.

Caradon then lamented the delay which had afflicted the
Security Council's moves. "Had there not been delay last month,
delay in endorsing the Secretary-General's appeal, delay which
we strenuously opposed from the first, we might have been able
to avert and prevent the war altogether." [39] Sensibly, he expressed the strong hope that the Council would not sink back to
its lax attitude in May when some members refused to take the
situation seriously. "No one should doubt the urgency of the
work ahead of us, work which will urgently occupy us for
long to come."

Broken down, this meant that the Council should devise some
steps leading in the direction of a final solution but not getting

[39] *Ibid.,* p. 31.

there in one or two leaps. Though he did not say so, part of his statement was, to say the least, a dissociation of his view from the kind of wide-ranging texts which had been introduced by the super powers, one of them being a close ally and friend.

Third, Caradon revealed a most important element in the negotiations of the past week. He stated: "We were ready to make provision in a first resolution not only for a cease-fire, but also for disengagement and withdrawal." [40] This revelation indicated that rigidities had obstructed a much more substantial first step than the Council in fact took in Resolutions 233 and 234. Those rigidities, as became known and as we have indicated, were related to the nature of withdrawal and disengagement. Precisely they raised the questions as to whether Israel and the UAR troops should again be massed along their common frontier and whether UAR troops should point their guns at the narrow channel of navigation in the Strait of Tiran. The only sensible course, in the interests of peace, would have been to insist that the forces of the two sides should not stand facing each other along the border. Indeed, as we have already observed,[41] the UAR by its acceptance of Resolution 1000 (ES-I) had undertaken not to introduce military equipment into the Sinai region. Israel should have been made to act in the same spirit, as, indeed, it was bound to do in terms of the Armistice Agreement. The withdrawal of UAR forces from Sharm el Sheikh would not have meant the renunciation of sovereignty— no sovereign power keeps its forces on every square inch or mile or even every 100 square miles of its territory. Such a withdrawal would have meant simply an indication of a statesman-like choice in favor of peaceful negotiation as opposed to a less well considered decision in favor of conflict. Lord Caradon pointed out that on June 5 there was a chance of getting disengagement and withdrawal on terms which were not only in consonance with the Charter and the bounden duty of the Se-

[40] *Ibid.*   [41] Page 18 *supra.*

curity Council but in the best interest of the parties themselves
and in conformity with strict observance of the Armistice Agreement. Taking into account these factors, he said that the Council should give urgent consideration to "ways and means to put
the demand [for a cease-fire] into effect and of how we could
go on to the next stage of disengagement." [42] Again he was
thinking in terms of small practical steps.

The fourth point in the British statement called attention
to the parties to the conflict. "It must be said too that the
parties to the conflict have fallen far short of readiness to respect
and employ international authority." [43] This was a pregnant
sentence and yet it was an understatement. As we have observed,
from the beginning the parties in their insistence either on their
rights as belligerents or on their right to use counterforce were
in fact disregarding their UN Charter obligations and were making a mockery of the UN machinery carefully developed in
1949 and again in 1956 to help *them* toward the maintenance of
peace in their own area of the world. Lord Caradon, who was
perfectly right in drawing attention to this matter, went on to
state that "it is on the ground, in the deserts, in the hills and the
villages and cities of the Near East that action is required." [44]

Caradon's final substantive point was a fair and humane sum-
ming-up of the tasks ahead:

What are those tasks? They are to stop the fighting, and we pray
that the fighting may very soon be stopped; to ensure and secure
disengagement; to bring relief and succor to the wounded and the
homeless; and then to move to the greater tasks of conciliation and
the establishment of order and justice.[45]

It is permissible to interpret the reference to "disengagement"
as one to "disengagement and withdrawal," since Caradon had
in the same statement already spoken of the willingness of his
delegation to attain these objectives. Lord Caradon's last plea
was directed especially to the permanent members of the Coun-

[42] S/PV.1351, p. 32.   [43] *Ibid.*, pp. 33–35.   [44] *Ibid.*   [45] *Ibid.*

cil, as well as to his other colleagues. It was a call for abandoning old prejudices in trying to reach sensible solutions.

Perhaps it is unfortunate that for speeches such as this the Council, in situations of urgency, waives consecutive interpretation. It is unfortunate because the members of the Council should have had some time to ponder over the highly constructive and reasonable remarks which the representative of the United Kingdom had made. However, procedures are not so easily adjustable and the Council next listened to Foreign Minister Eban, who with his own eloquently prepared text before him did not even mention Caradon's statement. He was not, at this stage, oriented to the strategy of pacification. His competently performed purpose was to deliver before the Council a chapter in the contention between the Israelis and the Arabs.

The only Council members to speak thereafter that afternoon were those of the United States, the USSR, and Bulgaria. As might have been expected, Bulgaria found the U.S. draft resolution unacceptable and in particular complained that its main operative paragraph calling for negotiations would have left the Israelis sitting on Arab territory for an unspecified and possibly endless period. Ambassador Goldberg rebutted this view but at the same time pointed out that the United States draft "asks them [the parties] to get together to resolve those problems," [46] thus making it clear that the extent and the nature of withdrawal and other problems were to be worked out by the parties themselves. The Council, in this view, was not to take a position on territorial problems. Clearly this was not a view which would be universally acceptable.

Ambassador Fedorenko of the USSR continued to ignore the United States text—as indeed had Lord Caradon. This ignoring of a text is an interesting diplomatic device. It means different things at different times. In the case of the United Kingdom, it

[46] *Ibid.*, p. 66.

indicated no great enthusiasm for the United States proposal. In the case of the Soviet Union, it would be fair to suggest that Fedorenko's silence meant that he was not willing to foreclose the possibility of negotiation with his U.S. colleague on the formulation of a mutually acceptable text. The UN position, then, when the Council rose for the day in the late afternoon of June 8, was one of clear divergences of position, but not of deadlock. The fact that so close an ally of the United States as the United Kingdom had not associated itself with the U.S. text, and the further fact that none of the other Western states had spoken in its support, would undoubtedly be taken into account by the United States and would stimulate the possibilities of movement toward compromise formulations.

The night of June 8–9 was to be a restless one for the President of the Council. At 1 A.M. he was informed of a cable from the Syrian Foreign Minister to the effect that Syria had decided to accept the two cease-fire resolutions of the Council, provided that "the other party" agreed upon a cease-fire.[47] At 5:30 in the morning he received a communication from Israel informing him of the shelling of sixteen Israeli villages along the northern frontier with Syria.[48] When the Council met shortly after noon on June 9, the situation it faced was one of severe conflict between Israel and Syria, borne out by a report from UNTSO officers which the Secretary-General made known to the Council.

Ambassador Tabor had used the morning in contacting his colleagues and efficiently had obtained their agreement to a resolution directed toward the situation between Israel and Syria. In his capacity as President, he presented the draft of this resolution shortly after the Secretary-General had reported on the situation. The text of the resolution, which was adopted immediately and unanimously, is as follows:

[47] S/PV.1352, p. 6.　　　[48] *Ibid.*

The Security Council,

Recalling its resolutions 233 and 234,

Noting that the Governments of Israel and Syria have announced their mutual acceptance of the Council's demand for a cease-fire,

Noting the statements made by the representatives of Syria and Israel,

1. *Confirms* its previous resolutions about immediate cease-fire and cessation of military action;

2. *Demands* that hostilities should cease forthwith;

3. *Requests* the Secretary-General to make immediate contacts with the Governments of Israel and Syria to arrange immediate compliance with the above-mentioned resolutions, and to report to the Security Council not later than two hours from now.[49]

There were some new elements in the latest resolution adopted by the Council. First, it noted the mutual acceptance by Israel and Syria of its demand for a cease-fire. In other words, by implication it accepted the view that there was an inherent mutuality in the process of achieving a cease-fire. The second new point was that the Secretary-General was to arrange compliance with the cease-fire resolutions instead of simply reporting on the situation as had been the previous arrangement. Third, by immediate compliance the Council apparently meant what it said: the Secretary-General was to report on compliance within a mere two hours of the adoption of the resolution. It is noteworthy that he was able substantially to comply with this demand during the course of the afternoon. By 4 P.M. the Secretary-General reported that both Syria and Israel were ready to stop immediately their military operations.[50]

Finally, it was significant that, though divergences of view had been crystallized in highly differing draft proposals, all the members of the Council were still able to agree on short-term measures. Immediately after the adoption of the resolution Ambassador Goldberg made a statement for the United States

---

[49] Security Council Resolution 235 (1967), June 9, 1967.
[50] S/PV.1352, pp. 86–87.

which, while not saying so in direct terms, seemed to reflect some of the considerations to which Lord Caradon had drawn attention in his valuable intervention of June 8:

We are not doing credit to the United Nations by the manner in which we have been proceeding. . . . If we go back . . . and consider what happened in this situation, we shall see that there has been a lack of ability to concert our actions here so that conflict may be avoided . . . to stop the fighting so that there can be a sorting-out of the problems that develop whenever fighting takes place.

Goldberg went on to say:

My Government is willing to concert its actions with every member of this Council so that we can bring the fighting to an end, so that we can start consideration of all that we need to consider, so that we can make a major contribution towards the restoration of peace in the area.[51]

These remarks implied a certain degree of acceptance of the gradualness that had been the theme of Lord Caradon's statement. Furthermore, the emphasis on concerting of actions—and it was so strongly emphasized that it could not possibly be missed—was another way of saying that the United States was willing to seek mutual accommodations of its own point of view and those of other members of the Council. This process would clearly have involved some departure from the formulations already made by the United States. Here, then, was a constructive statement which had in its tones and overtones much for the Council carefully to consider.

Again it was unfortunate that the Council had no time to digest these remarks. Without the pause afforded by consecutive interpretation, it went on to hear a statement by Ambassador Fedorenko the main points of which were directed toward condemnation of Israel and general criticism of United States policy. As regards Israel he said, "The aggression of Israel must be severely punished, and we have not the slightest doubt that this

[51] *Ibid.*, p. 27.

will be done." [52] In this statement Nikolai Fedorenko was undoubtedly expressing the view of his government, but in doing so he was again adopting the negotiating tactic of going far ahead of the immediate requirements of the situation. This was an approach entirely different from the practical approach advocated by Lord Caradon on June 8. It is understandable that a government may have strong views about the actions of another state. It is even conceivable that a government might believe that some retributive law is at work which will certainly punish the other state concerned. But, again, this does not appear to be the method which has been enshrined in the Charter by the representatives of the Soviet Union themselves at the Bretton Woods Conference and the United Nations Conference on International Organization at San Francisco. At the United Nations, as in any other organization or club, it is necessary to work on the basis of certain accepted norms in regard to both procedures and objectives. The United Nations is fortunate in that these norms were drafted by a large number of states and obtained their common adherence. This being so, it is necessary that in the day-to-day work of the Organization, and more particularly when crises arise, the founding powers in particular should conform to the accepted norms. This is not to suggest that those norms are unalterable. They certainly may be modified if consensus can be reached for change. This is inevitably a gradual process and one that does not drastically alter well-considered foundations. It is not consistent with this process for one state, no matter how powerful and sincerely motivated, to demand action which would constitute drastic alteration of the accepted and well-founded norms. To do so merely arrests the process of joint action in the United Nations, action which, it must always be remembered, can only be concerted.

The more tangible point raised by Fedorenko was that of

[52] *Ibid.*, p. 41.

withdrawal. He demanded that Israel "must also immediately and unconditionally withdraw its troops from their [the Arab states] territories. . . . We cannot allow the forces of aggression to remain on the territory seized by them. This situation brooks of no delay." [53] The Soviet pressure for withdrawal was mounting.

On the same afternoon the Indian representative made a series of proposals; among them were two practical ideas which seemed to fit the needs of the situation. The first was "to reactivate and strengthen United Nations machinery in the area to enforce the cease-fire and secure withdrawal on the lines proposed by the Secretary-General in his report of 26 May." [54] The other was that the Council might consider "whether the Secretary-General should not . . . depute a personal representative to the area to help in reducing tension and restoring peaceful conditions." There were two other points in the Indian proposals: one was that the Council should call for the withdrawal of armed forces, while the second was that after the withdrawal the Council "should consider earnestly the steps to be taken to stabilize peace in the area." [55] Thus, in addition to two useful practical suggestions the Indian approach sought to take in the substance of both the Soviet and the United States positions. In attempting so much, though it did foresee all this in stages, it might be said that the Indian proposal also was cast too widely.

By now there was no lack of proposals before the Council. What it needed was a clearer sense of direction. To some extent that continued to be provided by the fact that all fighting had not yet ceased, but an end to hostilities was now in the offing and it was thus becoming increasingly important that a new effort be concerted by the members of the Council to find a common approach to the next salutary step in solving the complex Middle East problem.

[53] *Ibid.*   [54] *Ibid.,* p. 51.   [55] *Ibid.*

CHAPTER V

A Firm Cease-Fire

HAVING GIVEN the Secretary-General two hours in which to arrange a firm cease-fire between Israel and Syria (Resolution 235), the Security Council took steps to attest the implementation of its instructions. Adjourning its 1352d meeting at 4:30 P.M., it reconvened on the same day (June 9) at 7:15 P.M. The Secretary-General was able to report that at 5:30 P.M. the Syrian representative had informed him in writing that orders had been issued to the Syrian armed forces to stop military operations forthwith, and at 6:05 he was informed by Ambassador Gideon Rafael of Israel that corresponding orders had been issued to the Israeli armed forces. However, the message from the Syrian permanent representative and another one at 6:50 P.M., together with a message received at 7:05 P.M. from the Syrian Minister of Foreign Affairs, all complained of new attacks by Israel.[1] Ambassador Rafael countered by confirming the issue of orders to the Israeli armed forces for the cessation of hostilities and charging that three Israeli villages were being heavily bombarded by Syrian artillery. To these countercharges of continuing aggression Ambassador El-Kony of the United Arab Republic contributed the information that "only a few hours ago, and during the meeting of the Security Council, many parts of the United Arab Republic, notably Cairo, came under heavy bombing."[2] This charge was described by Ambassador Rafael as a "malicious fabrication." "I categorically deny it. The spreading of irre-

[1] S/PV.1353, pp. 12-15.   [2] *Ibid.*, p. 16.

sponsible and false charges of this kind only aggravates the already tense situation in the Middle East." [3]

It now appeared that though the cease-fire had been accepted the fighting was still spreading on the Israeli-Syrian front. This prompted Fedorenko's fourth intervention of the evening's meeting and his most important one. Repeating charges of U.S. instigation, he again asked for condemnation of Israel's refusal to comply with the Council's decisions, and demanded, for the first time, that Israel be warned "that the Security Council will be compelled to use the powers which are invested in it by the Charter of the United Nations to deal with such situations." [4] Immediately thereafter, and presumably with intent to indicate that there were other measures which could be taken to compel Israel's compliance, Fedorenko read into the record the communication issued by the seven Eastern European governments of Bulgaria, Czechoslovakia, Hungary, East Germany, Poland, the USSR, and Yugoslavia on that very day (June 10, Moscow time). This communiqué stated that "the Socialist countries declare that they fully and completely make common cause with their [the Arab states'] just struggle and will render them assistance in order to repel the aggression and defend their national independence and territorial integrity. . . . If the Security Council does not take the proper measures, great responsibility will rest on those States which fail to fulfill their duties as members of the Security Council." [5]

There are four points to note about this communiqué: first, it raised the level of adherence to the Arab cause from general support to assistance in repelling aggression. The word "assistance" was not defined but implied was "effective" assistance; about this time some of the Communist countries started to hint privately that volunteers from certain states might, after all, go to the assistance of the Arab states. This was a far cry from earlier private expressions of Eastern European diplomats that it

[3] *Ibid.*, p. 18.   [4] *Ibid.*, p. 27.   [5] *Ibid.*, p. 31.

was out of the question for any of their forces to go to the Middle East to fight against Israel, and it still seemed a little far-fetched. Second, and as a delimitation of the purposes for which assistance would be given, it was made clear that the interest of the Communist countries was to repel aggression and to defend national independence and territorial integrity. This delimitation meant that the Communist countries were not going to assist the more extremist Arab opinion. There would be no question of destroying Israel or even of cutting it down to a smaller size than before the hostilities began. Third, there was a vague threat that the Communist states realized that their new position, taken together with the lack of "proper measures" by the Security Council, could lead to widespread conflict. Hence the phrase in the communiqué about the "great responsibility" which would rest on the other members of the Council. Fourth, and most important, the communiqué was meant to give the leaders of Syria and the UAR a boost in the Arab world: they had powerful and trusty friends, and therefore the leaders should not be lightly exchanged for others. In this respect the communiqué was a move to uphold the Soviet position in the region.

Ambassador Georges Tomeh of Syria gave the debate an even greater flavor of urgency by asserting that the real purpose of Israel's massive attack on Syria was to overthrow the Syrian government. He insisted that Damascus had been bombed. These charges were denied categorically by Ambassador Rafael, but the tension in the Council was now at a new height and its capacity to contribute to the maintenance of international peace and security became temporarily frozen.

To break out of this impasse, Arthur Goldberg offered some suggestions. Basing himself on the position of his government that it was "of the gravest importance that the Security Council's resolutions shall be complied with in letter and spirit by Israel and the Arab countries involved," [6] he proposed an impartial

6 *Ibid.*, p. 42.

investigation by the Secretary-General of allegations regarding violations of the cease-fire. He then called for adequate United Nations machinery to implement the cease-fire resolutions.[7] These proposals opened the door to calmer consideration of the situation. Ambassador Tomeh stated that the Syrian authorities were "ready to facilitate any investigation to be carried out in order to give the Security Council the facts by which it can judge the situation." [8] Ambassador Rafael replied: "I find myself in singular agreement with the representative of Syria in stating that Israel will facilitate the investigation which the Secretary-General may wish to institute to find out the facts." [9] When, a few minutes later, Ambassador Tomeh requested the Secretary-General to contact United Nations personnel on the spot and to make a report, Ambassador Rafael said, "I second the motion made by the Syrian representative." [10] Here, then, common ground was emerging, though of course without any credit being given to Ambassador Goldberg or to Ambassador Parthasarathi, who had made proposals which facilitated this new development.

The Secretary-General responded by urging that Israel and the Arab states take effective steps to ensure full cooperation with the United Nations observers, including the returning to UNTSO of Government House, Jerusalem, without which there were no UN wireless communication facilities for contacting the observers. He also stressed the need for freedom of movement for the observers.[11] Ambassador Fedorenko broadly supported the Secretary-General and specifically supported the Syrian request for investigation. It then fell to Lord Caradon to give his diplomatic and persuasive assistance to the effort to formulate the proposals toward which the Council was groping. Attempting to find a consensus (and therefore not mentioning

---

[7] *Ibid.*, p. 47; this second proposal was in line with one made earlier in the day by the representative of India. See page 76 *supra*.

[8] *Ibid.*, p. 82.   [9] *Ibid.*   [10] *Ibid.*, p. 86.   [11] *Ibid.*, pp. 87–90.

those states in regard to whose position there was no doubt), elegantly he said: "The idea came from the representative of the Soviet Union, the enthusiasm from the representative of the United Kingdom, and the precision from the representative of France." [12] Actually it was Caradon himself who had given the main push. He strongly backed the Secretary-General's recommendations and asked the Council to stand ready to receive the report which the Secretary-General would make to the President. The implication was that until then the Council members and the Arabs and Israelis should hold their charges and counter-charges, which were not assisting the situation. This enabled Ambassador Tabor, the President, to ask the Council to agree to the following: "that we request the parties concerned to extend all possible cooperation to the United Nations observers in the discharge of their responsibilities; that we request the Government of Israel to restore the use of the Government House in Jerusalem to General Odd Bull and to reestablish freedom of movement for United Nations observers in the area; and that we then decide to adjourn." [13] The Council agreed to this formulation and adjourned after a long day's work at about 11 P.M., having taken a not very spectacular but nevertheless a useful step forward.

This phase of the Council's work clearly illustrated a phenomenon which may sometimes be seen in international affairs, and even in situations of extreme tension, when the crucial factor becomes the ability and capacities of an individual diplomat to resolve issues on his own initiative. Lord Caradon could not have had any last-minute clear-cut instructions to help the Council resolve the immediate clash between the positions of the USSR and Syria on the one hand and that of Israel on the other. But by associating himself with some aspects of Fedorenko's position and by calling in the assistance of the French—who indeed had said very little—he was able to close the gap be-

[12] *Ibid.*, p. 101.   [13] *Ibid.*, pp. 102–3.

tween West and East by finding a slender piece of middle ground. The implications of what had been achieved that night on June 9 were to become clearer later, and, as we shall see, they proved to be very considerable.

It was hoped that the Secretary-General might be able to get some information by 10:30 A.M. on June 10, but he regarded this as a somewhat too optimistic view, and consequently the Council decided to allow U Thant some flexibility in this regard and did not fix the hour at which it would reassemble.

However, other events were to supervene. At 2 A.M. on June 10 the Prime Minister of Syria instructed his representatives to ask for an emergency meeting on the ground that Israel had occupied the town of Kuneitra and was pressing forward toward Damascus. The Council members returned to their seats at 4:30 in the morning on June 10. Already the Secretary-General had received some information from the UN observers and the latest flash was that an air raid had taken place on the Damascus airport area. He could not confirm whether Kuneitra was in Israeli hands but reported warfare in that area.[14] Fedorenko now held that it was quite clear that Israeli forces were already some way into Syrian territory, were bombing the capital, and were continuing to fight. He claimed that Ambassador Rafael had sat "five hours among us and openly misled the Council and tried to divert the attention of the Security Council and play for time, for the annexationist purposes of the Israeli hordes." [15] This, then, was the latest Soviet stance: a sense of outrage, continued demands for condemnation of Israel, and a pillorying of the country and its representatives for their aggression: "The criminal bandit activity against Syria must be condemned immediately and unreservedly." [16] The Arabs were now pressing hard for Council action, asserting the capture of Kuneitra by Israeli forces. But Arthur Goldberg contended that the Council was still awaiting a report on the essential point which had brought

14 S/PV.1354, pp. 6–7.   15 *Ibid.*, p. 17.   16 *Ibid.*, p. 21.

them into session that morning. "Let us have General Bull's representative go to Kuneitra and report to this Council. Is Kuneitra in the possession of the Syrian forces or is it in the possession of the Israeli forces? When we get that information the Council will know what to do." [17]

Twenty minutes later the Secretary-General read to the Council a further report from General Bull: "Most immediate from Bull. Report received from Chairman of Israeli-Syrian Mixed Armistice Commission. Damascus at 0923 hours GMT. Air attack on Damascus going on." [18] Fedorenko triumphantly asked Arthur Goldberg "whether he could find it possible to express his views now on what we have just heard from the Secretary-General." [19] His calmness unshaken, Goldberg replied:

It is not entirely clear to me whether this report is based on first-hand observation or not, but I say specifically that a bombing if it is going on is in violation of the orders. . . . Any firing from gun emplacements into Israeli villages would be in violation of the cease-fire order and likewise could not be condoned. . . . We need, it is perfectly obvious, a comprehensive report as to what is going on in the entire area.[20]

Ambassador Rafael of Israel said he had contacted his government again and categorically denied that any Israeli aircraft had attacked Damascus or the airport or the vicinity of Damascus at any time. "My Government has launched a strong protest against that sort of reporting which has been transmitted by the Chairman of the Israeli-Syrian Mixed Armistice Commission." [21] He added that his government was in touch with General Bull and had requested him "urgently to dispatch observers to the frontier line to verify the situation so that reliable reports can be transmitted to the Security Council." [22] Nevertheless, again the Secretary-General reported that UNTSO observers stated that "Damascus has been bombed by Israel air force." [23]

[17] *Ibid.*, p. 27.   [18] *Ibid.*, p. 36.   [19] *Ibid.*, pp. 37–40.
[20] *Ibid.*, pp. 41–42.   [21] *Ibid.*, p. 46.   [22] *Ibid.*, p. 51.
[23] *Ibid.*, pp. 52–55.

The striking fact in the gray early hours of the morning of June 10 was the alertness with which the Council was now following developments in the Middle East almost from minute to minute. Before the session rose at 7 A.M. for a brief break, the Secretary-General read out another cable from General Bull which transmitted a report from Mr. Sasson of the Israeli Foreign Office: "There have been and are Israeli aircraft in the vicinity of Damascus; they are there as protective cover for the Israeli forces in the area." [24] This statement in itself indicated that Israeli forces had in fact advanced to the vicinity of Damascus. The report from General Bull also stated that the Tiberias Control Center had seen clouds of smoke "rising from side of hill in Israel," which indicated the shelling of Israeli villages by Syria.

The capacity of UNTSO, even with scant facilities for observation, to transmit information to the Security Council was of immense value at this juncture. It also indicated how dependent the Security Council was on reports from the area of conflict. The members of the Council from Ambassador Goldberg to Ambassador Fedorenko referred to the reports and asked the Secretary-General for more of them, thus reinforcing the move initiated by India, the United Kingdom, and others for the strengthening of UN machinery in the area. Already in the total UN effort, the Council was but the visible part of the iceberg, the submerged part being persistent UN activity in the field. If it were true that Israel was trying to overthrow the Syrian government, then UN observer activity on the spot, by exposing the situation, would be a counteracting factor. If it were not true that Israel was advancing rapidly in Syria, then, too, UN observers would soon confirm the facts. Similarly, they would deal with the countercharge of Syrian shelling of Israeli territory. What had so far emerged was that Israeli forces were advancing in Syria and that there was also some Syrian shelling

24 *Ibid.,* pp. 63–65.

of Israeli territory. In this military activity by both sides, one was gaining more successes than the other. The Council adjourned briefly to enable its members informally to discuss this very situation.

It reassembled after a brief hour of respite at 8:10 P.M. on June 10. By now the injunction of Resolution 235 of June 9 asking the Secretary-General to arrange compliance with the cease-fire orders within two hours, i.e., by about 4 P.M. on June 9, was, in strictly literal terms, a thing of the past. However, it had stimulated UN activity on the spot. It had furnished General Bull and his observers with the authority to present the governments concerned with demands in connection with UN observation. But it was clear that the Security Council would have to act more effectively in order to secure even the first step toward pacification—a real cease-fire.

The Secretary-General opened the resumed proceedings by reading another message from the Chairman of the Israeli-Syrian Mixed Armistice Commission: "Confirming attack at 7:35 GMT in area—repeat area—of Damascus airport. A second air attack south of Damascus at 8:55 GMT. And a further attack at 9:19 GMT north of Damascus. All strikes appeared to be outside the city of Damascus and based on UNTSO observation." [25]

Ambassador Fedorenko immediately intervened in indignation: "The circle is complete. The perpetration of the crime is proved. . . . We are compelled to note the inexplicable position adopted by . . . especially the representative of the United States." [26]

The United States representative did not rise to this bait. It again fell to Caradon of the United Kingdom to try to point the way to concerted Council action. He described the information given by the Secretary-General as "most important and very serious." [27] His proposal was that the Council should in the

[25] S/PV.1355, pp. 3–5.   [26] *Ibid.*, p. 6.   [27] *Ibid.*, p. 27.

strongest terms "condemn any and every breach of the cease-fire, without exception." [28] He wanted the Council to authorize the Secretary-General immediately to communicate both to Israel and to Syria the insistence of the Council "on full and immediate compliance with the cease-fire orders; and then the insistence of this Council on freedom of movement and communication for all United Nations staff; and certainly also the insistence of this Council on the return to the UNTSO of the Headquarters from which General Bull is not able at present to operate." [29]

Thus, once more, Caradon had sought to give perspective and direction to the Council; his timing, too, was right, for the exposure of the facts of the situation in the area concerned was compelling movement in the direction that Caradon demanded. Immediately after this statement, the Secretary-General reported that General Bull had been asked to meet General Moshe Dayan, the Israeli Defense Minister, to make proper arrangements for the cease-fire and to determine the time at which it would go into effect.[30]

In spite of continuing recriminations between Israeli and Arab representatives, Lord Caradon's move stimulated an intervention by Ambassador George Ignatieff of Canada. He repeated the proposal already made by others for an immediate strengthening of UNTSO and again urged, as had the Indian representative on June 9, the dispatch by the Secretary-General of a special representative to the area. In this further crystallization of the movement forward, Ambassador Ignatieff did not name the representatives who had previously made these proposals. His first proposal had already been put to the Council by the representatives of India and the United States, while the second proposal had also been made by the Indian representative. In not naming his colleagues Ambassador Ignatieff was not ignoring authorship of the proposals; he was deliberately refraining from mentioning

[28] *Ibid.*   [29] *Ibid.*, pp. 28–30.   [30] *Ibid.*, p. 31.

the originators because he was seeking not their support but the support of the Soviet Union, and it would not have helped to emphasize American support for these proposals.

In the course of the same Council session Ambassador Rafael reported on the meeting between Generals Dayan and Bull. The Israeli Defense Minister had told General Bull that Israel would accept any proposal made by Bull for implementing and supervising the cease-fire. General Dayan had said that the cease-fire could enter into force at any hour decided upon by General Bull.[31] There was also a promise of assistance in transportation, communications, and equipment but there was no word on the return of the Government House in Jerusalem. Shortly thereafter the Secretary-General reported from General Bull that Syria was being told that Israel was prepared to cooperate on a cease-fire provided Syria would do the same and that Bull had proposed a cease-fire effective at 1630 hours GMT on June 10.[32] On this note the Security Council was able to adjourn so as to allow time for another report to come from the Secretary-General on the implementation of the cease-fire.

However, the Soviet Union demanded a meeting again that evening. The Council reassembled at about 9 P.M. on June 10 and Ambassador Fedorenko stated that he had been obliged to ask for a meeting because Damascus was being bombed again and there was fighting in the region of Kuneitra. The remedy urged was immediate Council condemnation of Israel. This, then, was a move away from the more constructive steps which had been developing that morning mainly as a result of the urging of India, the United States, the United Kingdom, and Canada.

There was still one way in which the Council could return to those steps, namely, to call for another report from the Secretary-General. The President wisely took this course. U Thant made a report to which he attached a caveat, pointing out that it was fragmentary and therefore would have to be construed with

[31] *Ibid.*, p. 76.   [32] *Ibid.*, p. 92.

caution. His report indicated that there had been some bombing seven to ten kilometers south of Damascus, about fifteen minutes after the agreed cease-fire time of 1630 hours. It also indicated that an hour and a half after the agreed cease-fire time there was continued artillery fire from Syria on positions in Israel.[33] "Both Israeli and Syrian authorities" confirmed Kuneitra's occupation by Israeli forces. It had proved to be impossible for UNTSO observers to reach Kuneitra because another town en route (Sasa) had been invested by Israeli forces. Really, then, although the Israeli-Syrian cease-fire had been accepted almost two days previously, fighting was still going on, but it was now sporadic rather than along the whole frontier.

The issue now was: Should the Council condemn or take steps further to strengthen the cease-fire? The Soviet Union and Ambassador Tarabanov asked for condemnation, with Tarabanov adding that "the occupation troops [must] be withdrawn from the territory they have usurped, and this immediately." [34] Here was an indication that the Communist states would add to condemnation the demand for full-scale withdrawal. It should be noted that this proposal also had been made by Ambassador Parthasarathi of India on June 9, but again the Communist states were not attributing it to him. They were determined to play the role of the main supporters of the Arab cause and to appear in the position of initiators of demands against Israel. Ambassador Goldberg countered that the immediate question before the Council was still a cease-fire order, and he looked forward to an early report from the Secretary-General that the cease-fire was fully in effect.[35] Goldberg proceeded to introduce a draft resolution [36] embodying some of the points which had been suggested to the Council by other delegates. First, he incorporated Lord Caradon's recommendation that the Council should condemn any and all violations of the cease-fire; second, he asked the

[33] S/PV.1356, p. 18.   [34] *Ibid.*, pp. 38–40.   [35] *Ibid.*, pp. 43–45.
[36] *Ibid.*, p. 46. See Appendix 7.

Secretary-General to make a full investigation of reports of such violations. This was a refinement of proposals which had been made by India and others. Unfortunately the new draft resolution did not give the Secretary-General any additional staff or demand cooperation by the parties with UNTSO. In these respects it fell short of the requirements of the situation.

However, soon afterward Ambassador Roger Seydoux of France asked the Secretary-General whether General Bull had adequate staff. The Secretary-General replied that he would immediately inquire from General Bull, but he thought that the efficiency and promptness in reporting depended primarily on freedom of movement and of adequate security measures for the observers.[37] In any event the French effort, which a little later took the form of asking for steps to reopen the Kuneitra UNTSO Center, was directed to practical steps, which were precisely the need of the hour.

But Ambassador Fedorenko chose to ignore these practical suggestions and directed a question to the United States, namely, whether Ambassador Goldberg would condemn the bombing of Damascus and other military activities by Israel.[38] To this Ambassador Goldberg replied in two sentences: first, his own draft resolution condemned all violations of the cease-fire; second, he asked Ambassador Fedorenko whether he was prepared to condemn all violations confirmed by the Secretary-General. Ambassador Fedorenko stated that he would reply to his American colleague. However, he spent some fifteen minutes further accusing Israel of aggression and insisting that the United States draft was aiding the Israeli aggressor in legitimizing the occupation of Arab territory, but he did not answer Ambassador Goldberg's question. The latter did not press it. The lack of an answer was itself significant, indicating that the representative of the Soviet Union could not deny that there was military activity in both directions. But in focusing on the occupation of

[37] *Ibid.*, p. 56.   [38] *Ibid.*, p. 61.

Arab territory by Israel he was hoping that the posture of championing the cause of the conquered would gather Council sentiment in favor of the Arabs. The Communist states insisted that a resolution lumping together all violations of the cease-fire was not fair. Ambassador Tarabanov went so far as to say: "It is even a crime to submit a draft resolution of this nature to the Security Council, because it already gives us a yardstick of what the Security Council is going to be called upon to do and of how far the Security Council is to be pushed." [39]

"No Arab breaches of the cease-fire," [40] reported General Bull's cable which U Thant read to the Council. He also gave details of the efforts of UNTSO teams to deploy themselves in the area but said that the move to Kuneitra from Tiberias had "been delayed pending the decision of the Israeli Minister of Defense regarding this move." [41]

On the whole the Secretary-General's report indicated that, though the Security Council had been unable to arrive at a common position, the United Nations observers in the area were on the move even if they were still encountering obstacles. They were contributing tangibly to the cause of peace. This at least was clear, so clear that no member of the Council commented on the Secretary-General's report. Theirs was the silence of approval. At 2:39 A.M. the Council adjourned, hoping that the cease-fire would now end such military activity as had stubbornly continued.

Sunday, June 11, was the fifth day after the first Security Council call had gone out for a cease-fire (Resolution 233), and it was the fourth day after the four main combatant states in the Middle East had signified acceptance of the cease-fire. All the Council's three resolutions had been adopted unanimously and had the stupendous weight of the backing of the United States, the Soviet Union, and thirteen other states. Progressive steps to achieve a full cease-fire had been taken, and yet late on Sunday not all the fighting had ceased.

[39] *Ibid.*, p. 106.   [40] *Ibid.*, p. 107.   [41] *Ibid.*

Late that evening Syria asked for an immediate reconvening of the Council. The members gathered at 10:30 P.M. to listen to the Syrian assertion of the advance of Israel's forces in the area of Rafid toward the headwaters of the Yarmuk River, the largest tributary of the Jordan.

The Secretary-General made a report which did indicate some Israeli movements in the Rafid area, but pointed out that "the key point in connection with the observance of the cease-fire is the question of whether the Israel troops were in Rafid and environs before 1630 hours GMT on 10 June, or whether they had advanced to that sector after the time fixed for the cease-fire to go into effect." [42] The report left this crucial point undetermined, with the result that the ensuing debate consisted of bitter assertions and counterassertions.

To the Syrian allegations Ambassador Rafael of Israel replied by saying that all movements after the cease-fire in the Rafid area had taken place within "the truce lines." He claimed that there was no fighting or firing anywhere along the frontier line and that the cease-fire was being scrupulously observed. He also informed the Council that the Kuneitra Control Center had been reopened with the cooperation of the Israeli authorities and that United Nations observers were functioning from there.[43]

But some delegations chose to widen the issues under consideration. Fedorenko charged the Israelis with defiance of the United Nations and the Security Council: "We hear insults . . . ," he said. "General Moshe Dayan . . . says that the map of the Middle East will be rearranged and that the Israeli State will have new frontiers. Moshe Dayan stated: 'I certainly cannot recall that any problem was ever settled by diplomacy or through the United Nations.' " [44]

Assuming that this was the mood of Israel—and no one, not even the Israeli representative, contested the cynical statement about diplomacy and the United Nations attributed to Dayan—

[42] S/PV.1357, p. 6.   [43] *Ibid.*, p. 17.   [44] *Ibid.*, pp. 22–25.

what was the Soviet remedy for the situation? It was a repetition of the demand to condemn Israel and to take "decisive and immediate measures to ensure the implementation by Israel of the resolutions adopted by the Security Council." [45] Though these were forthright suggestions, they did not amount to a spelling-out of measures such as those envisaged in Chapters VI or VII of the United Nations Charter. Fedorenko rounded out his intervention by referring to the Soviet draft resolution (S/7951) which asked for condemnation of Israel and the withdrawal of its forces.[46] However, he did not demand a vote on his draft, which, judging from the attitudes and statements of Council members, would not have secured the necessary majority.

Lord Caradon again appeared in a constructive role. He invited the Council to focus its attention on the specific complaint by Syria which had brought the members together at a very late hour of the night on Sunday; since Syria wished the Council to deal with this complaint and this alone, the Council could turn its attention to other matters at its next meeting.

As to the Syrian complaint, he said: "If the suggestion was that under cover of the cease-fire and following the cease-fire agreement there had been an advance to Sheikh Meskine and Dara and the Yarmuk, this would be a question which would require immediate and drastic action by the Security Council." [47] This was an appropriate verbalization of the issue before the Council. Syria was the complainant and to a complainant's ears Caradon's approach was both reassuring and conciliatory. Since, however, there was no clear evidence as to whether the complaint was justified, Caradon made a precise, clear, and peaceable suggestion: the Council should insist that there should be no breach whatsoever of the cease-fire and that "if there were any breach, we in the Security Council would take the most serious and grave view of any such breach of any kind, and that we would not tolerate any advance beyond the points which were

[45] *Ibid.*, p. 26.   [46] See Appendix 9.   [47] S/PV.1357, pp. 28–30.

set down in the arrangements, which were made by General Bull on our behalf." [48] He urged that this stand be communicated to General Bull and to the parties concerned.

Caradon's statement had a determining effect on the course of events as the night wore on. Ambassador Goldberg, in substance, repeated Caradon's proposal when he said "that any forward movement of troops beyond positions held at 1630 GMT on June 10 is simply not acceptable, and that if any such movements had been made, the units must be returned to the positions prevailing at that time." [49]

There was also a chorus of agreement with Caradon that Bull and his men were doing a splendid job: France, Canada, India, and Argentina expressed this view. To it France added a demand for the return by Israel of Government House, Jerusalem, to UNTSO, a move supported by Canada and Argentina.

Meanwhile, there were statements again by the representatives of the USSR, Bulgaria, and Mali, who insisted on a more generalized resolution by the Security Council. These statements too had their effect. For when at Lord Caradon's demand the Council recessed briefly, they influenced the outcome of consultations among the members.

The President of the Council, Ambassador Tabor, was again active in driving toward unanimity and at 3 A.M., with the consent of most members of the Council, he was able to introduce a draft resolution. The first operative paragraph condemned any and all violations of the cease-fire. This is what Lord Caradon had suggested two days previously and had repeated during the current session of the Council. The next paragraph requested the Secretary-General to continue his investigations and to report as soon as possible. This formulation was necessary, as some crucial facts had been left unclear in the brief reports from General Bull. The next operative paragraph affirmed that the cease-fire included a prohibition of any forward military move-

[48] *Ibid.*, p. 31.   [49] *Ibid.*, p. 57.

ment and it called for the prompt return to cease-fire positions
of any troops which may have moved beyond them. Finally the
text called for full cooperation with UNTSO. This draft resolution, like the three preceding ones on the cease-fire, was adopted
unanimously and became Resolution 236 of June 12, 1967.[50]
The resolution fell far short of the demands of the Soviet Union
for specific condemnation of Israel and for an immediate call for
withdrawal to the armistice lines. However, it was firm and
clear, in the manner that Lord Caradon had suggested, on strict
observance of the cease-fire. Also, it introduced the concept of
condemnation and in this sense may be regarded as having
moved somewhat in the direction for which the Soviet Union
had been pressing ever since the outbreak of hostilities on June
5. These facts explain the unanimity in the vote.

That unanimity was, however, more grudgingly given than
in the case of the three previous resolutions. On June 6 and 7 it
was clear to all, including the most ardent supporters of the
Arab states, that the immediate necessity was a cease-fire. The
Soviets saw that their massive military aid had not enabled the
Arabs to stem the Israeli tide. There was no alternative to a
cease-fire, even if that involved loss of Arab territory. However,
by June 10 the demand for the next step had been mounting. All
three cease-fire resolutions had referred to the end of hostilities
as a first step, thereby indicating clearly that other steps were
to come. By June 10 the Soviets had decided that it was time for
the next step to be taken.

The resolution of June 12, necessary though it was, did not
constitute a discernibly new step. That explains why, when
the Council reassembled for its 1358th session in the afternoon
of Tuesday, June 13, matters moved to a climax. This turned
out to be, in fact, the longest of the Council's series of sessions
on the 1967 Middle East crisis, and at it both the United States
and Soviet representatives made their longest statements. Since

[50] For text see Appendix 8.

it was the Soviet position which had been least reflected in the resolution of June 12, it was the Soviets who asked for the convening of the 1358th meeting. Ambassador Fedorenko opened the meeting with a statement of some five thousand words that brought into the open a number of the Soviet Union's main concerns. First and foremost, it revealed that the Soviet Union saw Israeli action as an attempt to change "the so-called balance of power in the Near East" to the detriment of "the national liberation movements of the Arab peoples." [51] All this was being done, asserted Fedorenko, to secure advantages for imperialism, "particularly for United States imperialism," and the object also was to weaken "the progressive regimes in the United Arab Republic, Syria and other Arab countries." [52] Here we see a convergence of two primary Soviet motives: an expression of Soviet national interests—the Middle East is a close neighbor of the Soviet Union and what goes on there is of interest to the USSR—and ideological considerations related to the theory of liberation movements. There are regimes in the Middle East which though not Communist have been injecting increasing doses of socialism into Arab society. Moreover these injections have come largely through authoritarian actions unlike the socialistic developments in, say Sweden or India. In other words, they are more in keeping with the Marxist tradition. These two factors of national interest and mutual understanding between certain Arab regimes and the Soviet Union of concepts of the development of society were given primacy by Fedorenko in his delineation of the situation in the area. Together with the favorable references he made to Arab nationalism, these indeed were the basic ideas which he developed.

Coming to his conclusion, Fedorenko stressed that the cessation of hostilities had been but the first step, and he construed Resolution 236 of June 12 as in fact condemning Israel because Israel alone, he argued, had been defying the decisions of the

[51] S/PV.1358, p. 11.   [52] *Ibid.*

Security Council in continuing to pursue its activities.[53] He asked the members of the Council what the consequences would be if international law and the United Nations Charter were brushed aside on a wide scale and conquest was made the basis of territorial expansion. This was an appeal to the generality of United Nations membership, which includes many states with misgivings about their more powerful neighbors. All this background having been developed, Fedorenko introduced a revised text of the Soviet resolution calling for condemnation of Israel and demanding immediate and unconditional withdrawal to the armistice lines.[54] As if to clinch his case, Fedorenko turned to Goldberg and quoted from the latter's statement to the Council on May 24 to the effect that the United States was "firmly committed to the support of the political independence and territorial integrity of all the nations in the area." He asked Goldberg whether that statement was still valid and whether the United States was "prepared to affirm that it is against the territorial claims of Tel Aviv." [55] He went on to ask ancillary questions, such as whether the United States and the other Western delegations would agree to immediate withdrawal and would acknowledge that occupation of Arab soil by Israel was "illegal, criminal, contrary to the United Nations Charter and the elementary principles of contemporary international law." [56]

Finally, Fedorenko asked the President immediately to put the draft resolution of the Soviets to the vote, if possible at that very meeting. In this connection he referred to the heavy burden of responsibility on the members of the Security Council, which, if they failed to discharge by accepting his resolution, would make it "necessary to seek other ways and means to see to it that the United Nations does its duty under the Charter." [57] Thus was concluded Ambassador Fedorenko's detailed and extremely strong speech setting out the Soviet position. Strong though it was, was it persuasive? Was it not so strong that it

[53] *Ibid.*, p. 21.   [54] See Appendix 9.   [55] S/PV.1358, p. 26.
[56] *Ibid.*   [57] *Ibid.*, p. 27.

would harden positions all around and be, in fact, counter-productive? Would it not have the effect of inducing the mood among many other members that they were not going to be pushed around by veiled threats?

Ambassador Goldberg responded with his longest statement during the Middle East crisis. He saw the Soviet draft resolution as a proposal which would take matters back to the confrontation of June 5 immediately before hostilities erupted. "If ever there was a prescription for renewed hostilities, the Soviet draft resolution is that prescription." [58] He said that it was precisely a fourth round in the Arab-Israeli conflict that the Council should concert its efforts to avoid. He refused to accept the view that solutions in the Middle East were impossible. He realized that "agreements between the parties on these profoundly contentious matters will take a long time but the United Nations, speaking through this Council, has an urgent obligation to facilitate them and to help build an atmosphere in which fruitful discussions will be possible." [59] This would require primarily consultation and negotiation among the members of the Council so as to evolve new positions of consensus to put to the parties. Goldberg's approach was different from that of Fedorenko. The latter's long statement had led to the conclusion that the Council must either adopt the Soviet text or new ways would have to be found to see to it that the United Nations did its duty. Fedorenko had held out no hope, and had given no indication, of further efforts within the Council. Not to be ruled out was the likelihood that Fedorenko's tactic was designed to pressure the Council in the direction of his draft resolution while keeping in the background the possibility of flexibility in regard to further Council discussion. We will soon see in which direction the Soviets were leading.

Goldberg described the policy of his delegation as a search to ensure political independence and territorial integrity to all

[58] *Ibid.,* pp. 48–50.   [59] *Ibid.,* p. 52.

the states in the area and an end to acts of force, a humanitarian and equitable solution of the problems of refugees, the development of the resources of the Jordan River and the rights of all nations to innocent passage of the Suez Canal and the Gulf of Aqaba, and, finally, the conversion of the Armistice Agreement of 1949 into a permanent peace.[60] In this statement was contained an answer to some of Fedorenko's queries, particularly those in which he had challenged the United States on the question of the territorial integrity of the Arab states.

Goldberg quoted from the United States draft resolution before the Council (S/7952/Rev.2), drawing attention to the call for prompt discussions after the cease-fire among the parties concerned through the use of such third-party or United Nations assistance as they might wish; this draft resolution looked toward the establishment of viable arrangements encompassing the withdrawal and disengagement of armed personnel, the renunciation of force regardless of its nature, the maintenance of vital international rights, and the establishment of a stable and durable peace in the Middle East.[61] He ended his statement with a plea to pursue these tasks.

We have already noted the comprehensive character of the United States proposal, of its sweep toward what are obviously desirable ultimate objectives. We have seen how this differed from the more practical step-by-step approach of Caradon and some other members of the Council. In repeating the United States proposal Goldberg was in a sense expressing his awareness of the climax to which the Council was now coming: either it must move forward toward peaceful settlement or its effort would be stunted and matters might even be left where they were, including the occupation by Israel of four times as much Arab territory as its area on June 4. The real task of the Council would be whether it could find a *via media* between the comprehensive proposals of the United States on the one hand

[60] *Ibid.*, pp. 43–45.   [61] *Ibid.*, p. 51.

and the sharp, forthright proposals of the Soviet Union, which if accepted would, as Goldberg had pointed out, take matters back to the unsatisfactory position of June 4, 1967.

How did the Security Council respond to this confrontation of irreconcilable positions? Immediately it reacted by silence. It showed no capacity to move into the situation and demand moderation and the approach of limited steps forward. It listened to five long statements by representatives of the Arab states and Israel, each repeating well-known positions. The Israeli representative, Reginald Kidron, rejected the Soviet Union's draft resolution as destructive.[62] El-Kony of the United Arab Republic countered by describing the United States draft enjoining discussion between the parties as an acceptance by the Council of Israeli aggression.[63]

As the six-hour meeting neared its close, Fedorenko demanded again that his draft resolution be immediately voted upon. However, by a vote of ten in favor and three against (Bulgaria, Mali, and the USSR) with two members abstaining (India and Nigeria), the Council decided to adjourn to the next day. Immediately thereafter the Syrian representative, who had not made a statement, was permitted to speak. There were a few other brief speeches and the Council finally adjourned at about 11 P.M., having begun its marathon session at 3 P.M. that day.

The next morning Caradon again took the initiative when the Council reconvened, attempting to place before his colleagues some basic thoughts on the responsibilities of the Security Council. He urged acceptance of the important principle that members of the Council "are not here only to express our national policies and to defend our national interest. . . . we are not here to take sides, to score off one another, to poison relationships, to intensify distrust."[64] Coming from an outsider or from a man with less experience or even from a representative of a smaller state with admittedly narrower responsi-

[62] *Ibid.*, p. 113.   [63] *Ibid.*, p. 162.   [64] S/PV.1360, p. 6.

bilities with respect to the maintenance of international peace
than those given by the Charter to a permanent member of the
Security Council, these ideas might have appeared to be unrealistic. However, with Caradon's ripe experience and his position they had no such ring. They set out a basic tenet which
must underlie Security Council deliberations at all times. He
went on: "We have all accepted very different obligations. We
have tasks much more difficult. We are here to practice tolerance . . . to find common ground . . . to seek just and honor-
able solutions, to establish and keep a peace firmly based on international authority." These *are* the realities of the Security
Council, even though members may lose sight of them and of
the Charter injunctions on which they are based. When achievements are made, it is because these tenets are observed. Caradon
differed from the representative of Mali, who had said that the
Council was achieving nothing and getting nowhere. "On the
contrary, the series of actions we took following the first cease-
fire resolution last Tuesday has been necessary and right and
timely. What is more: it was successful." [65] Moreover, there was
the successful and valuable part being played by General Bull
and his men to bring about and maintain a cease-fire. These were
the achievements to the credit of the Council.

What of the future? Characteristically, Caradon said it was
"essential that we should give our minds to the practical prob-
blem." [66] This problem was how best the Council should work
for disengagement and withdrawal. What should the Council do
to achieve these steps? Caradon supported two recommendations
of the representative of India: the strengthening of United Nations machinery and the appointment of a special representative
of the Secretary-General in the area. To these he added a third:
the Council should consider also the appointment of a mediator
to "undertake discussions with the Governments concerned so

[65] *Ibid.,* p. 11.   [66] *Ibid.,* pp. 13-15.

that an immediate start can be made in setting the foundations for a just and lasting peace." [67] These were the three modest steps that he recommended; modest in relation to the total problem but great steps in that they would demand intensive consultations among the members of the Council before agreement could be reached, and great steps because if agreement on them were reached, it would set the compass in the direction of forward movements which in their turn could gradually affect crucial attitudes and relationships in the Middle East itself. The countries there would still be exercised by anxiety, by considerations relating to their security, dignity, independence, and territorial integrity. All these attitudes would have to be brought into and reflected through the tangible steps which the Council would proceed to devise. None of them could be lost sight of, and there was no reason why they should be if a beginning were made in the manner suggested by Caradon.

Caradon's final point was that it was only by working together that the Council members could achieve their purpose. This would require "a great effort together to give our minds to practical means of overcoming the formidable barriers before us. . . . I trust that we shall never abandon the determination to make the United Nations an effective instrument for that purpose [of establishing order and justice throughout the Middle East]." [68] These were wise and necessary words.

However, the Soviet Union was insistent that a vote be taken on its draft resolution, and the Council members felt bound to state their positions. Argentina said that it could not condemn Israel while the facts were not clear, and in this view it was followed by China, Japan, and Brazil. The Argentine representative added that in order to create conditions for negotiations there must be withdrawal on the one hand and free transit through international waters on the other.[69] Ethiopia and Ni-

---

[67] *Ibid.,* p. 16.   [68] *Ibid.,* p. 17.   [69] *Ibid.,* p. 32.

geria took a midway position, but Mali strongly supported the Soviet draft, being the first of the nine states that had so far spoken to do so.[70]

The French position was clear in principle, but somewhat obscure on specifics. Ambassador Seydoux stated: "On the level of principles we can only support the Soviet draft resolution." [71] But then he asked what one could expect from such an initiative and whether indeed the proposed resolution had any chance of being carried out. Perhaps the basic French point was that "we must strive together to facilitate, when the time comes, conversations that could lead to agreements acceptable to all parties." He announced that it was on this basis that his delegation would finally cast its vote.[72]

Speaking for the United States, Arthur Goldberg did not comment on the Soviet draft resolution. It was unnecessary to do so. The opposition of the United States to the Soviet approach had come out clearly through several days of intensive debate. Throughout this period Ambassador Fedorenko was unwilling to consider any changes in the formulations contained in the Soviet draft proposal. Aware of this fact, Ambassador Goldberg stressed that, for its part, the United States was quite willing to see its draft proposals amended and made more acceptable: "Although we have proposed a draft resolution which expresses our sincere convictions in the matter, we are open-minded and would be glad to consider constructive suggestions for improvement in the United States text." [73] At the same time Goldberg informed the Council that the United States was not asking for an early vote on its draft resolution in order to permit time for fuller consideration by Council members. He opened the door to alteration of the draft by saying, "Some members have indicated that they will wish to suggest certain changes in our text." [74] Finally, he said that the Council had "far from exhausted

<hr />

[70] *Ibid.*, p. 72.   [71] *Ibid.*, pp. 33–35.   [72] *Ibid.*   [73] *Ibid.*, p. 82.
[74] *Ibid.*

its possibilities of contributing to the construction of a stable peace in the Middle East. . . . we are not at the end of our work; we are only at the beginning." [75] These brief phrases were more important than some members of the Council realized. For the United States delegation to state so clearly that the work had just begun meant that the situation was not to be left at the cease-fire and the occupation of territory by conquering armies. Implicit here were such steps as withdrawal of forces, freedom of navigation, and hopefully a permanent peace.

The vote on the Soviet draft resolution came immediately after Goldberg's statement. Only four Member States—Bulgaria, India, Mali, and the Soviet Union itself—favored the first operative paragraph condemning "Israel's aggressive activities and its violations of the aforementioned Security Council resolutions [Resolutions 233 and 234], of the United Nations Charter and of the United Nations principles." None of the other eleven states on the Council voted against this paragraph. They all abstained in the vote. The abstention meant that not all the states concerned had made up their minds as to whether or not to condemn Israel. We have observed that in some cases representatives had stated that the issues were not clear; in other cases no such statement had been made. Of primary consideration was the fact that if, for example, the United States had voted against the Soviet proposal this negative vote of a permanent member might have been interpreted as a veto in spite of the fact that the proposal had already failed because it had been unable to muster the minimum of nine votes required by the Charter. Stating this consideration in another way, the fact that the paragraph had gained only four votes made it unnecessary for those who did not subscribe to its contents to cast negative votes; abstention would serve the purpose just as well. The second paragraph of the Soviet proposal on the withdrawal beyond the armistice lines obtained six votes, Ethiopia and Nigeria

[75] *Ibid.*, p. 83.

joining those who had voted for the condemnation of Israel. Again, and for similar reasons, all the other nine members of the Council abstained.

Thus the Soviet proposal did not come near adoption. Had the Soviet Union been willing to negotiate a different kind of proposal, one in which the condemnation applied to all violations of the cease-fire and—very important in the Middle East— to all threats of the use of force, and if it had agreed to interpolate respect for international obligations in the second paragraph, the resolution might have become the basis of further negotiation toward a settlement. After the vote the Soviet representative again alluded to the "extreme measures by the United Nations" which would have to be taken for "the immediate and decisive cessation of the continuing aggression in the Near East." [76] He did not indicate precisely what these extreme measures would be, but at the very end of his statement he expressed his government's "conviction that all peace-loving and progressive forces, all those who hold dear the cause of freedom and independence of peoples" would join together to attain their objectives.[77] This phrase, in spite of its vagueness, indicated the excessive confidence with which the Soviet Union tends to predict the direction and effect of "world opinion."

Arthur Goldberg made a final attempt to get the Soviet Union to look in another direction. "What are needed are not condemnations, which are rarely effective diplomatic actions." And again: "I interpret the remarks of the representative of the Soviet Union to mean that . . . there is an attempt to build a case for some other move which has been published in the Press in reports about Soviet intentions." [78] Goldberg was referring to press rumors that the Soviet Union was about to ask for an emergency session of the General Assembly. He added: "We are interested in a genuine effort to arrive at real peace in the Middle East and to work together in this Council to that end."

[76] *Ibid.*, pp. 88–90.   [77] *Ibid.*, pp. 91–92.   [78] *Ibid.*, pp. 93–95.

Ambassador Fedorenko did not respond to these remarks, and the meeting closed with no sign of a tangible likelihood that the Council would move on to another agreed step to resolve the Middle East situation.

It was in this frustrated frame of mind that the Council met again later that day (June 14) in the last of the series of meetings on the Middle East that had commenced on May 24. This meeting was necessary because there was still before the Council a draft proposal on the refugees and prisoners of war, introduced by the delegations of Argentina, Brazil, and Ethiopia. This proposal—which called attention to the Geneva Convention of 1949 on the Treatment of Prisoners of War—asked Israel to ensure the welfare and security of the inhabitants of the conquered areas and to facilitate the return of refugees, and asked the Arab governments also to respect the terms of the Geneva Convention. It was quickly supported by a number of Council members and was adopted unanimously, to take its place as Security Council Resolution 237.[79]

Thereafter Ambassador Fedorenko announced that from the point of view of his delegation "the Security Council has in fact concluded its examination of this problem at the present stage." [80] Thus he reiterated that there would be no shift in the Soviet position on the possibility of compromise solutions. As for the United States draft resolution, he clearly implied that it would be vetoed. "The Soviet Union will exercise its right in the Security Council when the United States draft resolution is put to the vote." [81] When the United States representative again drew attention to the open-mindedness of his delegation about the text of its resolution, Ambassador Fedorenko rejoined: "It is quite clear that there can be no basis for an understanding between our positions." [82]

The representative of Canada made a final effort on behalf of

[79] See Appendix 10.   [80] S/PV.1361, pp. 58–60.   [81] *Ibid.*
[82] *Ibid.*, p. 61.

the Council members, stating it to be his impression that the majority of the members wished to continue consultations for further constructive efforts. The Soviet delegate did not respond, but Ambassador Tarabanov of Bulgaria did: "We believe that we ought to declare our work concluded and find other solutions elsewhere within the framework of the United Nations." [83] This statement indicated more clearly than any of the Soviet statements that the Soviets and their associates would restrict themselves to peaceful UN measures rather than join in the conflict in the Middle East.

It was just barely possible that there still remained one door to the Council chamber that might be left ajar. It was a slim possibility, and one which would remain in the realm of theory rather than of fact unless it could muster wide support, but it was worth mentioning, and Lord Caradon drew attention to it before the meeting adjourned. "It is open to any member of this Council to ask for a meeting whenever he considers it necessary. . . . We should not assume that the attitude of some members of the Council means that the rest of us are not free to pursue in this Council the efforts to make a valuable contribution in dealing with the grave situation which is before us." [84]

In practice, however, meetings of the Council, as long as the mood of certain important members remained unchanged, would be an exercise in frustration. It was in these circumstances that the Council adjourned shortly after 8 P.M. on June 14, 1967, with a cease-fire barely established in the Middle East, a greatly changed territorial mosaic, and a future potentially as menacing as the past had been at any time. The Council had missed its most constructive opportunities when it had failed to act in May, and thereafter it had never really caught up with the flow of events in the region.

[83] *Ibid.,* p. 66.   [84] *Ibid.,* p. 67.

CHAPTER VI

Observations on the First Phase of
the Security Council's Effort

FROM MAY 24 to June 14, 1967, the Security Council convened twenty-one meetings on the Middle East crisis and spent sixty-seven and one-half hours in verbal battles to deal with it.

This phase of the Security Council's work falls into two parts, the first being the six meetings held from May 24 to June 3 before the outbreak of hostilities. During this period the initiative came from the Western powers who hoped to stem the rising tide of belligerent actions, which was becoming increasingly menacing with the concentration of forces around and within Israel's frontiers, the recall of UNEF, the blockading of the Gulf of Aqaba, and new restrictions on navigation in the Suez Canal. The initiative to convene the Council was taken by Canada and Denmark, and only the Western powers introduced draft resolutions for the Council's consideration. The Western members made twenty-eight interventions on matters of substance at these six meetings. Thirteen of these interventions were made by the United States alone. On the other side, the Soviet Union and Bulgaria made eighteen interventions and introduced no proposals. Thus the preponderance of activity during this phase was with a group of states directing their efforts to restraint and the removal or containment of factors which could erupt in hostilities. The Communist states directed their attention mainly to rejecting the Western position and to claiming that the actual situation in the Middle East was being overdramatized and would not in fact lead to war.

The role of the other members of the Council was characterized by their recognition that the Middle East situation involved the vital interests of the great powers and was, therefore, only marginally the concern of the lesser powers. As a result, Argentina, Brazil, and Taiwan China made only one intervention each in the first series of six meetings, while Japan made two. Even the African states of Mali and Nigeria, which might have been expected to be exercised over the situation because of geographical and other factors, made only three interventions each and did not greatly affect the main trends of discussion. Of the nonaligned states, Ethiopia with five and India with four interventions were the most active. Neither of them, however, made proposals in the form of draft resolutions.

While the great powers were undoubtedly deeply involved in the Middle East situation, the states directly concerned were not great powers. Some of these states, particularly the United Arab Republic, were prominent in the nonaligned world. This being so, it might have been expected that the nonaligned, together with the less aligned members of the Security Council such as Nigeria, Japan, Denmark, and perhaps Brazil, would have attempted to make a joint effort in the form of a draft resolution on certain aspects of the situation. No state could be blind to the threats of force and to the actions which had been taken to the detriment of the United Nations machinery in the area. If the nonaligned and others did not react to this situation with moves to reverse the accelerating deterioration, this was because the Arab states directly involved did not wish friendly Council members to act in this direction—not that this absolved any member of the Council of its responsibilities, but it was there as a fact of the situation.

Indeed, the most striking fact during the first six meetings was the lack of interest in UN action on the part of the states directly involved. None of those six meetings was requested by any of the Arab states or by Israel. The United Arab Republic did suggest a draft resolution asserting the validity of the General Armistice Agreement, respect for it by all concerned, and reactivation of certain aspects of United Nations machinery in the Middle East. This proposal (Document S/7919 of May 31, 1967), however, did not deal with several of the currently obtrusive elements in the situation, and though India gave notice that it would ask for a vote on the proposal, the draft resolution had not been fully discussed by the Council when the nature of the situation was totally altered by the outbreak of hostilities. The main reason for the failure of the Council to take measures to prevent this outbreak was the almost complete lack of interest in such measures on the part of the Middle East states themselves.

There was no serious evidence during this part of the series of meetings that the recent (1966) increase in the number of nonpermanent members of the Council from six to nine meant an increase of the interest of this group in the affairs and deliberations of the Council. Even granting that in this organ of the United Nations five states have a special position, there is room for useful contributions by other states, including mediatory functions. This type of functioning was not sufficiently in evidence in the crucial stage when hostilities could have been prevented.

On June 5 hostilities broke out in the Middle East. The situation demanded an immediate initiative to restore the peace. The logical expectation would have been an immediate demand for a Security Council meeting by one or more of the states involved in the conflict. This did not occur. The President of the Council, Ambassador Hans Tabor of Denmark, took the initiative and convened the Council, stating: "I felt it my duty, in the exercise of my responsibilities as President of the Security Council, to convene the Council for this urgent meeting." At this stage the contestants seemed willing to leave the issue to the fortunes of war. Both sides were apparently confident of their capacities.

War now raged in the Middle East. Inconceivable as it may seem, after meeting for no more than an hour on the morning of June 5, the Council adjourned and was not able to meet again until 6:30 P.M. in the early evening of the following day, June 6. Then, too, it met on the momentum of the initiative of the President and not at the request of the parties to the conflict. It immediately adopted its first cease-fire resolution, again on the initiative of the President and on the basis of consultations largely generated and directed by him. Thus, the second part of this phase of the Council's meetings was again initiated by the West.

Soon the fortunes of war were going clearly in favor of one side and against the other. This factor had a profound effect on the Council and on the nature of its deliberations. The next meeting, held on June 7, was convened at the request of the Soviet Union, and Ambassador Fedorenko immediately introduced a draft resolution, thus indicating that the initiative had passed in some degree to those who were especially concerned about the fate of the Arab states involved in the war. That concern was not entirely in one political camp. One meeting of the Council was called at the request of both the United States and the Soviet Union.[1] However, in this second part of the series of meetings, the largest number of requests came from the USSR. The representative of that state asked for four meetings, while the representative of Syria requested three. The other meetings were convened to continue discussions initiated at meetings which had been specifically requested as indicated. Thus, in the second half of the Security Council's deliberations (the fifteen meetings held from June 5 to June 14), there were altogether nine initiatives to hold meetings; seven of these came from the USSR and Syria, one was made by the President, and one by the United States of America.

In this part of the meetings the North American and Western

[1] The 1351st meeting of the Council held on June 8, 1967.

powers made sixty-four interventions; of these the United States made thirty, the United Kingdom twelve, and France and Canada eleven each. Against this participation were the seventy-four interventions made by the Soviet Union and Bulgaria. The Soviet Union intervened forty-seven times, while the Bulgarian representative spoke twenty-seven times. These figures relate to substantive interventions and not, of course, to mere procedural points raised by Council members. We see that the thrust was no longer mainly from the West, having largely passed to the other side.

Three other factors were especially striking in regard to the participation of members of the Council. First, Taiwan China, though formally a permanent member and therefore charged with a very special responsibility for the maintenance of international peace and security, intervened only once in the fifteen meetings after the outbreak of hostilities. It is clear that this permanent member is not as active in the Council as its status would lead one to expect.

Second, Argentina, Brazil, Japan, and Nigeria continued to regard themselves as being on the periphery of the debate. Each of these states intervened but thrice in these important and generally lengthy meetings. Furthermore, the interventions of Argentina and Brazil concerned mainly the problem of refugees. This problem is of course important, but it was neither the central issue nor directly part of the primary responsibility which devolves on members of the Council in accordance with the provisions of Articles 23 and 24 of the Charter. There is not necessarily a direct or standard relationship between the number of interventions and the utility of a member of the Council. The nature of the Council's proceedings is such that consultations behind the scenes also play a role, and since every vote is valuable, every member of the Council is brought into behind-the-scene consultations in some degree. Nevertheless, the degree of open participation is of significance, and that of the group of states just mentioned remained lower than should normally be expected of Council members in connection with a major problem of tensions and conflict.

Even Ethiopia, a close neighbor of the Middle East and an active member of the nonaligned group of states, made only four substantive interventions. Indeed, of the nonpermanent members only Canada and India spoke at a majority of the meetings. Each spoke at eight of the fifteen meetings from June 5 to June 14, Canada with eleven interventions and India with nine.

Proposals for the Council's acceptance bearing directly on the crucial issues of war and peace were made by the Soviet Union, the United States, and the President of the Council. During this period the Security Council adopted five resolutions, of which the majority were introduced by the President, Ambassador Tabor. These were Resolutions 233, 235, and 236, all dealing with the cease-fire. In addition to these three resolutions, President Tabor also formulated and introduced a consensus of the Council, at its 1353d meeting, which we have noted in Chapter V. The remaining resolution on the cease-fire, Resolution 234, was introduced by the Soviet Union. The fifth of the Council's resolutions, on the problem of refugees and prisoners of war, was an initiative, as we have observed, of Argentina, Brazil, and Ethiopia. All five resolutions were adopted unanimously, an action in keeping with the Council's traditions. Most resolutions adopted by the Council secure the votes of all or very nearly all its members. The reason is simply that most of the nonpermanent members are friends or allies of one or more permanent members. When they are not allies, as for example the nonaligned states, they are glad to see agreement reached among the great powers, and for that reason alone tend to cast their votes in favor of proposals to which these powers have jointly subscribed.

The only resolution to be put to the vote and defeated was the Soviet proposal on condemnation and withdrawal. It embodied characteristics which were at once too drastic and too exclusive to qualify for acceptance as a compromise solution. Although the United States draft resolution (S/7952) was not put to the vote and although the United States representative stressed that his delegation was prepared to consider amendment of the proposal, it also was too sweeping to be readily acceptable as a compromise measure. As a general rule, the greater the power of a state, the more sweeping or drastic its proposals tend to be. It is the middle powers and the smaller powers that tend to concentrate on smaller steps, and it is these smaller steps that have a chance of gaining the adherence, reluctantly or otherwise, of opposing great powers. The great powers may call the tune: generally a dissonant one. But it is not to them that ordinarily the international community can turn for the most acceptable formulations of solutions to problems unless it happens, which is very rarely the case, that their views coincide.

It is this factor which both enables and requires the lesser powers to play a constructive role in international affairs. And it is because this is so that it becomes a matter of regret when the nonpermanent members of the Security Council do not show vigor and imagination in presenting ideas, suggestions, and proposals.

It would be premature to reach the conclusion that the present nonpermanent members are not able to fill adequately the role which the foregoing circumstances indicate for them. The Council meetings were abruptly cut short by the decision of the Soviet Union to shift consideration of the issue to the General Assembly. Had the meetings continued it is conceivable that the nonpermanent members would have made further initiatives such as the four suggestions of the representative of India, at least two of which were widely supported: his suggestions for the strengthening of United Nations machinery and for the appointment of a special representative of the Secretary-General.[2] The

[2] S/PV.1352, p. 51.

United Kingdom and Canada particularly spoke in favor of these proposals, which could have eventually found their place in a resolution aimed at taking small rather than drastic or sweeping steps.

A final observation on the functioning of the Security Council in this period relates to the abrupt termination of its sessions. A basic reason for this termination was the fundamental belief of the Soviet Union and Bulgaria in what they regard as world opinion. The implication was that "world opinion" was not adequately represented around the Council table. This should not have been the case in a Council which had recently been expanded from a membership of eleven to fifteen states. However, too many Council members were missing opportunities for participation. In the first phase of Council meetings, before the outbreak of hostilities, as many as seven of the fifteen members were silent at a majority of the meetings. And precisely the same number were silent at a majority of the meetings in the second phase of fifteen meetings.

If, when it was first rumored that the Soviet Union would ask to shift consideration of the crisis to the General Assembly, most of the members of the Council had urged the Soviet Union to continue discussions in the Council, it is possible that the meetings would have gone on for at least a few weeks. In point of fact, however, of the nonpermanent members only Canada urged continuance of the meetings, and of the permanent members only the United Kingdom supported the United States view favoring further Council activity. If all the other members (excluding Bulgaria, which could not in the circumstances be expected openly to disagree with the Soviet Union) had urged the continuance of Council consideration of the issue, would not the Soviet Union have taken into account this manifestation of world opinion? Unfortunately there was no such move in the Council, even though it should have been clear to the members that certain relevant factors pointed in the direction of continuance of Council consideration. First, there was the relatively small size of the forum, which is more conducive to the emergence of agreed conclusions than is a body such as the General Assembly; second, some of the important powers, including the United States, were keen to continue Council consideration and were showing willingness to modify the draft proposals which they had submitted. To cut off this momentum was to lose the possibilities of constructive development. Third, powerful pleas were being made, in particular by Lord Caradon of the United Kingdom, for the taking of small steps, and in the debate several small steps had been identified by Council members. If the non-permanent members and some of their permanent colleagues had pressed vigorously for continuing discussions, progress along the lines of small steps and the enunciation of the appropriate basic principles might have been attained in the Council, where success was more likely than in the General Assembly. In the latter body small steps tend to be less acceptable because large steps are more dramatic, and small powers coalesce to form large groupings with some of the characteristics of individual great powers, including a strong penchant for large dramatic steps which have a fine sound and look well on paper, but most infrequently are translated into reality.

These reflections on the possibilities of the Security Council should not, however, close our eyes to the constructive achievements of the meetings which concluded on June 14, 1967. These included a cease-fire, achieved as a result of much discussion and four unanimously adopted resolutions. Second, although there had been no expansion of UNTSO, it had been reactivated with the consent of both the Arab states and Israel. Third, the parties to the conflict had been reminded of their obligations toward refugees and prisoners of war.

CHAPTER VII

The Convening of the Fifth
Emergency Special Session
of the General Assembly

THE FIFTH EMERGENCY SPECIAL SESSION was called as a result of procedures initiated by a letter addressed to the Secretary-General on June 13, 1967, by Andrei Gromyko,[1] Minister for Foreign Affairs of the USSR. In some ways the procedures in this case marked a departure in regard to the initiation of special sessions of the General Assembly.

The basis of procedure for calling such sessions is the UN Charter itself.[2] A specific procedure is prescribed by General Assembly Resolution 377 A (V) of November 3, 1950. That resolution defines certain circumstances in which emergency special sessions of the Assembly may be convoked within twenty-four hours of a request therefor, namely, a lack of unanimity among the permanent members of the Security Council leading to failure by the Council "to exercise its primary responsibility for the maintenance of international peace and security in any case where there appears to be a threat to the peace, breach of the peace, or act of aggression."[3] In these circum-

[1] A/6717, June 13, 1967.   [2] Article 20 of the Charter.
[3] General Assembly Resolution 377 A (V), Part A, par. 1. The relevant provisions of this resolution are incorporated in Rules 8 and 9 of the Rules of Procedure of the General Assembly.

stances an emergency special session shall be called if requested by the Security Council on the vote of any seven members (raised to nine on the expansion of the Security Council membership to fifteen), or by a majority of the members of the United Nations.

The first four emergency special sessions were called in cases of clear emergency on the basis, in each case, of a resolution by the Security Council in terms of the relevant provision in Resolution 377 A (V). Those calls by the Council showed the wide use that could be made of the procedure that had been devised to initiate emergency special sessions.

The resolution in the Security Council asking for the First Emergency Special Session, in the Suez crisis of 1956, was introduced by Yugoslavia and was adopted on October 31, 1956, although two permanent members (France and the United Kingdom) voted against it.

Four days later, on November 4, 1956, the Security Council adopted a resolution calling another emergency special session of the General Assembly to consider the Hungarian question. In this case it acted on the initiative of a draft resolution introduced by the United States, and the emergency special session was called although the Soviet Union voted against the resolution in the Security Council.

In the third case, on August 7, 1958, the Security Council considered a request by the Soviet representative for the calling of an emergency special session of the General Assembly following the failure of the Council to agree on the conditions and modalities in connection with the withdrawal from Lebanon and Jordan of U.S. and U.K. armed forces respectively. The Council also considered a draft resolution introduced by the United States and on August 7 adopted it, rather than the Soviet proposal, as the basis of convoking the Third Emergency Special Session of the General Assembly.

In all three cases permanent members of the Security Council had been directly involved, and in two of them one or more such members had voted against the proposed calling of an emergency special session of the Assembly. In the third case, the country which was directly involved, and in regard to which there was a demand that its forces be withdrawn from Lebanon, itself introduced a draft resolution enabling an emergency session of the Assembly to be called to consider, mainly, possible ways and means to extinguish its military presence in the Middle East. In short, the United States initiated the call for the session to deal with a situation in which the main focus of UN effort was directed against its own actions.

In the fourth case (the Congo) none of the permanent members of the Council were directly involved. The resolution in the Council calling for an emergency special session was introduced by the United States, and was adopted although the Soviet Union and Poland voted against it.

In the case of the Middle East crisis of 1967 there had been several weeks of meetings in the Security Council during which five resolutions (Nos. 233–237) had been adopted, all of them unanimously. One of these resolutions had been introduced by the USSR. However, another resolution introduced by the USSR had, as we have seen, been rejected by the Council. A number of other resolutions, including texts introduced by Canada, the United States, and the UAR, were awaiting consideration by the Council. In these circumstances it was doubtful that nine members of the Council would have voted for the calling of an emergency special session of the Assembly. A debate would moreover have ensued on whether the governing provision in Resolution 377 A (V) had become operative: failure by the Security Council to exercise its responsibilities for the maintenance of international peace and security. In these circumstances the USSR, which had decided to call an emergency special session, chose not to follow the practice which had become established in the four previous cases. It did not ask the Security Council to adopt a resolution calling for an Assembly session. Instead, the Soviet Foreign Minister addressed a letter to the Secretary-General and simply asked for an emergency special session to be convened within twenty-four hours. The letter did not refer to General Assembly Resolution 377 A (V) but rather to Article 11 of the United Nations Charter, which empowers the General Assembly to consider any question relating to the maintenance of international peace and security, except that when the Security Council "is exercising in respect of any dispute or situation the functions assigned to it in the present Charter, the General Assembly shall not make any recommendations with regard to that dispute or situation unless the Security Council so requests." [4]

By citing Article 11 of the Charter the Soviet Union was, by implication, advancing one of two views: either that the General Assembly should make no recommendations or that the Security Council was not exercising its Charter functions regarding the Middle East. It was the latter view which had been implicit in remarks made by Ambassador Fedorenko in the Security Council. Furthermore, Gromyko's letter of June 13 asked that the General Assembly "should consider the situation which has arisen and should adopt a decision designed to bring about the liquidation of the consequences of aggression and the immediate withdrawal of Israel forces behind the armistice lines." [5] Thus the Soviet Union made it quite clear that the Assembly was to adopt resolutions making recommendations to Member States. We will see, however, whether the Soviet Union and indeed the membership of the Council in general really subscribed to the view that the Council was no longer exercising its proper functions.

As later events will show, an element of fiction has crept into UN practice in regard to compliance with the jurisdictional injunctions in Articles 11 and 12. Issues such as those relating to

[4] Article 12 of the Charter.   [5] A/6717, June 13, 1967.

the Congo and the Middle East have been before both the Security Council and the General Assembly for the adoption of resolutions in circumstances which have not been in strict conformity with the provisions of these articles.

We have observed that Gromyko's request (Document A/6717) did not mention General Assembly Resolution 377 A (V). It had not become the invariable practice to refer to that resolution in calling for emergency special sessions. In the case of the first, second, and fourth such sessions the bidding resolution of the Council had referred specifically to Resolution 377 A (V), but the text of the Council resolution calling for the Third Emergency Special Session had not mentioned it.[6] Article 20 of the Charter does not rule out the calling of emergency sessions of the Assembly, and it may be argued that its provisions are in themselves sufficient legal basis for calling such sessions without any recourse to procedures set out in a resolution of the Assembly. Article 20 states that "special sessions shall be convoked by the Secretary-General at the request of the Security Council or of a majority of the members of the United Nations." It might be argued that, if a member of the UN asks the Secretary-General to convoke an Assembly session with all speed because the situation concerned is one of extreme urgency, the Secretary-General could or should take urgent steps to sound out the members of the United Nations. If a majority of members so sounded agreed to the calling of an emergency special session, such a session should in fact, be convoked. We might also note that Resolution 377 A (V) provided that an emergency special session would be convened within twenty-four hours of the receipt by the Secretary-General of a request, whether by the Council or by a majority of UN members. However, in the case of the Fifth Emergency Special Session this provision was only nominally put into effect, if at all. The Soviet request was received on June 13, telegrams were dispatched by the Secre-

6 S/4056/Rev. 1.

tary-General immediately, and a majority of affirmative replies had been received by 0930 hours on June 16. However, the Assembly did not meet until the afternoon of June 17 and then did so purely formally, deferring the commencement of its substantive work to June 19. Indeed, the state which had initiated the call for the urgent convening of the Assembly addressed a note verbale to the Secretary-General requesting that the Assembly should not be convened until June 19.[7] Thus the Soviet Union, while asking for an emergency session, was not maintaining its request for one within the terms of General Assembly Resolution 377 A (V). Although the Secretary-General in his telegram to Member States referred to the General Assembly rules of procedure, which mention that resolution, the UN may have witnessed a new procedural development in the manner of the calling of the emergency special session, and one that indicates that such sessions may be convened without reference to General Assembly Resolution 377 A (V) and without compliance with its provisions. The Charter itself could be made the basis for the calling of a special session within ten days, a week, or less, depending upon the urgency of the situation involved.

Procedurally, then, the calling of the Fifth Emergency Special Session of the General Assembly marked in some respects new developments in United Nations practice. In this connection note should be taken of the fact that the United States did not accept the view that the Security Council had failed to discharge its proper functions. In his letter of June 15, 1967, to the Secretary-General, Ambassador Arthur Goldberg pointed out that the Council had adopted five resolutions and that several others were under consideration. In these circumstances

the United States Government does not believe that a situation has arisen in which the Security Council, in the words of General Assembly Resolution 377 A (V), "fails to exercise its primary responsibility for the maintenance of international peace and secu-

[7] A/6719.

rity." Accordingly, the United States is not able to concur in the request for the holding of an Emergency Special Session at this time.[8]

The U.S. letter could have gone further and pointed out that since the Security Council was still exercising its functions Article 12 of the Charter would inhibit the General Assembly from making any recommendations. Certainly there had been no vote in the Security Council by which that body had divested itself of its agenda item concerning the Middle East crisis. However, the United States was not disposed to be too strict about the relevant Charter provisions. Having stated its view against the convening of an emergency special session, Arthur Goldberg's letter went on: "If, nevertheless a majority of the Membership decides to convene such an Assembly, the United States hopes that any discussion will have a helpful influence in encouraging and enabling all States concerned to deal effectively with the underlying causes of tension and conflict in the Middle East." By "all States concerned" the United States meant what it said. The U.S. delegation was to play a significant and active role at the Fifth Emergency Special Session even if it had not been of the view that such a session should be called. Certainly, the calling of the session involved improvisation and ingenuity in regard to both the interpretation of the circumstances and the plain meaning of the law of the United Nations.

[8] A/6718, June 15, 1967.

CHAPTER VIII

The Statement of Positions
in the Assembly

THE FIFTH EMERGENCY SPECIAL SESSION of the General Assembly, in an effort to maintain the fiction that it was meeting in full accordance with the terms of Resolution 377 A (V), convened briefly on June 17, heard a wise and interesting statement by its President, Ambassador A. R. Pazhwak, and promptly adjourned for two days to the unurgent hour of 10:30 A.M. on Monday, June 19.

The atmosphere of the opening of the session was in some degree analogous to that at the Third Emergency Special Session. On that earlier occasion the United States, the super power which was directly involved, had taken the unusual step of presenting its position through its head of state, President Dwight Eisenhower. At the Fifth Emergency Special Session, though neither of the super powers was directly involved, the Soviet Union regarded the situation as one that closely concerned it. It accordingly sent its Chairman of the Council of Ministers, Alexei Kosygin, to make its first statement of case. Moreover, by raising the Assembly to summit level the Soviet Union increased the expectation that it intended to work toward the achievement of results that would serve its interests.

Chairman Kosygin opened the substantive discussions on June 19 with a detailed statement of the position of the Soviet government. But this statement did not bring a novel point of view to the Assembly. It revealed that the approach of the Soviet government remained broadly that which it had been in the Security Council. The demand was for immediate withdrawal of Israeli forces to the armistice lines and for full "elimination of the consequences of the aggression" against the Arab states. At the same time there were fresh nuances encompassing expressions of both the hopes of peace and the possibilities of renewed and more serious military conflict. Also noteworthy was some indication of confidence in the United Nations. In this vein, Kosygin early in his statement referred to the cease-fire and said, "It also does considerable credit to the Security Council." [1] Though he was not satisfied with this achievement, the admission that the Council had worked well in achieving the cease-fire was an important one. Indeed, throughout the speech there were positive references to the United Nations which seemed to imply that present-day Soviet policy values this international organization and regards it as a significant factor in the maintenance and restoration of international peace and security. At no time did Kosygin threaten to take the issue out of the United Nations and at no time did he threaten withdrawal from or noncooperation with the Organization if the case he brought before it was not accepted. On the contrary, he ended on a note of confidence in the United Nations:

If . . . the General Assembly should find itself incapable of reaching a decision in the interests of peace, this would deal a heavy blow to the expectations of mankind regarding the possibility of settling major international problems by peaceful means, by diplomatic contacts and negotiations. No state which genuinely cares for the future of its people can fail to take this into consideration. *The peoples should rest assured that the United Nations is capable of achieving the aims proclaimed in its Charter, the aims of safeguarding peace on earth.* [2]

This welcome faith in the United Nations was the most significant revelation contained in Kosygin's statement. It does not

[1] A/PV.1526, p. 2.   [2] *Ibid.*, p. 26; italics added.

of course follow that long-term Soviet policy is committed to the United Nations. The long-term policy of all states is largely uncommitted. What is important are the discernible trends of policy, and Kosygin's statement revealed a trend favorable to the United Nations which clearly other states should take into account.

Another nuance conducing toward peaceful settlement, and one that was directly relevant to the Middle East situation, was contained in remarks which Kosygin made about Israel as a state. Although there was no logical compulsion that he should raise this issue, he said:

Every people enjoys the right to establish an independent national State of its own. . . . It is on this basis that we formulated our attitude toward Israel as a State when we voted in 1947 for the United Nations decision to create two independent States, a Jewish one and an Arab one, in the territory of the former British colony of Palestine. Guided by this fundamental policy, the Soviet Union was later to establish diplomatic relations with Israel.[3]

Finally, the more positive nuances—which were new in that they had not appeared in the numerous Soviet statements in the Security Council phase of consideration of the crisis—related to the future arrangements in the Middle East. Kosygin stated: "The government of the Soviet Union expresses the hope that the General Assembly will take an effective decision ensuring . . . the restoration and consolidation of peace and security in the Middle East."[4] These words must have been carefully weighed. Kosygin could have stopped at the restoration of peace, but he spoke of its consolidation and he brought in the concept of security. Implicit in this thought must have been some recognition that the Assembly would have to do more than merely restore the status quo as it had been on June 4, 1967.

There were also nuances which moved in the direction of greater severity than even the forthright statements of Ambassa-

[3] *Ibid.,* p. 13.   [4] *Ibid.,* p. 26.

dor Fedorenko in the Security Council. While the Ambassador
had contented himself with a demand for condemnation of
Israel, complete withdrawal to the armistice lines, and punishment of the Israelis, Kosygin stated: "Elimination of the consequences of aggression also means restituting the material damage inflicted by the aggressor upon those whom it attacked and
whose lands it occupied and pillaged." [5] Perhaps it was natural
for the Soviet Union to raise this point. Most of the goods cap-
tured by the Israelis consisted of Soviet equipment that had been
supplied to the Arabs. Foreign Minister Eban of Israel asserted
that $2 billion worth of Soviet equipment had been abandoned
by the Egyptians in the Sinai during the armed conflict.[6]

Finally, the new points in Kosygin's presentation included
another which was directly relevant to the United Nations. The
draft resolution which he introduced, after its clauses on condemnation, withdrawal, and restitution, contained the following
clause:

"4. *Appeals* to the Security Council to take for its part immediate effective measures in order to eliminate all consequences
of the aggression committed by Israel." [7]

This clause of the Soviet proposal indicated that though the
Soviet Union had called the Assembly into session it had not
forsaken the Security Council, and that it continued to regard
the latter body as the appropriate one to take active measures in
regard to the Middle East crisis.

Kosygin attempted to rouse the sympathy of the small and
weak powers of the United Nations—the vast majority—by
drawing attention to the fateful repercussions of permitting territorial changes as a result of armed conflict:

If Israel's claims do not receive a rebuff today, tomorrow a new
aggressor, big or small, may attempt to overrun the lands of other
peaceful countries. . . . If we here, in the United Nations fail to
take the necessary measures, even those states which are not parties

[5] *Ibid.,* p. 23.   [6] *Ibid.,* p. 51.   [7] A/L.519. See Appendix 11.

to the conflict may draw the conclusion that they cannot expect protection from the United Nations.[8]

This analysis of the new elements in Chairman Kosygin's statement of June 19 before the General Assembly gives some indication of the present attitude of one of the super powers toward the United Nations that is relevant to that body's handling of the Middle East crisis. It does much to ensure, though it does not guarantee, that the crisis will continue to be handled within the United Nations and will therefore tend not to erupt in a wider military conflict. Of course the Soviet Union alone is not the determining factor in this regard; but it is an important one which will influence the course of events.

As was to be expected, the Soviet statement also contained material which ranged beyond the Middle East issue. It attacked U.S. policy in Vietnam, and in general terms it attacked U.S. policies toward Cuba, the Congo, and the Dominican Republic. It also attacked the policies of the West German Republic and accused the United States and the United Kingdom of complicity on Israel's side in the armed conflict in the Middle East. These situations were part of the recent or current international scene and it was no surprise that they were brought into play by Chairman Kosygin. Goldberg dealt with these parts of Kosygin's statement in a manner which befitted the United Nations. He deeply regretted the charges of complicity; as regards Vietnam, he offered to join with the Soviet Union either in the United Nations or outside it in an effort to promote negotiations to bring peace; and the other charges he regarded as irrelevant.[9]

So far as the Middle East crisis itself was concerned, the Kosygin statement set out one of the seven approaches which were to be contained in statements made in the next three days of Assembly sessions. These seven approaches comprised those

[8] A/PV.1526, p. 21.   [9] *Ibid.,* pp. 63–66.

of the states most closely involved in the issue. They did not embrace the approaches of other states, such as France, Rumania, and the Latin American countries. The Soviet approach, as we have seen, retained its main lines as expressed in the Security Council debates, but there was the added indication, though vaguely stated and not contained in the Soviet draft resolution, of a perception of the necessity to take steps to consolidate peace and security in the Middle East.

This approach was not an exact homologue of the Arab approach. The latter stood uncompromisingly in a position of no negotiations, direct or indirect, with Israel; a return to the situation as it existed on June 4, 1967, including, presumably, maintenance of the blockade of Aqaba; no renunciation of belligerence; and, of course, no recognition of Israel. Some elements of this position were bluntly stated by Jamil Baroody of Saudi Arabia at the Assembly's first substantive meeting on the morning of June 19. On the basic question of the presence of Israel as a Middle East state, Baroody said:

The leader of my country [Saudi Arabia] has time and again made it explicit, in various capitals of Western Europe, that the Arab world cannot accommodate Zionism in our midst. . . . If our leaders did not reflect the mood of the Arab people, they would not remain leaders.[10]

The Arab position was stated more fully by the Chief of State of Syria. Dr. Noureddin Atassi drew attention to past condemnations of Israel by the Security Council. He then claimed: "It was after we informed Secretary-General U Thant that we had ceased fire as from 1630 hours GMT, 10 June, that the Israeli invasion of our territory began." [11] He called on the United Nations to reject firmly the logic of Israeli conquest, of which "the result would be that we admit the right of the stronger to conquer the lands of the weaker and retain them by force." [12] He added: "We shall reject any conditions or discussions based on an invasion. We ask you to firmly condemn

[10] *Ibid.*, pp. 68–70.   [11] A/PV.1527, p. 26.   [12] *Ibid.*, pp. 33–35.

aggression and to immediately liquidate its traces." [13] The Syrian Chief of State also welcomed the draft resolution introduced by Chairman Kosygin (A/L.519).

The difference between this position and that of Kosygin was not negligible. The Soviet leader had expressed the hope that the General Assembly would take decisions which would, *inter alia*, consolidate peace and security in the Middle East. The Syrian leader asked only for condemnation, punishment, and immediate liquidation of all traces of invasion. In the past, among the basic factors arresting any progress in the direction of a firm peace in the Middle East had been the unacceptability of the fact of Israel to the Arab states, an unacceptability which Ambassador Jamil Baroody had restated. There was no evidence of any change of that attitude in Dr. Atassi's speech. This position was distinguishable from that of the Soviet Union. Kosygin had reiterated Israel's right to exist, a view for which no Arab counterpart was forthcoming.

A more guarded statement of the Arab position was made by the *doyen* of Arab diplomats, Mahmud Fawzi, on June 21, 1967. Fawzi is too skilled a diplomat to weaken his own position by the injection of extremist attitudes in regard to issues on which the UAR's position is unconvincing. While he was critical of the United States, insisting that it had supported the Israeli armed attack through the activities of the Sixth Fleet,[14] his statement was, on the whole, replete with benignity and the wounded feelings of the nationalist who saw his country's territory and the rights of his people trampled upon.

The most persuasive and comprehensive statement of the Arab position was made by the Prime Minister of Sudan, M. A. Mahgoub. He argued at length the legalities of right of passage through the Gulf of Aqaba. In support of the UAR he asserted:

Israel claimed a belligerent's right of retaliation on Syria in April 1967. The United Nations found that Israel was not justified in this,

---

[13] *Ibid.*, p. 36. [14] A/PV.1529, p. 31.

and censored Israel. But even if it were justified, the United Arab Republic could certainly exercise a comparable—and less bloody—belligerent right, namely to close the Strait of Tiran to strategic cargo for Israel.[15]

This argument draws heavily on the concept that belligerent rights continue to vest in the two sides in the Middle East, the UN Charter provisions on the nonuse of force and threats of force notwithstanding. But Prime Minister Mahgoub did not depend only on this argument. He asserted that Elath had been occupied a month after the signing of the Armistice Agreement in February, 1949.

Turning to the outbreak of hostilities, Mahgoub argued that even conceding the provocation caused by the massing of Arab troops on its frontiers, "the action taken by Israel was not legitimate self-defense within the meaning of Article 51 of the Charter because no armed attack on her territory had in fact occurred." [16] He also pointed out that Article 51 of the Charter of the United Nations stipulates that measures undertaken in exercise of the right of self-defense are to be reported to the Security Council. It is indeed true that the parties made no report accompanied by specific requests that the Security Council take action to restore peace and security. However, it may be argued that the terms of Article 51 were complied with by the reports of the outbreak of hostilities which both Israel and the UAR made to the President of the Security Council on the morning of June 5, 1967.[17]

Mahgoub avoided statements of total incompatibility between the positions of the Arab states and the United States. Referring to the policies of the United States in the 1956 Suez crisis, he said: "The United States then insisted, as it is doing now, that certain arrangements must be made to establish a permanent peace in the Middle East. That is creditable and necessary." [18]

[15] A/PV.1530, p. 28.   [16] *Ibid.*, p. 36.   [17] S/PV.1347, p. 3.
[18] A/PV.1530, pp. 49–50.

Implicit in this statement was the need for permanent peace in
the Middle East, and by referring favorably to the far-reaching
proposals made by the United States in 1956 the Prime Minister
of Sudan seemed to be opening the door to similar possibilities
now. He insisted, however, that the first order of business—as
in 1956—should be the withdrawal of foreign forces from Arab
territory. The position of the Sudan appeared to be closer to
that of the Soviet Union than to that of the Arab states, which
gave no indication of possibilities of compromise in regard to
Israel. Two other statements from countries neighboring on
the Middle East approached closely the less extreme version of
the Arab position. There was the statement of Iran, whose Foreign Minister, Ardeshir Zahedi, demanded immediate withdrawal. This could lead to the creation of a "climate for reason
and a viable peace keeping arrangement." [19] There was an implication here that the situation could improve so that "reason"
—which would presumably lead to the application of such processes as mediation or even negotiation between the parties—
could assert itself. The second such statement was that of the
Foreign Minister of Pakistan, Sharifuddin Pirzada. After asking
for outright condemnation of Israel and the immediate withdrawal of forces, on the long-term issues he said:

Another suggestion . . . is that we should take advantage of this
Assembly session and examine all outstanding issues in the Middle
East. Pakistan, for one, is anxious that no issue should escape examination, but the question is: are we to examine all outstanding
issues while the aggressor remains on the victim's soil? [20]

Here was an indication that the time for examination of the
long-term issues would come later. However, there appeared to
be a certain regression from this approach in the immediately
following thought expressed by the speaker:

We here have only one frame of discussions, and only one basis of
action. That is the Charter. Let us apply the provisions of the Charter

[19] *Ibid.*, p. 57.   [20] A/PV.1531, pp. 66–67.

to the present situation. If we do so, the only course of action for us is to condemn the aggression launched by Israel on 5 June and to demand the withdrawal of Israeli forces from Arab territories, including the Holy Places, to positions prior to hostilities. . . . The wrongs done to the Arabs must be righted. Only thus will conditions be created for a just and durable peace in the region.[21]

There are elements of ambiguity in this statement. It could be interpreted to mean that the full requirements of the Charter would be met by condemnation and withdrawal and that these developments would establish the necessary conditions for a durable peace. In this meaning, the statement is in accord with the more extreme Arab position. However, since the Foreign Minister had mentioned previously the examination of all issues at a later date, it would seem that he left the door open for further measures to strengthen and secure peaceful conditions in the area.

We have examined in some depth two of the seven positions which emerged in the initial meetings of the Fifth Emergency Special Session of the General Assembly: the Arab position in its two versions and the somewhat more farseeing Soviet position.

A third position was enunciated by the Prime Minister of Yugoslavia, Mika Spiljak, whose country had been and remains a staunch supporter of the UAR, Syria, and some other Arab states. This position differed from the two previous ones. First, it differed fundamentally from the Arab position in regard to the general approach of Yugoslavia toward Israel, "whose existence we have never questioned," said the Prime Minister.[22] It approximated the position of both the Arabs and the Soviet Union in that Yugoslavia demanded immediate and unconditional withdrawal of Israel's forces, condemnation of Israel's aggression, and indemnities to the countries that had been invaded. However, it differed from the Soviet position in the

21 *Ibid.*, p. 67.   22 A/PV.1529, p. 51.

degree to which it appeared to favor negotiation for a long-term settlement:

> There can be no negotiations prior to execution of the withdrawal, nor can there be any search for arrangements that would otherwise be necessary for the long-term stabilization of the situation in the Near East and securing of the independence and territorial integrity of the countries of that region, as long as the forces of the aggressor are not withdrawn from the occupied territory.[23]

This is a clearer commitment to negotiation for a long-term settlement than had appeared in the Soviet statement made by Kosygin. The Yugoslav position was espoused by others. For example, the representative of Tanzania spoke of his country's recognition of Israel, but he supported the Soviet draft resolution and expressed the apprehensions of "the third world" which was just freeing itself from the chains of colonialism, imperialism, and racial and economic degradation. "It has already been suggested in some British and other Western papers that Smith, Vorster and Salazaar might pursue similar courses vis-à-vis independent African states." [24] This expression of almost personal apprehension arising out of a recognition of weakness explained the general approach of Tanzania and many similarly placed new small countries.

A fourth position to emerge was that of India. The Indian Foreign Minister, M. C. Chagla, speaking on June 21, 1967, did not join in or ask for the condemnation of Israel. He called for immediate and complete withdrawal of Israeli forces, but added: "We have no quarrel with the people of Israel, and our record shows the objective attitude that we have adopted towards the State of Israel." [25] India is the only large state in western, southern, and southeast Asia to recognize Israel.

The Indian position also differed from the previous three positions in that it saw a certain urgency in moving toward a durable and just peace: "Unless and world community can arrange

[23] *Ibid.*, p. 52.   [24] A/PV.1530, pp. 22–25.   [25] *Ibid.*, p. 76.

—and arrange firmly and speedily—a durable and just peace, it is not inconceivable that a world conflagration may follow," [26] said Foreign Minister Chagla. Finally, the Indian delegation had some suggestions to make regarding measures to be taken immediately after withdrawal, namely, the strengthening of the United Nations Truce Supervision Organization and the appointment of a special representative of the Secretary-General to help reduce tensions in the area and to facilitate the return of refugees to their homes. Such pragmatic measures had not characterized any of the three approaches previously analyzed.

The fifth approach was stated with great succinctness by Jens Otto Krag, Prime Minister of Denmark. He put in the forefront "two main considerations." The first of these was the acceptance of the aim "not to re-establish the unstable conditions existing before the outbreak of hostilities." [27] The second was that "the United Nations consequently must contribute to laying the foundation for a lasting peace based upon just and equitable solutions which are acceptable to all concerned." [28] These considerations also implied certain objectives. How were the objectives to be achieved? The answer was that two basic principles would have to be borne in mind by the United Nations. First, "Military action should not lead to territorial gains." [29] Thus, without reservations the Prime Minister enumerated clearly the principle of the full withdrawal of conquering troops. He pointed out that it was not a question of a country not gaining the fruits of aggression. Military action, whether in self-defense or as aggression, was not to lead to territorial aggrandizement. He did not, however, envisage withdrawal as an isolated step. Another principle was laid down: "We cannot accept that any member of the United Nations should base its foreign policy on the assumption of the non-existence of an-

26 *Ibid.,* p. 71.   27 A/PV.1529, p. 37.   28 *Ibid.*   29 *Ibid.*

other Member State." [30] Once these principles were firmly accepted there would follow the safeguarding of the political and territorial integrity of all the states of the Middle East. There should also be international guarantees and provisions for halting an arms race; the refugee problem must be given a high priority; there should be free passage through international waterways, a matter of concern not only to the parties but to all nations. Pending the achievement of these long-term goals, there would be United Nations observer teams, demilitarized zones, and possibly another peace-keeping force. Prime Minister Krag's relatively brief statement had the great merit of seeing the necessities of the future while providing for detailed measures to meet the immediate obstacles to the movement forward to a peaceful future.

With much greater rhetoric, the Foreign Secretary of the United Kingdom, George Brown, stated what in essence was a very similar position to that of Denmark. He too laid down firmly the stipulation that there should be no territorial acquisitions for Israel as a result of the war. He quoted Article 2 of the Charter and stated: "Here the words 'territorial integrity' have a direct bearing on the question of withdrawal. . . . I see no two ways about this; and I can state our position very clearly. In my view, it follows from the words in the Charter that war shall not lead to territorial aggrandizement." [31] On the other hand, he made it clear that "any settlement must recognize the right of all states in the area to exist in true dignity and real freedom, and that must include the ability to earn their living in assured peace." [32] Immediately following this sentence George Brown interpolated a sentence which showed parliamentary skill and also had an overtone of readiness for negotiation among the great powers. He added: "I understood this to be the view of Mr. Kosygin, and I hope my understanding was correct." With

[30] *Ibid.*, p. 41.   [31] *Ibid.*, p. 11.   [32] *Ibid.*, p. 12.

this sentence George Brown was attempting to move the Soviet position more clearly toward a durable peace in the Middle East which would be fair to all the states concerned, including, of course, Israel. There was no comment by the Soviet delegation on this sentence, a silence which may be fairly interpreted to mean that it did not dissent. Brown also spoke of the necessity of the right of free and innocent passage through international waterways for the ships of all nations and for steps to arrest an arms race in the area. Like India, he suggested the nomination by the Secretary-General of a representative and the strengthening of the United Nations Truce Supervision Organization. "What everyone wishes to see, what everyone expects now, what is desperately required is some immediate, positive, practical action." [33]

Thus two Western European powers, Denmark and the United Kingdom, took a clear position on withdrawal, asked for urgent steps to help deal with the immediate situation, and looked ahead to a just settlement in the interests of all the countries of the Middle East. This position was broadly and quickly ratified by the Prime Minister of Italy and the Foreign Minister of Belgium. The Italian Prime Minister, Aldo Moro, said that "the withdrawal of troops is certainly a necessary step," then added, "but it is not sufficient." The United Nations would have to give thought to creating conditions for a settlement. Not to do so "would be compromising its very reason for existence." [34] He mentioned the points which the other Western European delegates had stressed: the refugees, the right of navigation, and the ending of the arms race. He referred specifically to the suggestion which had been made by the representative of India for a special representative and to the similar United Kingdom suggestion and said that these proposals deserved to be explored. Foreign Minister Pierre Harmel of Belgium stressed the same points, referring specifically to the in-

[33] *Ibid.*, p. 17.   [34] A/PV.1530, p. 66.

terventions of the representatives of the United Kingdom and Italy.

The position of the United States fell into a sixth category. As we have observed in analyzing the proceedings of the Security Council, the super powers tend to favor comprehensive and even drastic solutions to problems. In their own way the proposals made by Kosygin were certainly drastic. Looking in another direction the proposals of the United States, too, were in a sense drastic, and they were certainly comprehensive. Speaking for the United States early in the debate, on June 20, 1967, Ambassador Arthur Goldberg referred to the five comprehensive principles enunciated by President Johnson in his address on June 19, 1967, at the National Foreign Policy Conference for Educators. President Johnson had said:

Our Country is committed—and we here reiterate that commitment today—to a peace that is based on five principles:
First, the recognized right of national life.
Second, justice for the refugees.
Third, innocent maritime passage.
Fourth, limits on the wasteful and destructive arms race.
And fifth, political independence and territorial integrity for all.[35]

Goldberg stated that "these principles, if implemented, offer a solid basis for a durable peace in the future." [36]

Turning to the Soviet proposals made by Kosygin, Goldberg commented: "Israel alone is to be condemned as an aggressor—though surely in the light of all the events, both recent and long past, that led up to the fighting, it would be neither equitable nor constructive for this Organization to issue a one-sided condemnation." Going on to what he called the heart of the Soviet proposal, Goldberg described it as follows:

"Israel, withdraw your troops and let everything go back to exactly where it was before the fighting began on 5 June." In other words,

[35] New York *Times*, June 20, 1967.   [36] A/PV.1527, p. 12.

as I said in the Security Council, the film is to be run backwards through the projector to that point in the early morning of 5 June when hostilities had not yet broken out.[37]

The short-term drastic action proposed by the USSR was unacceptable, as Goldberg said: "Surely it is not an acceptable approach for the United Nations." [38] The acceptable approach was that which had been written into the Armistice Agreement of 1949, Article XII of which stated that the purpose of the Agreement was "to facilitate the transition from the present truce to permanent peace in Palestine." On the basis of President Johnson's five principles and having regard to the injunction in the Armistice Agreement, Goldberg introduced a draft resolution by which the United Nations General Assembly would endorse the cease-fire and decide that its objective must be a stable and durable peace in the Middle East; this peace should be achieved through negotiated arrangements with appropriate third-party assistance and be based on the five principles enunciated by President Johnson. Such was the United States proposal.[39] It differed from the approach of the Western European states in that it made no mention of the interim pragmatic steps which would be required to alleviate the situation, to reduce tensions, and to help the movement in various ways toward a more stable peace. Moreover, the first principle of President Johnson was elaborated so as to read, "Mutual recognition of the political independence and territorial integrity of all countries in the area, encompassing recognized boundaries and other arrangements, including disengagement and withdrawal of forces, that will give them security against terror, destruction and war." [40] This formulation did not state precisely what the recognized boundaries were to be and whether withdrawal would be complete in the sense of returning Israeli forces to positions within the armistice lines of 1949. Presumably these matters

[37] *Ibid.*, p. 16.   [38] *Ibid.*, p. 17.   [39] A/L.520. See Appendix 12.
[40] A/L.520.

were to be subject to negotiation between the parties. Here, then, was a difference from the clear-cut principle of full withdrawal enumerated by most of the Western European representatives. Another difference was that while those representatives had generally expressed the hope that direct negotiations could, at some time, be achieved, they had not asked immediately for such negotiations. There was not a great difference in final objectives, but the divergence of modalities was wide and arose from the more forthright approach of the United States, as a very great power, to world affairs. In many respects the approach of the United States commanded a wide measure of general sympathy and acceptance. This was true in regard to most of the final goals implicit in the principles enunciated by President Johnson, but in its totality the United States approach remained in a sense beyond the grasp of the rank and file of the membership of the United Nations. Smaller powers were unable to imagine that the bold and comprehensive design of the United States could be espoused as the immediate recommendation of the General Assembly.

The seventh position tended to be more unique than that of the United States. This was the position enunciated by Foreign Minister Abba Eban on behalf of Israel. Speaking on the first day of the substantive proceedings of the General Assembly, June 19, 1967, Foreign Minister Eban said: "In free negotiations with each of our neighbors, we shall offer durable and just solutions redounding to our mutual advantage and honor." [41] He went on to say:

For the first time in history no Mediterranean nation is in subjection. All are endowed with sovereign freedom. The challenge now is to use this freedom for creative growth. There is only one road to that end: the road of recognition, of direct contact and of true cooperation, of peaceful coexistence.[42]

A little later in his statement Abba Eban said:

[41] A/PV.1526, p. 58.   [42] *Ibid.*, pp. 59–60.

Peace and security, with their juridical, territorial, economic and social implications, can only be built by the free negotiation which is the true essence of sovereign responsibility. A call to the recent combatants to negotiate the conditions of their future coexistence is surely the only constructive course which this Assembly could take.[43]

Here too was a forthright approach and one that in a conceptual sense had many elements—negotiation, cooperation, coexistence, and creative growth—to which no one could object. Even the strong pitch for free and direct negotiation was worth the making even though most Member States would regard it as too much to expect, in the circumstances, of the Arab states concerned. However, in substance this approach left undefined such important matters as withdrawal from the conquered territories of three states. In the light of the Charter of the United Nations, to which Israel is a party, a matter such as withdrawal falls within the clear directions of the law of the United Nations. It is not one that can be left to negotiation unless those negotiations are circumscribed within the framework of the accepted legal position, which, of course, would take care also of Israel's legitimate rights and interests. Would it not have been wiser for Israel at this juncture to make specific its adherence to the principles and injunctions of the Charter and to pledge itself to act accordingly? A plea for negotiations within this framework would have had much more impact on the General Assembly. As it was, the approach of Israel, stated with great eloquence and containing elements which could have been acceptable, remained unique and, to most states, so far as the Charter was concerned, in some degree off course. At the other extreme was the position of some of the Arab states. They too gave no specific assurance of compliance with the clear injunction of the Charter that there is to be no threat of the use of force. Prime Minister Krag of Denmark implied this when he said: "We can-

[43] *Ibid.,* p. 61.

not accept that any Member of the United Nations should base its foreign policy on the assumption of the non-existence of another Member State." Such an approach obviously cannot square with the obligations that all Member States of the United Nations have undertaken, through the Charter, in their dealings with one another. The positions of both the Arab states on the one hand and Israel on the other represented the extremes within which the United Nations would have to endeavor to find its way toward solutions or, at the very least, viable adjustments of the situation.

The seven approaches which we have discussed covered the attitudes of most member states of the United Nations—except the Latin Americans—to the Middle East crisis. However, a few countries, the most important of which was France, approached the problem in ways which were in some respects unique. In the long run the French position tended to converge toward goals which many other states—most of the Western European states, some Asian states, and Canada—had mentioned or were to mention.

Maurice Couve de Murville, the Foreign Minister of France, said: "The basic facts—they are still the same. The question is still that in the East Jews and Moslems be able to live side by side in peace, in tolerance and in reciprocal respect." [44] Later he said: "Only a freely negotiated settlement accepted by all the parties concerned and recognized by the international community could one day solve these problems as a whole. Obviously, we are far from this, and the French delegation knows this as well as anyone." [45] Since negotiation lay, in the French view, in

[44] A/PV.1531, pp. 33–35.

[45] Ibid., p. 41. We might note that Foreign Minister Eban did not accept this assessment. At the 1536th meeting of the General Assembly on June 26 he said: "I venture to express a lesser pessimism than did our eminent French colleague on the chance of an early dialogue, provided that everything is done to promote it. For both parties have an objective need for peace." (A/PV.1536, pp. 57–58.)

the distant future, the problem would fall in the meanwhile to the great powers for their consideration and for a decision by them:

In this community [the international community], it would be up to those whose special responsibility for the maintenance of peace and security is recognized in the Charter to play their role. Besides, we know that nothing will be done without these Powers nor, with all the more reason, against them or against any one of them.[46]

A concert of the four great powers (China, as represented at the United Nations, was excluded; moreover, the Peking government of China was also excluded as being unacceptable to the United States) would have to be reestablished and in that concert apparently France would play a distinctive and unique role in the reestablishment of peace in the Middle East.

France feels that it can claim to be entirely impartial and that its sole purpose in the Middle East, as everywhere else, is none other than peace. It has never—and I say this first to the Israelis—known racism, and today knows it less than ever before in its history. It maintains age-old relations with the Arabs, based, as far as it is concerned, on respect for their dignity and on the awareness that their first needs are the affirmation of their national personality and their economic and human development.[47]

The putting aside of negotiation until a long-deferred and unknown date in the future and the postulation of a special role for the great powers were not exclusive to the French position. They were points too realistic not to be mentioned by other representatives. Though his government had called for a special General Assembly meeting on the issue of the Middle East, Kosygin recognized that the great powers had a special role to play: "Much depends on the efforts of the great powers. It would be good if their delegates as well found a common language in order to reach decisions meeting the interests of peace in the Middle East and the interests of universal peace." [48]

---

[46] A/PV.1531, pp. 41–42.   [47] *Ibid.*, p. 42.   [48] A/PV.1526, p. 23.

Several other countries referred to the role of the great powers. Foreign Secretary George Brown of the United Kingdom drew attention to Kosygin's words and asked for further elaboration of the role of the great powers.[49] Perhaps Paul Martin, the Foreign Minister of Canada, expressed the most realistic point of view when he said: "There is no doubt in my mind that the permanent members of the Security Council must work together if any settlement is to be durable."[50] The Foreign Minister of Belgium, Pierre Harmel, had also drawn attention to Chairman Kosygin's remarks.[51]

What made the French approach unique, however, was that it went far beyond the recognition of a special responsibility resting on the great powers: four of those powers were to take upon themselves the settlement of the issue under the leadership of one of them (France). This was a suggestion not for United Nations diplomacy but for great-power diplomacy in which the forums of the United Nations would play no role, except perhaps, in the final analysis, the role of attestation. It might still be argued that this is, broadly speaking, a realistic point of view. But the fact remains that it is not in keeping with the major arrangements and procedures which the great powers and other states have together formulated. Moreover, it is not in keeping with widely accepted notions of our time such as the rights of states and regions to share in international decision-making on issues of direct concern to themselves. Finally, the insistence on the role of four or five great powers overlooks, in several ways, the realities of the dispositions of power which exist at the present time. First, the disparity in power between the United States and the Soviet Union, severally and jointly, on the one hand, and any other power or combination of powers, on the other hand, is so great that the mention of four great powers together, as if they were all peers, is artificial. Second, both in

[49] A/PV.1529, pp. 10–11.   [50] A/PV.1533, pp. 48–50.
[51] A/PV.1531, p. 27.

historical terms and in potential there are other claimants in the world to the title of "great power." Third, and most important of all, difficult though it is with all the weight and authority of the United Nations and its Charter to move toward negotiation of issues, this is a procedure and practice which the world is increasingly accepting. To suggest a regression exclusively to great-power politics would only greatly increase the obstacles to international understanding and negotiation; for in the final analysis good negotiation involves the participation of the states directly concerned. In its essential concept of great-power diplomacy, removed from the forums of the United Nations, the French position remained unique and without support from the 121 states represented at the Fifth Emergency Special Session of the General Assembly.

As the debate proceeded, heads of state or government, foreign ministers, and other representatives of the Member States came to the podium and took up positions which conformed generally to one or another of the seven approaches which this analysis has identified. Thus Mauritania, through its Foreign Minister on June 22, expressed an opinion in line with the strongest Arab position, as did the representative of Cuba on June 23. On the other hand, on June 23 the Prime Minister of Afghanistan and the Chairman of the Council of Ministers of Hungary expressed positions which approximated those of Yugoslavia. In each case, though there was fervent support of the Arab cause, there was also clear indication of the need to negotiate. On June 22 the Chairman of the Council of Ministers of Mongolia and on June 23 the Foreign Minister of Guinea and the Chairman of the Council of Ministers of Poland all aligned themselves with the Soviet approach. On the other hand, the Foreign Minister of Indonesia and the Foreign Minister of Turkey, speaking respectively on June 22 and 23, expressed positions which, though supporting the Arab states, did not explicitly favor condemnation and were on the whole assimilable to the

Indian approach. The Western European approach, the main framework of which had been first stated by Denmark and the United Kingdom, was broadly followed by Italy on June 21, Belgium on June 22, Sweden on June 23, Nepal on June 26, and Nigeria on June 27. This approach, which in many respects shared with the Indian approach the middle-of-the-road position, gained adherence from several continents.

Two interesting and significant variants of the Western European approach were expressed by the Foreign Minister of Canada, Paul Martin, and by Ion Gheorghe Maurer, Chairman of the Council of Ministers of Rumania, both on June 23. Canada is a country which has played an active and valuable role in regard to Middle East affairs. The first point of significance in the statement of Paul Martin was his view that the Security Council should continue its activities in regard to the crisis. He revealed that consultations had been in progress to make a Canadian draft resolution on the implementation of the cease-fire more widely acceptable and he stated:

In our view, these consultations should continue. The Security Council should deal with the draft resolutions before it. As we have often been reminded, the Council has the primary responsibility for the maintenance of peace and security. Here in this Assembly I would hope that we could establish some guidelines to assist the Council when it resumes its work.[52]

This was the clearest statement made regarding the importance of the role of the Security Council in the Middle East Crisis. On the question of the withdrawal of the Israeli forces Canada took a stand in line with the Western powers. Paul Martin quoted from the statement made ten years earlier by Lester Pearson, then Foreign Minister and now Prime Minister of Canada: " 'We cannot but agree that if Israel has a right to live and prosper free from the fear of strangulation from its neighbors, the Arab states also have a right to feel confident that

[52] A/PV.1533, p. 42.

Israel will not attempt to expand its territory at their expense.' " [53] Martin emphasized this matter in putting first among his four suggested principles the need for "respect for the territorial integrity of the nations of the area including provisions for the security and international supervision of frontiers." [54] His other principles were the right of all nations to innocent passage through international waterways, an early and just solution of the refugee problem, and international concern for the preservation of the special spiritual and religious interests in Jerusalem. The Canadian position taken as a whole lay somewhere between the position of the Western European states and that of the United States, though it was nearer to the former than the latter. Like most of the Western European states, Canada also envisaged the appointment of a special representative to the Secretary-General. In brief, the United Nations was kept in the foreground throughout in the Canadian approach. In this respect it was essentially an antithesis of the French approach.

The attitude of Rumania was of special significance because of its possible influence among other countries of Eastern Europe. The Chairman of the Council of Ministers of Rumania departed from the explicit position of the Soviet Union and most other Eastern European states by expressing a view in favor of direct negotiations between the parties concerned. "When circumstances prevent direct contact between the parties, it is then incumbent upon the international community to create a propitious climate for such a future dialogue." [55] However, for such a dialogue to take place, the Rumanian view was that there should be a withdrawal of forces so as to place the parties in a position of equality. Ion Gheorghe Maurer went on to say: "The necessary condition for the initiation and progress of any negotiation is that of perfect equality between the parties, and the avoidance of any attempt to impose solutions or, to that end, to exploit advantageous military situations." [56]

[53] *Ibid.*, pp. 43–45.   [54] *Ibid.*, pp. 48–50.   [55] *Ibid.*, p. 66.
[56] *Ibid.*

In asking for withdrawal, Rumania was taking the same position as the Western Europeans; in asking for direct negotiations, Rumania had taken a step in advance of some of the Western Europeans. But Rumania was disposed to go further in its policy of conciliation. "Relations of cooperation should be established in that area [the Middle East] in order to ensure the economic, national and social progress of those countries." [57] Indeed, in the Rumanian view all matters would be settled by an arrangement between the parties to reach "rational and equitable agreements that would take into account the legitimate rights of the people concerned." [58] Here, then, an East European state, a member of the Warsaw Pact, adopted a position in which the rational elements in a solution were very little distorted by partisanship. Israel's war gains were to be renounced and the Arabs were to receive security within their frontiers while, in exchange, they would negotiate with Israel for mutually beneficial arrangements. If more countries had been able to press for approaches similar to this, the Fifth Emergency Special Session could have done more toward the achievement of just and peaceful arrangements for the Middle East. Harsh partisanship, extreme positions, and the blurring of principles such as those contained in Article 2 of the Charter of the United Nations prohibiting the use of force or the threat of force do not serve the basic interests of peace or of equity. Fortunately, the Charter wisely awards the major responsibilities for resolving disputes to the Security Council. Both because it is considerably smaller than the Assembly and because its members cannot but be aware of the special responsibilities with which they are vested, the Security Council is less subject to the strong and destabilizing winds of partisanship than is the General Assembly. The Rumanian approach was worthy of the United Nations and of consideration by the Security Council and its members.

As was to be expected, the Arab states, including Yemen and

57 *Ibid.*, pp. 57–60.   58 *Ibid.*

Jordan on June 26 and Morocco and Iraq on June 27, all supported the position of full withdrawal, condemnation, restitution,
and no negotiations. However, the approach of King Hussein of
Jordan, as stated in his address to the Assembly on June 26,
contained features which illuminated the Arab position and
brought certain aspects into clear relief for the other members
of the Assembly. First, he stressed the relationship of peace to
justice. To the Arab mind justice inevitably must conjure up
the plight of well over one million refugees. But the problem
goes deeper than that. The sense of injustice seems to demand
that the refugees return to the territory of Israel and by doing
so diminish the size of Israel to something considerably less than
that which resulted from the Armistice Agreement of 1949. This
view explained King Hussein's statement: "Today's war is not a
new war, but part of the old war, which will go on for scores of
years if the moral and physical wrong done to the Arabs is not
righted." [59] Irredentism among the Arabs of Palestine and their
other Arab supporters is stronger than irredentism anywhere else
in the world. There have been movements of refugees on a far
larger scale than in Arabia—in parts of Europe and Asia—but
irredentism has generally become subordinated to other human
urges. In the deserts that surround Israel it is more difficult, apparently, for other human urges to assert themselves. There
seems to be a tenacious determination that other urges should
remain subordinate to that of irredentism. An even more striking
and portentous part of King Hussein's statement related to the
lessons of the Israeli-Arab war:

If there is one military lesson to be learned from the recent battle it is
that victory goes to the one who strikes first. This is a particularly
ironic and dangerous lesson to establish. But one way of establishing
it is to reward the aggressor with the fruits of his aggression. The
members of this Assembly should ponder well this point, or
they will surely risk setting a precedent which will haunt these
halls and the world for decades to come.[60]

[59] A/PV.1536, p. 6.   [60] *Ibid.*

Here was stated bluntly the doctrine of a tooth for a tooth, a doctrine which, Middle Eastern in its origin, apparently flourishes with special vigor in the region of its birth. But it is also a view which is broadly shared by many peoples, and King Hussein was undoubtedly right in drawing attention to the repercussive implications of a war of conquest, particularly among Member States of the United Nations which have voluntarily accepted a law that rules out any gains being derived from the use of force. The weakness of King Hussein's argument was not in what he stated but in what he left unsaid. In order that the law of the United Nations should be respected it was equally required that the threat of the use of force against the existence and presence of a Member State should also be fully eliminated. Indeed, the argument must necessarily be pushed to this point. Otherwise the process, which King Hussein wisely engaged in, of indicating the repercussive effects of certain actions is arrested at mid-point. In the Middle East it is clear that movements toward peace must go beyond the mid-point of this argument and must comprehend not only the use of force but certainly overt preparation for the use of force and threats to use force which have been the foundation for inevitable eruptions of conflict.

As to the task of the United Nations, King Hussein posed and answered the question very simply: "What, then, is the duty of the United Nations? It can be nothing else but the swift condemnation of the aggressor and the enforcing of the return of Israeli troops to the lines held before the attack of 5 June." [61]

There was no word of strengthening UN machinery in the area, no talk of navigation, no talk of even tacit acceptance of the configuration of states in the area, and of course no indication of negotiation. Indeed, before he closed the King returned to the condemnation of Israel's aggression and the return of all Arab territory. If this was not done there would be war once more and the United Nations would, in the future, never again

[61] *Ibid.*, p. 11.

be obeyed if it called for a cease-fire.[62] The King's speech was a sobering one, but its logic was such that it could only lend support to those very different approaches based on the strict insistence by the United Nations that the process of conciliation in the area proceed at least to the point of recognition of the existence of all the present UN members, based on a territorial configuration prior to the outbreak of hostilities on June 5, 1967.

We have already noted that Cuba had stepped out of line with the other Communist Member States by adopting a position at least as adamant as that of the Arabs. But the Arabs themselves were outdone by another uniquely placed state—Albania. The Foreign Minister of Albania, Nesti Nase, roundly abused the Soviet revisionists. Although the Arab states had acknowledged the assistance they had received from the Soviet Union and had expressed their support for the draft resolution which had been introduced by Kosygin, the Albanians found that resolution too mild and introduced one containing a more bitter attack against the Western powers and an adamant expression of the exclusive right of the United Arab Republic to determine the use of the Suez Canal and the Strait of Tiran.[63]

Although they approximated, in a basic sense, the approach of the Western European states, there were interesting singularities in the statements made by the representatives of Finland and Ireland. The Finnish Ambassador to the United Nations, Max Jakobson, began by saying that because Finland was neutral its best contribution would be to "refrain from taking sides in the disputes between the great powers." He pointed out that a neutral state has a special obligation

to retain the confidence of all parties and thus . . . to perform such peaceful services as may be required, including the modest yet indispensable service of maintaining contact between states that have broken off diplomatic relations. This is an obligation which the Finnish Government is accustomed to assume.[64]

[62] *Ibid.*, p. 12.   [63] A/L.521.   [64] A/PV.1537, p. 61.

However, with this disclaimer Ambassador Jakobson went on to reiterate Finland's commitment, and that of all Member States, to the Charter of the United Nations. On this basis he stated a position which was close to that of the Western European states: full withdrawal by Israel, United Nations participation in Middle East arrangements as long as a lasting political settlement was not achieved, urgent attention to the problem of refugees, the need for effective measures to prevent the spread of nuclear weapons, a balanced reduction of conventional armaments, and, finally, great-power cooperation to maintain the peace. The element of difference between this approach and that of most other Europeans was that the Finnish representative refrained from making statements about the contents of a long-term settlement in the area.

Deputy Prime Minister and Foreign Minister Frank Aiken of Ireland is one of the stalwarts of the United Nations scene. Ireland's brand of neutrality is far from one of removal from the affairs of the world. Frequently Ireland has a significant contribution to make and on June 27, 1967, Frank Aiken made a distinctive and important statement. It was perhaps the most far-reaching of all those made in the Assembly's debate. He stated its purpose as being to suggest

for the consideration of the Assembly the basis for a treaty of peace which we believe would give a fair and reasonable chance of preventing another clash every few years, or perhaps a conflict in which nuclear weapons would be used. Indeed, I am convinced that if a stable peace cannot be secured, the race for the bomb is bound to begin in real earnest.[65]

The two essential elements in Aiken's plan were

First, the withdrawal of Israeli forces to the 4 June line in an orderly and controlled manner . . . ; secondly, the treaty should be legally and firmly guaranteed by the United Nations including a majority, if not all of the great Powers in the Security Council.[66]

[65] A/PV.1538, pp. 16–17.   [66] *Ibid.*, p. 17.

He hoped that the Secretary-General could assist in the initiation and conduct of negotiations on a permanent treaty of peace and he set out some of the matters which should be covered by such a treaty: division of the Jordan waters, freedom of navigation in the Suez Canal and Aqaba, air rights, wayleaves for pipelines carrying oil and water, surface traffic rights to the Mediterranean for Arab states, and the prohibition of hate propaganda.[67] Frank Aiken had an imaginative and valuable suggestion to make to Israel. He hoped

that the government of Israel would announce without delay that one of her contributions to a treaty of peace and non-aggression, signed by herself and her Arab neighbors, and guaranteed by the United Nations, including the great Powers of the Security Council, would be the withdrawal of her forces to within the boundaries of 4 June last. Anything less than a complete withdrawal would be intolerable on the part of a signatory of the United Nations Charter. Agreed adjustments of the boundaries for economic reasons, such as the improvement of road communications, would not, of course, be excluded at a later stage.[68]

Unfortunately Foreign Minister Aiken's ideas have not yet been translated into reality by the Arabs and the Israelis.

[67] *Ibid.*, p. 21.   [68] *Ibid.*, pp. 18–20.

The Latin American Position

THE TWENTY-THREE Latin American states that are members of the United Nations, excepting Cuba, refrained from participating in the debate for more than a week. Thirty-seven other countries had expressed their points of view and some of them had spoken more than once before the Argentinian delegate entered the debate in the late morning of June 27, 1967.

The Latin Americans might be likened to the European neutrals twice removed. Being geographically remote from the Middle East and without any significant trade with that area, they are able to be more detached from the Middle East crisis than any other considerable group of states. At the same time, Hispanic culture has had an injection from the Arab world and the Latin Americans have a certain psychological interest in the Middle East. There are, moreover, both Arab and Jewish peoples living in many of the Latin American countries. Finally, and perhaps most important of all to the Latin Americans, the problems of the Holy Land evoke a strong emotional response.

We have noted that in the Security Council the participation of the two important Latin American states, Argentina and Brazil, was peripheral. In the General Assembly, however, there are over twenty Latin American states and jointly they constitute an important voting group. The fact that in the Assembly there are no special categories of membership tends to free the smaller states from inhibitions which are, in some degree, operative in the Security Council. Another important consideration is that in recent years the Latin Americans have found themselves increasingly drawn into world affairs, and have consequently come to take a more active part in such affairs than they did in the earlier years of United Nations activities. For example, two Latin American states—Brazil and Mexico—are members of the Eighteen-Nation Disarmament Committee which for more than five years has been engaged in an almost continuous pursuit of agreements in the field of arms limitation and disarmament. So far as the Middle East is concerned, two Latin American states— Brazil and Colombia—were among the seven states that constituted the Advisory Committee created by the First Emergency Special Session of the General Assembly in connection with the establishment and continued functioning of the United Nations Emergency Force. It was to be expected that the Latin American states in the Assembly would have some part to play in the attempt to deal with the Middle East crisis. What was not initially known was that the Latin American role would become a highly significant one and would be of major importance in the negotiations, both behind the scenes and in the Assembly hall, for arriving at formulations which could be widely acceptable as a basis for steps toward the pacification of the Middle East. The general approach of the Latin Americans toward the formulation of a position was quite distinct from the approaches previously identified. This is not to say that the Latin American position was so unique that it had no points of similarity with the other approaches before the Assembly. On the contrary, the Latin Americans could not have played a significant role if one of their foremost objectives had not been to widen the area of consensus among Assembly members. There were, at the same time, certain definite principles involved in the Latin American approach, and the steadfast maintenance of positions of principle is what gives an approach its strength and its distinctive contribution.

Nicanor Coste Mendez, Foreign Minister of Argentina, the

first Latin American to participate in the debate, revealed the major aspects of the Latin American approach.

First and foremost in this approach was the strong emphasis on juridical principles. The first substantive point made by the Foreign Minister of Argentina was: "Time and again my delegation has stressed the need for a scrupulous respect for the legal principles that govern relations among states and gave its support to any resolution that bore with it their reaffirmation and application." [1]

In line with this thinking, Coste Mendez went on to say that "the essential meaning of the present session . . . is to put an end to all bellicosity and to organize peace." [2] How was this peace to be organized? So far as the Assembly was concerned this was to be done by a juridical approach: "By the definition and affirmation of certain general principles . . . this Assembly should once again reiterate the basic principles of the Charter." [3] It would then be for the Security Council—and again this was a procedural approach based on international law—to carry the task further.

When the Argentinian Foreign Minister went on to define the main lines of his country's position in detail he blended juridical points with the practical steps which could be taken in conformity with international law. The first step was support and maintenance of the cease-fire, which was both a practical necessity and a legal obligation of respect for the decision of the Security Council. His second point was rooted in the law of the United Nations. He believed that the Assembly should "draw the attention of the parties to the purposes and principles of Chapter I of the Charter of the United Nations." He pointed out that

respect for the juridical and political personality of States . . . the rule which enjoins on States mutual respect for their territorial

[1] A/PV.1537, p. 52.   [2] *Ibid.*, p. 53.   [3] *Ibid.*

integrity and political independence, and that which prohibits the use or the threat of force to impose solutions contrary to the principles of the Charter . . . constitute the ineluctable bases for international coexistence among States.[4]

Another point was: "The Assembly should once again ratify the principle of free passage in international waters." This again was a legal approach. Two of the Foreign Minister's points dealt with the return of the issue to the Security Council, and the steps which that body should take. His fifth point was "that withdrawal must be a condition concomitant with a cessation of the state of belligerency if it is to have a truly logical meaning and a juridical basis." [5] He indicated that this formula was an application of another fundamental principle which had been formulated in Article 2 of the Anti-War Treaty signed in Rio de Janeiro in 1933.

In closing, the Foreign Minister expressed his concern about, and made suggestions in regard to, the problems of the refugees and the Holy Places.

In this Argentinian statement was present a degree of emphasis on juridical principles which had been unmatched in any of the other statements which we have passed in review. Others had referred to the importance of the principles of the Charter of the United Nations and compliance with them by the parties to the conflict, but no other approach was so firmly rooted in the sustaining ground of international law. The positions of nine other Latin American states were presented to the Assembly in the period up to July 4 when votes were cast on the draft resolutions before that body. Most of those statements contained strong evidence of the importance which the Latin American states, particularly those of Hispanic origin, attached to juridical principles.

The second Latin American speaker was Ambassador Julio Caesar Turbay Ayala of Colombia. Again the first point to be

[4] *Ibid.*, p. 56.   [5] *Ibid.*, p. 57.

made concerned the importance of maintaining the rule of law. "Our only commitments are those born of respect for the rule of law, for our international obligations, and our duty as a Member of the United Nations and of the American regional system." [6] When he came to make his suggestions to the Assembly his prelude was that "the paths of understanding . . . lie rather along the middle line of law, reason and justice." [7] First, there was to be universal recognition of Israel, for the United Nations had given that country its juridical and political life. Second, practical attention was to be given to the problem of refugees. Third, "Colombia is committed by international agreements to total respect for the provisions on free navigation and innocent passage of ships through the waterways of the world." [8] Fourth, there could be no legitimate alteration of territorial boundaries by force, a position to which Colombia was committed not only as a member of the UN: "This traditional Colombian position stems from our own juridical conviction and from the clear and irrevocable commitments flowing from the *Carta de Bogotá*, by which the Organization of American States was constituted." [9]

Fifth, he proposed such practical steps as demilitarized zones and the appointment of a mediator or a representative of the Secretary-General. Among his final points was the advice that the General Assembly should entrust the Security Council with the strict fulfillment of its recommendations. This too was an expression of view based on the law of the UN Charter. In summing up the position of his country the Colombian Ambassador said that he had "expressed in this hall the views of a country which respects the law and which believes in the power of reason and the irresistible strength of the law." [10]

The most incisive legal interpretation of the situation and the problems to be faced was made by the next Latin American speaker, Ambassador Don Leopold Benites of Ecuador, an expert

[6] A/PV.1538, pp. 24–25.   [7] *Ibid.*, p. 27.   [8] *Ibid.*, p. 31.
[9] *Ibid.*, p. 32.   [10] *Ibid.*, pp. 33–35.

in United Nations affairs who has recently been chairman of the highly important First Political Committee of the General Assembly. The Ecuadorian Ambassador made a brilliant analysis of the applicability to the situation of charges of aggression or belligerency. He pointed out that the direction of international law would establish the activities of the combatants in the Middle East as belligerency rather than as aggression.[11] But ever since the Treaty of Paris (the Kellogg-Briand Pact) outlawing war, "there was then born an imperative norm of international law which would in due course become a principle of *jus cogens* in the American sphere." [12]

He traced the development of this principle through the Stimson Doctrine contained in the letter of January 7, 1932, addressed to China and Japan, the nonaggression and conciliation treaty of 1933 known as the Saavedra Lamas Pact, the Buenos Aires Convention of December 23, 1936, down to Article 5 of the Charter of the Organization of American States, the juridical distillation being "victory grants no rights." [13] He then traced how the League of Nations and the Charter of the United Nations had continued the same ideas and concluded that based on

the progressive development of international law . . . I have specific instructions from my Government to state that we openly reject any territorial conquest through force or the retention of territories that have been occupied as a means of exerting pressure on further negotiations for peace.[14]

Such was the heart—and it was a juridical one—of the statement of the representative of Ecuador. In its further development he continued his legal analysis, and we might note only that he directed his legal acumen also to paragraphs 3 (b) and 3 (c) of the United States draft resolution (Document A/L.520). Paragraph 3 (b) asked for "freedom of innocent maritime passage." Ambassador Benites pointed out that " 'freedom' refers to

[11] A/PV.1539, p. 7.   [12] *Ibid.*, pp. 8–10.   [13] *Ibid.*
[14] *Ibid.*, p. 11.

the high seas, while 'innocent passage' refers to territorial seas."
He then quoted from paragraphs 4 and 5 of Article 14 of the
Convention on the Territorial Sea and the Contiguous Zone of
1958. In regard to innocent passage of ships he pointed out that
the U.S. draft had taken two concepts, which should have been
kept separate, and fused them.

The next Latin American statement was made by Foreign
Minister José de Magalhaes Pinto of Brazil on June 28. Here the
Spanish tradition was not to the fore, and the Brazilian delegate's
views were more pragmatic. He regretted that the services of
the United Nations Emergency Force should have been terminated at a time when the Force "could still have fruitfully
discharged its peace-keeping functions." [15] The seven principles
which the Brazilian Foreign Minister announced contained three
formal guarantees, two by Israel, regarding the settling of the
problem of refugees and the withdrawal of its forces, and one
by the United Arab Republic to ensure free navigation through
the Strait of Tiran. His other principles included recognition of
Israel by the Arab states, the opening of the Suez to ships of
all flags, the placing of Jerusalem under permanent international
administration, and, finally, negotiations for the settlement of all
pending problems by the parties concerned with the assistance,
if required, of a representative of the Secretary-General. The
Brazilian Foreign Minister underlined the pragmatism of his
country's approach by adding that his government had no preference for any particular method of resolving the situation. It
would accept whatever formula was workable.[16]

The general approach of Brazil to international problems is
often more pragmatic than the approaches of the other Latin
American states. In this particular case there was an additional
reason for pragmatism. At this stage Latin American representatives, including the representative of Brazil, had been talking to
representatives of the nonaligned states such as India and Yugo-

[15] A/PV.1540, p. 2.   [16] *Ibid.*, pp. 6–7.

slavia about a possible convergence of points of view to form the basis of a joint draft resolution. These discussions had not resulted in agreement but they had brought to a head many of the practical issues which had to be resolved. At the very session at which the Brazilian Foreign Minister spoke, the Ambassador of Yugoslavia introduced a draft resolution (A/L. 522) on behalf of fourteen states, for the most part nonaligned.[17]

In view of their nonaligned origin, the draft proposals introduced on June 28, 1967, by Ambassador Danilo Lekic of Yugoslavia were regarded both by their sponsors and by a somewhat wider circle of members as an attempted compromise solution which would perhaps be acceptable to the Assembly. The details of these and other proposals before the Assembly will be discussed in the next chapter. At this juncture we notice mainly the effect of the nonaligned proposals on the posture and tactics of the Latin American states.

The Latin Americans increased the intensity of their participation in the Assembly's proceeding. At each of the following three sessions one of them spoke, responding to the mood of the Assembly by injecting into their largely juridical approach suggestions for practical steps to meet a situation clearly demanding not only theory but action. At the 1541st meeting of the Assembly on the morning of June 29, Ambassador Enrique Garcia Sayan of Peru chose as his basis respect for "the norms of international co-existence as set forth in the Charters of both these Organizations [the United Nations and the Organization of American States] . . . adherence to principles such as those which are at stake in the present crisis, namely, the peaceful settlement of disputes, and respect for the territorial integrity and political sovereignty of States." [18] How was the United Nations to deal with this crisis? In posing this question Ambassador Garcia Sayan indicated the lines on which the answer would have to be found. He said the situation had "raised the question

[17] For final text, see Appendix 14.   [18] A/PV.1541, p. 11.

. . . as to whether the United Nations will prove capable of resolving this crisis by maintaining and reaffirming the Purposes and Principles set forth in the Charter; and also as to whether it can reestablish law and justice." [19] Ambassador Garcia Sayan found the answer, as had all of his Hispanic colleagues, in terms of juridical concepts and their application. But because these concepts now had to be translated into realities he sketched out a number of points to serve as guidelines for the resolution to be adopted. These points were a full withdrawal of Israeli forces, demilitarized zones on both sides of the armistice lines manned by United Nations forces, a special United Nations Commissioner to deal specifically with the resettlement of refugees, free transit of ships, including those of Israel through the Suez Canal and the Gulf of Aqaba, a special regime for Jerusalem, and, finally, "to urge the parties in conflict, once they have implemented these prior provisions, to negotiate directly a halt to the state of belligerence and to agree upon a peace treaty." [20] This was an interesting inversion of the basic juridical position formulated by Peru itself and a number of other Latin American states. The Peruvian proposal suggested the taking of a number of firm practical steps which would have the effect of giving both sides the substance of what each of them regarded as essential. The legal component of the new arrangements would be the coping stone that would be placed in position by the parties themselves once they had tasted the fruits of a new regime of orderliness and quiet in their region. There was much to be said for this approach, which took into account the view frequently expressed both in the Assembly and in private that it was impracticable to expect negotiations among the parties so soon after their dramatic armed clash. It is often wise in international affairs to create new practical elements in a situation before expecting the states involved to get together to do that which they have long refused to undertake.

[19] *Ibid.*   [20] *Ibid.*, pp. 13–16.

Apart from its practical wisdom, the Peruvian approach served to answer the proposals of the nonaligned states with a clear indication that, though the Latin Americans were geographically remote from the Middle East, they had every intention of formulating proposals regarding the latest and most serious situation that had arisen in that area. Moreover, the Peruvian statement, together with those which had been made by the representatives of Argentina, Colombia, Ecuador, and Brazil before the introduction of the fourteen-power draft proposals, showed that the Latin Americans were not going to be able to welcome those proposals. Their own concept of the juridical necessities of the situation, in terms of the United Nations Charter, was such that the nonaligned proposals fell short of the needs of the case.

On the afternoon of the same day, June 29, Ambassador Luis Demetrio Tinoco of Costa Rica again laid down the juridical bases of a solution. The requirements of the situation from the point of view of juridical order were recognition of the existence of Israel, "its consequent personality as an entity in international law," [21] and recognition of the fact that membership in the United Nations creates "specific, consolidated juridical situations which pertain to all Member States." [22] Ambassador Tinoco expressed the adherence of his government to the view that in international relations every legally constituted state has a right to be recognized, a right which creates a reciprocal obligation to recognize it on the part of other states; in support of this view he cited Lauterpacht, Jiménez de Aréchaga, and Ricardo Alfaro. Other rights and duties which were applicable to this situation were those of freedom of transit through the Suez Canal and innocent passage through the Strait of Tiran. On the other side he directed Israel not to "forget that modern law has totally abandoned the ancient concept which caused so much suffering and bloodshed: that the spoils of war go to the victor and that the victor can dictate the terms of peace." [23] He affirmed that

[21] A/PV.1542, p. 57.   [22] *Ibid.*   [23] *Ibid.*, pp. 58–60.

the United Nations could not tolerate retrogression in this respect, and he went on to strip Israel of all legal rights to Jerusalem. "Israel cannot assume and hold the territory that its armies have occupied. The Knesset has no authority to decree the Old City of Jerusalem to Israel. . . . The decree of incorporation . . . has no juridical value." [24] The Ambassador of Costa Rica had not enunciated a practical program for the area, but his views again made it clear that the fourteen-power draft resolution would not meet even the minimal conceptual demands of the Latin American states.

The next Latin American speaker, on the morning of June 30, was Foreign Minister Hector Luisi of Uruguay. He said that he had come to contribute "to the search for the solutions that will ensure to the Middle East a just and stable peace under the rule of international law." [25] The Foreign Minister went on to state three essential juridical principles: the irrevocability of the existence as sovereign states of all the parties to the dispute, the right of all nations to freedom from aggression of all kinds as well as freedom from intimidation, and the principle that conquest does not engender rights or establish superior bargaining positions.

The legal basis having been laid down, the Foreign Minister of Uruguay called for withdrawal and then made novel suggestions of great value. He called for supervision of military installations in the territories of the parties and an international commission to "enforce an immediate freezing of the arming process being carried out by the parties" and to "institute procedures for the reduction of armaments." [26] These wise suggestions were, however, not immediately taken up either by the other Latin American states or by other sections of the Assembly membership. Foreign Minister Luisi's proposals included the other obvious necessities of the situation in regard to navigation, refugees, and Jerusalem. The groundwork had by now been well laid for an introduction by the Latin Americans of their version of proposals to deal with the Middle East crisis.

[24] *Ibid.*, p. 61.   [25] A/PV.1543, pp. 38–40.   [26] *Ibid.*, p. 41.

Behind the scenes more had taken place than in the Assembly itself. The Latin American group had met frequently and, by now, had had the advantage of listening to over sixty statements by representatives of the Member States of the UN. Moreover, some of the most highly respected and well-known Latin American diplomats had shown the admirable restraint of refraining from participation in the debate so as to keep an open mind until the last possible moment. In this way they felt they could best serve the cause of peace by being able to incorporate or take advantage of all possible avenues of constructive thinking. Prominent among those who so restrained themselves was the brilliant representative of Mexico, Ambassador Francisco Cuevas Cancino. Assiduous in his meetings with other delegates from all sections of the Assembly and making contributions of primary importance at the discussions in the Latin American caucus, Cuevas Cancino had not entered the battle of words in the Assembly.

The resolution which the Latin American states finally drew up and introduced in the afternoon of June 30, 1967, was presented to the Assembly, not by one of the older Latin American states, but by Dr. P. V. J. Solomon, the able lawyer who heads the delegation of the non-Hispanic state of Trinidad and Tobago. Dr. Solomon introduced a resolution on behalf of eighteen of the twenty-three Latin American states (Argentina, Bolivia, Brazil, Chile, Colombia, Costa Rica, Ecuador, El Salvador, Guatemala, Guyana, Honduras, Jamaica, Mexico, Nicaragua, Panama, Paraguay, Trinidad and Tobago, and Venezuela). In the next few days Barbados and the Dominican Republic joined the other sponsors, while Peru and Uruguay remained supporters but not sponsors of the draft.

Dr. Solomon did not deem it necessary to preface the Latin American proposals by a restatement of the juridical principles on which they were based. He introduced them, indeed, without any detailed discussion, claiming impartiality for the Latin Americans: "Because we are not immediately involved, we have been able to view the situation more objectively perhaps than those who are directly involved and whose personal feelings and national interests are implicated more deeply than ours are." [27] The delegations on whose behalf the proposals were introduced hoped that in them would be found reconciled the interests of the parties "with the fundamental principles of justice, freedom and equity, as outlined in our Charter." [28] With this brief pragmatic introduction, more in the Anglo-Saxon legal tradition than that of the Hispanic world, Solomon introduced the following text:

The General Assembly,

Considering that all Member States have an inescapable obligation to preserve peace and, consequently, to avoid the use of force in the international sphere,

Considering further that the cease-fire ordered by the Security Council and accepted by the State of Israel and the States of Jordan, Syria and the United Arab Republic is a first step towards the achievement of a just peace in the Middle East, a step which must be reinforced by other measures to be adopted by the Organization and complied with by the parties,

1. *Urgently requests:*

(a) Israel to withdraw all its forces from all the territories of Jordan, Syria and the United Arab Republic occupied as a result of the recent conflict;

(b) The parties in conflict to end the state of belligerency, to endeavor to establish conditions of coexistence based on good neighborliness and to have recourse in all cases to the procedures for peaceful settlement indicated in the Charter of the United Nations;

2. *Reaffirms its conviction* that no stable international order can be based on the threat or use of force, and declares that the validity of the occupation or acquisition of territories brought about by such means should not be recognized;

3. *Requests* the Security Council to continue examining the situation in the Middle East with a sense of urgency, working directly with the parties and relying on the presence of the United Nations to:

[27] A/PV.1544, pp. 6–7.   [28] *Ibid.*, p. 7.

(a) Carry out the provisions of operative paragraph 1 (a) above;

(b) Guarantee freedom of transit on the international waterways in the region;

(c) Achieve an appropriate and full solution of the problem of the refugees and guarantee the territorial inviolability and political independence of the States of the region, through measures including the establishment of demilitarized zones;

4. *Reaffirms*, as in earlier recommendations, the desirability of establishing an international régime for the city of Jerusalem, to be considered by the General Assembly at its twenty-second session.[29]

If Solomon's presentation of the Latin American proposals did not spell out their juridical basis, that was fully done immediately after the weekend by Ambassador Humberto Lopez Villamil of Honduras. In his exposition of July 3 Lopez Villamil disclosed that the Latin American meeting of minds on urgent and necessary measures in the Middle East had been arrived at "without renouncing the basic elements of international law and the principles of the Charter." [30] In thus giving priority to a reaffirmation of the juridical basis of the Latin American proposals, the Ambassador of Honduras was performing the task of maintaining the balance between the juridical and the practical which the new proposals were intended to convey. Dr. Solomon's presentation had been so pragmatic that the sponsors of the draft resolution now considered it necessary to complement it by a more legal approach. In doing so the Latin Americans were wisely widening to the maximum the potentialities of their own proposals.

Besides, Ambassador Lopez Villamil's presentation added a new line of persuasion. It was necessary for someone to act in the current Middle East situation. It would be best for the parties to negotiate, but in view of the history of the past twenty years "the present moment does not contain the necessary elements for direct understanding." [31] Therefore action had to be

---

[29] A/L.523. For final text, see Appendix 13.   [30] A/PV.1546, p. 66.
[31] *Ibid.*, p. 67.

taken by the organs of the United Nations, to fill the breach. To this end the Latin American group had resorted to elements of equity and justice.

The Honduran Ambassador pointed out that the very first operative paragraph expressed "the will of the quasi-unanimity of this Organization, since it urgently requests Israel to withdraw all its forces from all the territories of Jordan, Syria and the United Arab Republic." [32] This proposal was of course firmly rooted in the legal view, which had been repeated by a number of Latin American representatives, that conquest creates no rights and in the context of the law of the United Nations is absolutely impermissible. Moving to the second part of the first operative paragraph of the Latin American proposals, the Honduran representative pointed out that the cessation of belligerency also followed from the law of the Charter. The conditions of neighborliness and peaceful settlement of disputes called for in the same paragraph amounted "merely [to] asking the parties to fulfill the purposes of the Charter of the United Nations peacefully, with the assistance of the Organization or with whatever assistance the Organization may be called upon to give." [33]

Paragraph two of the new proposals relating to the threat or use of force being repugnant to international order was "definitely a principle of international law accepted by all States which reflects the purposes of the Charter." [34]

Similarly, the third operative paragraph of the draft resolution was based on the law of the Charter which had assigned to the Security Council the primary responsibility to maintain international peace and security.

In summing up his presentation Ambassador Lopez Villamil said: "The Latin American draft resolution is not meant to encourage aggression or territorial ambitions in the region, since this result would betray the juridical institutions established by the Organization of American States." [35]

[32] *Ibid.*   [33] *Ibid.*, p. 71.   [34] *Ibid.*   [35] *Ibid.*, pp. 73-75.

Thus the Latin American proposals were unfolded in full keeping with the high purpose of fidelity to modern international law which is becoming increasingly a part of the Hispanic-American tradition.

At the same session of the General Assembly the Peruvian representative explained that though his delegation would support the Latin American draft resolution it would have preferred a text which would have established demilitarized zones on both sides of the armistice lines and would have placed "greater emphasis . . . upon the need by the belligerents to recognize the juridical existence of all areas in the region of the conflict." [36] On the same day the Latin Americans also presented again to the Assembly a more pragmatic interpretation of their approach through Ambassador Manuel Perez Guerrero of Venezuela, a senior UN diplomat and a member of the committee then engaged in examining the situation in South Arabia. While stressing all the points in the draft resolution—no annexations, withdrawal, the setting aside of belligerency, freedom of navigation, the problem of Jerusalem, and the settlement of refugees—the Ambassador did not mention the juridical concepts which had inspired the practical suggestions contained in the draft resolution.

In all, ten Latin American representatives had taken part in the debate, and the result of their effort had been a bold and significant one: the presentation of proposals directed toward pacification of an area of the world with which they were not directly involved and which was situated thousands of miles away. This step did not by any means complete the contribution of the Latin American states to the Fifth Emergency Special Session. However, the later and perhaps even more significant steps of these states, being closely connected with the efforts of other sections of the Assembly, are best examined in subsequent chapters of this study.

[36] *Ibid.*, p. 62.

CHAPTER X

The Emergency Assembly
Fails to Act

BY THE END OF June the Fifth Emergency Special Session of the Assembly had before it all the likely draft proposals on the main issues that constituted the crisis and erupted in war. Chronologically these were:

a) The Soviet draft which Chairman Kosygin had introduced as early as June 19.[1] We have already noted its main characteristics of condemnation, full withdrawal, and restitution, with no mention of negotiations.

b) The United States proposals introduced the next day, June 20.[2] These proposals, which were introduced in Ambassador Goldberg's first substantive statement to the Assembly, have also been reviewed. Unlike the Soviet proposals, they looked to the establishment of a stable peace in the Middle East through negotiations between the parties, with outside assistance if necessary. The basis of Middle East stability was spelled out to include fixed boundaries, recognition of the political independence and territorial integrity of all the states in the area, disengagement and withdrawal of forces, freedom of navigation, settlement of refugees, and limitation of arms shipments.

c) On June 26 in his completely one-sided presentation the Foreign Minister of Albania had introduced a draft resolution couched in extreme terms. It condemned not only Israel but the United States and the United Kingdom and affirmed that

[1] A/L.519. See Appendix 11. [2] A/L.520. See Appendix 12.

the United Arab Republic alone had the right to determine passage through the Suez Canal and the Gulf of Aqaba.[3]

d) The fourth draft resolution was that of fourteen states, largely nonaligned Asian and African states but including also Yugoslavia and Cyprus,[4] which we have briefly mentioned in our examination of the Latin American position and to which we will return for a fuller analysis. Both Albania and Cuba submitted amendments to this set of proposals in order to introduce condemnation of Israel and the Western powers.[5]

e) The fifth and final substantive draft contained the Latin American proposal [6] which we have reviewed in Chapter IX.

A draft resolution of the fourteen largely nonaligned countries might normally have been expected to locate the middle ground between the parties. This has been the traditional role of the nonaligned states in regard to cold war issues such as disarmament, nuclear weapons testing, and outer space. On colonial issues the nonaligned have taken positions strongly opposed to the continuance of the remnants of European colonialism, some of which positions have been fairly widely supported.

The Middle East crisis of 1967 was a new kind of test for the nonaligned states. Some of the Arab countries directly involved, notably the United Arab Republic and Syria, were stalwart members of this group of states. Algeria and Iraq also belonged to this general grouping. The test of the nonaligned states as a whole became whether they could or could not take a strictly nonaligned position in the General Assembly on an issue which engaged some of their own members in conflict with another state—Israel. This is not to be construed to mean that neutrality was required of the nonaligned. They have never regarded themselves as neutral. They have been nonaliged with the power blocs but have professed to be for a lowering of tensions, peaceful settlement, disarmament, de-colonization, and equity and fair dealings among states.

[3] A/L.521.   [4] A/L.522. See Appendix 14.
[5] A/L.524 and A/L.525 respectively.   [6] A/L.523. See Appendix 13.

There had been no exact parallel to this situation in the Assembly. The 1956 Suez crisis had been significantly different. On that occasion the participation of France and the United Kingdom in the attack on Egypt had given the situation a close relationship with old-time colonialism. The United States had opposed its Western European allies and the super powers thus stood broadly together.

The closest parallel to the new test of nonalignment had been the international situation created toward the end of 1962 when the forces of Peking China had invaded northeastern India. At that time the nonaligned states had seen a leading member of the group, and by common consent *the* leading member, suffer invasion; but few of them—the United Arab Republic was a notable exception—had expressed their sympathy openly with India. However, six nonaligned African and Asian states—Burma, Cambodia, Ceylon, Ghana, Indonesia, and the United Arab Republic—had met together and attempted to conciliate the Sino-Indian dispute. In addressing themselves to the problem, although they were dealing with a situation that directly concerned one of their own leading colleagues they showed a meticulous care for equity and impartiality. They drew up proposals which in most respects were acceptable to both China and India, and which exercised a stabilizing influence in the area. In this difficult test it might be said that the nonaligned states had acquitted themselves in a manner which was in keeping with the basic tenets governing their general approach to international affairs.

The Arab-Israeli situation was even more difficult than the Sino-Indian conflict. The Arabs have never recognized the existence of Israel and therefore both the psychological and political complexities of the situation were much greater than those that existed in the case of the Sino-Indian conflict. In that case the main emphasis, though not the only one, was on withdrawal as a first step to negotiation on the general issue of the border between China and India. Nonaligned thinking regarded the complete withdrawal of invading forces as the *sine qua non* of any settlement. In the 1967 Arab-Israeli war the principle of withdrawal had been stated as a prime necessity by a number of Western states. Though in most cases, with the notable exception of France, withdrawal was to be followed or accompanied by negotiation with the objective of fixing the terms of a durable peace, Assembly sentiment seemed, to the nonaligned states, to favor a primary emphasis on withdrawal.

However, while the Indian government was willing, in a variety of circumstances, to negotiate with China, the Arabs had by and large made it clear that they would not negotiate with Israel. Behind the scenes individual Arab representatives would lean toward a peaceful settlement, but not through direct negotiation between the Arab and Israeli leaders. In these circumstances the nonaligned were not able to find a feasible formula giving negotiations between the parties even approximate parity with the withdrawal of Israel's forces.

This being so, perhaps the nonaligned states should not have ventured upon proposals to the Assembly. But international politics rarely allows of so logical a conclusion. Political ties compel a forward movement of events. The nonaligned states could not let down Egypt and Syria, especially when the territories of these countries had been occupied, thereby creating a tangible wrong that, in the view of the nonaligned, had to be urgently undone—whatever else might require attention. If they did so, other powers not nonaligned would champion the Arab cause and this could lead to political repercussions and realignments which governments would have to ponder over and could not accept at short notice.

To the nonaligned these considerations were paramount, and they swept the sponsors of Resolution A/L.522 into a more one-sided position than would normally be expected from states with their basic convictions in international politics. The result was that the nonaligned resolution, first introduced on June 28,

1967, by Ambassador Danilo Lekic of Yugoslavia, called for full withdrawal of Israeli forces and asked the Secretary-General to ensure compliance with this call; to this was added a request to the Security Council "to give consideration to questions pertaining to the situation in the area" after the withdrawal of Israel's forces had been completed.[7] This text called for withdrawal—which is what the Arabs wanted—plus practically nothing else. Consideration by the Security Council had been enjoined in numerous resolutions on the Middle East over the years and had amounted to precisely nothing in terms of measures to establish peace in the area. The first nonaligned draft proposal could hardly be read as a possible basis for fulfillment in the Middle East of all the relevant objectives of the Charter of the United Nations. Nonalignment had produced a proposal much less effective and less assimilable by both sides than the nonaligned proposal in the case of the Sino-Indian conflict of 1962. Nevertheless, the nonaligned proposal, being both less drastic than that of the Soviet Union and less sweeping than that of the United States, could be said to take a position different from that of either of the super powers. This posture, in itself, tends to acquire a certain degree of merit among some states at the United Nations.

The first calculation of the nonaligned states was that their resolution would be able to muster about sixty-five positive votes, and perhaps the abstentions would be so numerous that the resolution might even obtain the requisite two-thirds majority.

This was a short-lived dream. The Latin Americans, seeing that the nonaligned proposal was very much nearer the objectives of the Arab side than it was to those of Israel and that it did not comply with the juridical postulates which they had identified, realized that there was room for another set of equitable and challenging proposals. They discussed the matter with

[7] A/L.522, par. 5.

some of the nonaligned states but no agreement was reached on a joint text. However, the nonaligned states began to realize that their draft proposal could not attract the wide support on which they had counted. As a result, on June 30, 1967—the date of the introduction of the Latin American draft resolution—they considerably revised the text of their proposals. They introduced a paragraph requesting the Secretary-General to designate a personal representative who would have the functions of a mediator in the area. This indicated that they were willing to envisage negotiations between the disputants with third-party assistance. More importantly, they considerably expanded their final suggestion regarding the Security Council. That body,

immediately after the withdrawal of the Israel armed forces has been completed, [was to] consider urgently all aspects of the situation in the Middle East and seek peaceful ways and means for the solution of all problems—legal, political and humanitarian—through appropriate channels guided by the principles of the Charter of the United Nations, in particular those contained in Articles 2 and 33.[8]

Another change in the text was that Israel was not to withdraw to positions within the armistice lines but to the positions held prior to June 5, 1967. This too was a change somewhat in favor of Israel. Withdrawal behind the armistice lines raised the question of demilitarized areas which Israel had entered some years previously and had not surrendered.

These modifications of the fourteen-power resolution were meant to meet the challenge of the Latin Americans. The Latin Americans, by maintaining their original text, except for a minor verbal alteration immediately before the vote, showed how carefully they had thought through the issues involved before deciding upon the formulations which best expressed their own principles. The nonaligned, on the other hand, made further revisions of their proposal and finally significantly altered the paragraph dealing with the long-term issues. The Security Council was apparently to consider those issues without waiting for

[8] A/L.522/rev. 1.

the withdrawal of Israeli forces. At any rate, this was a possible implication of exclusion from the text of the paragraph of reference to the withdrawal of Israeli forces. In addition, the Secretary-General was to report to both the General Assembly and the Security Council on compliance with the terms of the resolution instead of, as previously proposed, on compliance by Israel alone. These were substantive modifications; if they had appeared in the first rendition of the draft resolution the nonaligned could have claimed that they had truly put forward a proposal for peace in the area. To establish this claim one or more of the sponsors of the text could have elaborated the principles underlying the proposals—as Ambassador Lopez Villamil of Honduras had done in respect to the Latin proposals. By leaving to the very last—just before the vote was taken—the final and most significant modifications of their proposals, the nonaligned had deprived those proposals of fixity of purpose and adherence to principle. Moreover, the changes did not obliterate the lingering doubt that the basic intentions of the sponsors remained those that had been expressed in the original draft of June 28. In short, the tactics of the nonaligned had unfortunately robbed what could have been very valuable proposals of much of their merit. This was especially unfortunate, for the final rendition of the proposals indicated that the nonaligned had been able to effect some movement toward negotiation by the Arab states. The emphasis on Articles 2 and 33 of the Charter contained in the nonaligned text was, for example, in line with what Foreign Minister George Brown of the United Kingdom had said on June 21.

I should like . . . to set out certain principles . . . for a lasting settlement. Clearly, such principles must derive from the United Nations Charter. Article 2 of the Charter provides that "all Members shall refrain in their international relations from the threat or use of force against the territorial integrity or political independence of any state." [9]

[9] A/PV.1529, p. 11.

This article of the Charter is, in fact, a statement of the current doctrine of compulsory nonbelligerency by which all Member States of the United Nations are bound, and the fourteen-power resolution in its final version asked for operative arrangements to be made by the Security Council without a tie-in with Israeli withdrawal (though of course, this too was to be achieved). Had the Security Council gone ahead on this basis the Arab states would have been both legally and morally bound to comply with the Council's decisions.

As it was, the nonaligned draft was not able to carry conviction in quarters where conviction was essential. Ambassador Goldberg, having seen the final revision of the nonaligned text, still was of the view that

It calls for withdrawal now and it leaves every other essential step to the uncertain future. In particular, it makes no connection whatever between withdrawal and the end of claims of belligerency. . . . We find vague references to legal and political problems and Charter principles, to be considered at some time in the future. This fuzzy treatment stands in strong contrast to the Yugoslav draft resolution's clear and concrete call for the immediate withdrawal of Israel's troops to the positions held before 5 June. That withdrawal—if it could be brought about at all under such conditions—can scarcely bring more than a pause between rounds in this long and terrible conflict.[10]

Foreign Minister Gromyko, speaking for the Soviet Union on the draft resolutions, supported the nonaligned proposal. "This draft resolution quite correctly puts into the first place the question of the withdrawal of Israeli troops from the territories they now occupy." [11] However, though in this statement on July 3—following Arthur Goldberg's statement of the same day—Gromyko naturally defended the Soviet draft resolution and in doing so restated the Soviet approach to the whole issue, there was no mention of insistence on condemnation of Israel. Furthermore, the Soviet Foreign Minister injected a significantly

[10] A/PV.1546, pp. 6–7.   [11] *Ibid.*, p. 26.

new idea when he said that after the withdrawal of Israeli troops "there will be a much more peaceful atmosphere than now in order to achieve progress in all other questions—I emphasize the word 'all' questions—which have accumulated on the sidelines." [12] The weight and meaning of a statement in international affairs differs with the source of its pronouncement. Coming as it did from the grand champion of the Arabs and in a situation in which efforts were being made behind the scenes to urge the Arabs forward to some accommodation with Israel, this statement by Gromyko could reasonably be interpreted as indication of acceptance by the Soviet Union of the need to achieve progress toward a durable peace in the Middle East. Privately, members of the Soviet delegation emphasized this point and hoped that it would throw some light on the role which the Soviet Union was willing to play in the Middle East.

However, countries which had been more or less in the middle, such as Ireland, announced that the Latin American text "conforms closely to the views of the Irish delegation." [13] Canada expressed a similar view,[14] as did the United Kingdom.[15] Referring to the nonaligned draft, Lord Caradon said he recognized "that there has been an effort to make substantial improvements. . . . We are specially glad that this draft resolution includes reference to the principles of the Charter, and in particular to those contained in Articles 2 and 33. . . . This seems to us a most valuable addition." [16] Nevertheless, he thought it was still an unbalanced draft.

On the other hand, France interpreted the nonaligned draft more along the lines that the "moderate" states among the nonaligned had hoped for. Ambassador Roger Seydoux said: "This new text has one advantage in the eyes of my delegation, and that is that it is limited to what we consider to be the essential: on the one hand, the withdrawal of forces, and, on the other,

12 *Ibid.*, p. 27.   13 *Ibid.*, p. 16.   14 *Ibid.*, p. 17.
15 A/PV.1547, p. 42.   16 *Ibid.*

the search for an over-all solution of the problems arising between Israel and the Arab States." [17] By accepting this interpretation of the nonaligned draft, France too, and somewhat more
clearly than the Soviet Union, appeared to be accepting a commitment to join in a meaningful search for a long-term settlement. Of course, such commitments cannot necessarily be regarded as hard and fast. Their interpretation is a question of
diplomacy, but active diplomacy would have indicated that on
July 3, 1967, there was a need for a private sounding out by
such states as Mexico, Italy, Austria, and, of course, the United
States of the meaning and possibilities of the French and Soviet
statements of that day.

France made it clear, at the same time, that the first paragraph
of the nonaligned draft gave rise to objections because it was
not realistic to ask the government of Israel to withdraw its
forces immediately. "If an amendment could have been submitted to this paragraph my delegation would have approved
it." [18] Seydoux particularly welcomed the expansion of operative
paragraph 6, relating to the long-term settlement, and he emphasized that it was a lasting peace that his government was
after: "My government is deeply convinced that the goal to
be attained is a system of true peace, allowing all States of the
Middle East, including Israel, to live in normal circumstances
and to have stability." [19] The French delegate considered the
nonaligned draft to be consistent with this objective, and he
announced that France would vote for it.

Thus, the nonaligned draft won the support of two of the
four important permanent members of the Security Council. It
failed, however, to find support among the Western Europeans
and the Latin Americans. More significantly, it even failed with
certain states in Asia and Africa.

That support went almost automatically to the Latin American draft. For example, Ethiopia, while appealing for a last effort

[17] A/PV.1546, p. 41.   [18] *Ibid.*   [19] *Ibid.*, p. 42.

to arrive at common ground for a wide consensus in the Assembly, stated that if such agreement was not forthcoming the Latin American draft could best "help the United Nations to start on the right foot in dealing with this grave and complicated crisis." [20] There were Africans who took a very different view. For example, the delegate of Guinea took a stand on a general theory of history:

My delegation believes that . . . our brothers and friends from Latin America should be able to march in step with history in the sense of being much more concerned with the future than with the present. . . . We are convinced that history will see to it that the facts of what occurred in the Middle East are properly put on record. [21]

The core of the difference between the Latin Americans and the nonaligned states was revealed by Ambassador Parthasarathi of India in his statement shortly before the Assembly voted on the various drafts on July 4:

We have in the last twenty-four hours tried hard with our Latin American colleagues to find a basis for a common approach, but regrettably we have failed because of a profound disagreement on the necessity of bringing about immediate withdrawals before consideration could be given to any other issue. This is an issue of principle for us, and therefore my delegation will vote against the Latin American draft. [22]

Arthur Goldberg summed up the position of the U.S. government in ten points, among which he gave priority of place to the following: "First: without delay, armed forces should be disengaged and withdrawn to their own territories; and without delay any claims to a state of war or belligerency should be terminated." [23] He announced that, taking into account his government's views, he would vote for the Latin American text. The United Kingdom also preferred the Latin American draft. Most of the other Western European countries expressed no preference one way or the other, but their original statements in

[20] A/PV.1547, p. 22.   [21] A/PV.1546, pp. 86–87.
[22] A/PV.1548, p. 47.   [23] A/PV.1546, p. 2.

the debate, which had linked withdrawal and a final settlement, pointed to the direction in which their preference would lie. The position of the parties to the conflict was not unexpected. Abba Eban, the Foreign Minister of Israel, maintained that even the revised nonaligned draft "requires Israel to act as though there were peace, while allowing the Arab States to act as though there were war." [24] He rejected the view that the expanded paragraph 6 of the draft would really help the situation:

Those delegations which attach importance to paragraph 6 of the Yugoslav draft resolution should, in all fairness, read the proceedings of the Security Council between 19 May and the first days of June in order to understand how slender and how fragile is the reliance that Israel can place upon such a discussion in the present mood and structure of great-Power relationships.[25]

As to the Latin American draft resolution, Foreign Minister Eban stated that his delegation would be guided by certain principles, among which was the principle that the arrangements to be made in a peace settlement must take account of vital security interests. Another principle was that "sovereign States have the right and duty to fix their permanent frontiers by mutual agreement among themselves." [26] Both these principles, particularly the latter, were couched in language of pre-United Nations Charter vintage. Of course, the system of international relations envisaged by the Charter takes into account the interests of states but it is not left to Member States to settle their disputes through armed conflict and then reach other settlements which would reflect the results of the use of force. Indeed, Foreign Minister Eban was stating principles which were not reflected in any of the draft resolutions before the Assembly, including the Latin American draft.

The Arab states maintained their firm opposition to the position of the Latin Americans and to their draft resolution. Foreign Minister Habib Bourguiba, Jr., of Tunisia—generally regarded as the spokesman of a more moderate Arab state—said:

[24] A/PV.1547, pp. 28–30.   [25] *Ibid.*, p. 32.   [26] *Ibid.*, p. 36.

Today, in spite of affirmations of support and sympathy, the horizon is clouded by the majority of nations represented here, and particularly by the four great Powers, none of which has ever called into question the actual existence of Israel as a State, whereas in our eyes it is the very existence of Israel which constitutes permanent aggression.[27]

This sentiment was a constant chorus in the Foreign Minister's speech, and he ended by saying that in the opinion of his delegation the only way of ensuring the survival of the United Nations would be "the restoration of the right of the Palestinian people to their homeland." [28] So clear-cut were these statements that Foreign Minister Abdelaziz Bouteflika of Algeria could not do more than repeat them, though he represents a country which is regarded as more extreme in its anti-Israeli posture. "If Israel was created through a specially peculiar kind of international situation, the objective conditions will occur one day which will provoke a movement in the direction of justice and the inevitable reversal of the situation." [29] The other Arab states too expressed themselves in terms which made it clear that they were united in their firm opposition to the Latin American draft resolution.

The Assembly moved to a vote in the late afternoon of July 4 when it was still far from a wide consensus. The Latin Americans and North Americans, the Western Europeans and the neutrals of Europe, together with some African states and such Asian states as Thailand, preferred the Latin American text. On the other hand, many of the Asian-African states, together with France and the Communists, were in favor of the nonaligned draft resolution. But the last-minute modification of that text for the most part miscarried.

Thus, the Italian delegate, Ambassador Piero Vinci, on July 5, 1967, stated:

I also gladly acknowledge the increasing efforts the 17 co-sponsors [the original 14 had been joined by three others] made up to the last

[27] A/PV.1543, p. 32.   [28] *Ibid.*, p. 37.   [29] *Ibid.*, p. 57.

minute in order to meet the views of other delegations, including my own, and to try to attract wider support. I can only regret that some moves came too late and were not brought to more logical and constructive conclusions.[30]

As the vote neared on the afternoon of July 4, Ambassador Solomon of Trinidad confirmed that strenuous efforts had been made through the previous twenty-four hours—there had been a meeting of Latin American and nonaligned representatives until late into the night of July 3—to bring together the views of the sponsors of the two main draft resolutions before the Assembly:

During the last twenty-four hours I have on three occasions delayed speaking from this rostrum . . . in the hope that some sort of agreement could be arrived at between what are now the only two opposing views before the Assembly: the views of the non-aligned delegations and the views of the Latin American delegations. Until just a few hours ago these discussions continued, and we still feel that at this late hour it might yet be possible to arrive at a consensus.[31]

Less than a half-hour later the Ambassador of India was to make the remarks which we have already cited and which indicated that the nonaligned position remained firm for full withdrawal of Israeli forces before consideration could be given to other issues. However, the text of the nonaligned draft resolution, as we have seen, had in fact been modified so as to omit reference to Israel's withdrawal in the paragraph dealing with the settlement of other issues. The latest version of that draft would not, in fact, delay Security Council action on the other issues involved in a peace settlement until after Israel had withdrawn.[32] The disparity between the wording of the draft resolution and the fundamental point of principle brought out by the Ambassador of India served to show that in the course of negotiation some countries had agreed to formulations in their draft proposals which in fact went beyond the limits of their own views. A resolution spon-

[30] A/PV.1549, p. 28.   [31] A/PV.1548, p. 21.
[32] For full text, see Appendix 14.

sored by a dozen or more Member States is rarely fully satisfactory to all the sponsors. It represents a compromise of differing points of view and is one stage in the enormous effort required in the General Assembly, particularly in contentious issues, to construct pyramidally a consensus among the members of the Organization. In this particular case, reading together the remarks of the Italian, Indian, and Trinidadian representatives, we see how close to success this effort came. The nonaligned played down some of their principles in order to establish peace in the Middle East—which was the fundamental objective of the Assembly, in spite of the extreme reluctance of some of the Arab states.

Had the nonaligned been able to move faster than they did, with very little change of their verbal formulations—and given some slight movement toward a more pragmatic approach by the Latins—a compromise text could perhaps have emerged. Timing is always a crucial and most difficult factor in the process of negotiation. Another way of stating the possibilities is that if there had not been so much pressure to wind up the proceedings and take a vote on July 4, it might have been possible for the two sides to come together. Certain factors were moving in this direction. The most important of these was that some of the Arabs were beginning to express willingness to make concessions to other views in the Assembly. Indeed, the progress of the nonaligned text had been made possible by behind-the-scenes urgings by the representatives of many countries which had been addressed to the Arabs and more particularly to the representatives of the United Arab Republic. Had the Assembly been able to hold the vote off for a week or so, the Latin Americans and the nonaligned, with the reluctant, but desirable, barely spoken consent of some of the Arabs, might have presented the Assembly with a compromise text.

Would such a text have been to the liking of Israel? The answer is to be found by making an incisive analysis of the texts of the Latin Americans and the nonaligned states as those two texts were actually presented for vote on July 4, 1967. The crucial clauses were the following:

6. *Requests* that the Security Council consider all aspects of the situation in the Middle East and seek peaceful ways and means for the solution of all problems—legal, political and humanitarian—through appropriate channels, guided by the principles of the Charter of the United Nations, in particular those contained in Articles 2 and 33.[33]

   1. *Urgently requests:*

· · ·

   (b) The parties in conflict to end the state of belligerency, to endeavor to establish conditions of coexistence based on good neighborliness and to have recourse in all cases to the procedures for peaceful settlement indicated in the Charter of the United Nations.[34]

The Latin American text also made a firm request to the Security Council to guarantee freedom of transit on the international waterways in the region and to guarantee the territorial inviolability and political independence of the states of the region. Clearly some further spelling out of the nonaligned text would have been necessary for a compromise. At the same time, as we shall see in succeeding chapters, a compromise did not necessarily have to state in detail all that was contained in the Latin American text. A little more movement by the nonaligned and there would have been important urgings to the Latins from the western Europeans and others to move a little from their clear-cut juridical positions into the realm of agreed pragmatism. Such a movement would have entailed a behind-the-scenes agreement between the super powers, an agreement which would have amounted to commitments regarding the exercise of sovereign discretion in the forum of the Security Council. These imponderables in turn would have depended upon other factors, including the impressions which President Johnson and Chairman

---

[33] A/L.522/rev. 3 (nonaligned text).
[34] A/L.523/rev. 1 (Latin American text).

Kosygin had gained about each other in their meeting at Glassboro on June 23 and 25.

As we have seen, the first draft resolution introduced at the Assembly had been the Soviet text presented by Chairman Kosygin on June 19 (A/L.519), followed by the United States draft resolution (A/L.520) and a set of proposals by Albania (A/L.521). None of these had figured in the behind-the-scenes negotiations leading up to the voting. Few if any Member States believed that they had any chance of being accepted by the Assembly, and most doubted that they would be brought to the vote. The next text to be presented was the nonaligned resolution and following it was the Latin American text. There was also a draft resolution on humanitarian questions relating to refugees and prisoners of war which had been moved by a number of countries from practically all the continents (A/L.526). Finally, there was a resolution originally introduced by Pakistan asking Israel to rescind its measures in regard to the status of Jerusalem (A/L.527).

The nonaligned states, through the representative of Yugoslavia, asked that priority in the vote be given to their resolution. The Assembly did not contest this request.

In the vote, the Assembly first disposed of amendments to the nonaligned text which had been moved by Cuba and Albania. Both these countries sought to introduce condemnation of Israel, while the Cuban text implicated the United States also. These amendments were rejected by large majorities, particularly that involving the United States: only 20 delegates voted for this amendment, whereas 78 voted against it. Those voting for it included nine of the thirteen Arab states (Lebanon, Libya, Tunisia, and Morocco abstained from voting), ten Communist-bloc states, and Mauritania. The condemnation of Israel contained in the Albanian amendment received 32 votes with 66 votes in opposition. To the twenty that had voted for the Cuban condemnation were added, on this occasion, Morocco, Pakistan,

Somalia, Zambia, Afghanistan, Burundi, Guinea, Lebanon, Libya, Malaysia, Mali, and Tunisia. It was clear that this did not amount to a widespread condemnation of Israel by the Assembly. On the whole, the nonaligned, including important members such as India and Yugoslavia, refused to vote in favor of condemnation.

In the vote on the nonaligned resolution there were 53 states in favor, 46 against, with 20 abstentions. Thus there was a voting majority for the nonaligned resolution, but not the two-thirds majority required by Article 18 of the Charter of the United Nations.

Before voting on the Latin American text the Assembly had to dispose of the forthright or sweeping texts of the Soviet Union, the United States, and Albania. There was not much point in pressing any of them to the vote. The United States wisely announced that it would not do so. The Soviet Union, however, insisted on a vote on its proposals. Each operative paragraph was voted on separately and received between 34 and 45 votes. Each of the paragraphs was defeated and the whole resolution failed. The Albanian resolution fared far worse, obtaining only 22 votes.

The Assembly then proceeded to vote on the Latin American text. It did better than the nonaligned proposal, receiving 57 favorable votes with 43 against, but failed to obtain the requisite two-thirds majority. The number of abstentions was again 20.

Though the numbers voting for and against the two major draft resolutions were approximately the same, the composition of the states in these two categories of voters differed considerably from resolution to resolution. The nonaligned resolution was supported by all thirteen Arab states and all ten members of the Soviet bloc (including Cuba). There were four votes from Europe—France, Greece, Spain, and Turkey—and the rest of the votes were those of the largely nonaligned sponsors, including Yugoslavia, plus a number of other Asian and African countries. In opposition were all the twenty-two Latin American states, most of the Western Europeans, the United States, Canada, Australia, and New Zealand, and, in Asia, Israel and the Philippines. Perhaps a surprise for the nonaligned was that as many as seven African countries voted against their text: Botswana, Zambia, Ghana, Lesotho, Liberia, Madagascar, and Malawi.

On the other hand, the Latin American resolution received, apart from the votes of twenty-two Latin American countries, the affirmation of almost all the Western European states, the Philippines, Thailand, China (Taiwan), and Japan. It also received seventeen African votes, including of course the seven that had been cast against the nonaligned resolution. Those in opposition now were the Arabs, the Soviet bloc, a number of nonaligned states, and Pakistan, which in this session had worked closely with the nonaligned countries.

There was more similarity in composition among those who abstained on both major draft resolutions. In both cases, twenty countries abstained, seven of which were common to both lists: Sweden, South Africa, Singapore, Kenya, Laos, Nepal, and Niger. These may be regarded as the states which were unwilling to sanction any major proposal which did not command the support of both sides. Israel too abstained in the vote on the Latin American resolution.

There was little problem in adopting the proposal on humanitarian measures. It received 116 votes with none in opposition—only Syria and Cuba, the diehards of this Assembly, abstaining.

The proposal that Israeli measures regarding the status of Jerusalem should be rescinded did almost as well.[35] Ninety-nine states voted in its favor, none voted against, while twenty (including the United States) abstained. Israel did not cast a vote on this resolution.

Thus, at its marathon voting session on July 4 which ad-

[35] For full text, see Appendix 15.

journed shortly after 8 p.m. the Assembly failed to adopt a resolution dealing with the major issues arising out of the Arab-
Israeli crisis and conflict. The humanitarian resolution was an
obvious step to take. In the case of Jerusalem a resolution was
again obvious—even if unimplementable in isolation—because
of widespread sentiment regarding the Holy Places. The core of
the problem, however, remained intact because of the failure of
the Latin Americans and the nonaligned states to resolve their
differences.

The Middle East situation was too critical and too fraught
with destructive possibilities, capable of affecting both the peace
of the world and the United Nations itself, to be left entirely
unresolved. When the Assembly reconvened on July 5, 1967, its
President, Ambassador Abdur Rahman Pazhwak, made a statement with an important twofold purpose. First, he interpreted
the results thus far achieved so as to give them the utmost possible substance. Second, he looked hopefully to the immediate
future, in which he still saw the possibility of remedial Assembly
action.

President Pazhwak performed the difficult task of offering, not
a consensus which from time to time presiding officers of United
Nations organs have attempted, but an interpretation of the
work of the Assembly that covered three major points. First, regarding an established peace in the Middle East, he said: "They
[the members of the Assembly] have agreed that the time has
come when peace in the Middle East must be made, finally and
for all time." [36]

Second: "There is virtual unanimity in upholding the principle that conquest of territory by war is inadmissible in our time
and under our Charter." [37]

Third: "There was in addition a broad consensus that the
political sovereignty and territorial integrity of States allow
them a rightful freedom from threat of belligerency." [38]

[36] A/PV.1549, p. 11.   [37] *Ibid.*   [38] *Ibid.*

The formulation of these points was primarily an attempt by the President to point the way in which the Assembly should develop its subsequent steps. As to the future, he said:

It is my strong hope that, even at the eleventh hour, we shall be able to grasp the very serious moments that we might have at our disposal and use them to bring about something that we may be able to refer to as a fruitful result, in the interest of peace and in the interest of this Orgainzation.[39]

Eighteen representatives went to the podium of the General Assembly following President Pazhwak's statement. The first of them was the Prime Minister of Sudan, M. A. Mahgoub, who was not able to accept the presidential summing up: "Mr. President, I am extremely sorry to have to disagree with the theme which emerged from your brilliant statement at the beginning of the meeting." [40] Mahgoub went on to predict the doom of the United Nations, and, indeed, to pronounce an elegy:

When we mourn the fate of the United Nations, when we predict its extinction, we do so with a heavy heart. For this is the edifice that embodied the hopes and aspirations of all humanity. The Charter of the United Nations, which we are pledged to support, now lies in ruins, ravaged by those mighty nations which ought to have been its main supporters.[41]

This gloomy and bitter mood reached an apogee when the Prime Minister of Sudan blamed the great powers for the march toward the final failure of the United Nations. His bitterness was directed to all the great nations because, in the last analysis, none of them had been able to support the logic of the Arab case, which could reach only the conclusion of the removal of Israel from the scene. The Prime Minister warned that there was great danger of a war of annihilation and that "when the catastrophe overwhelms us, the smaller nations will not lose a great deal. We do not have much to lose. We shall be reduced in equal measure to the state of utter ruin that those who trade in ruin will bring

---

[39] *Ibid.*, pp. 13–15.   [40] *Ibid.*, p. 17.   [41] *Ibid.*, p. 21.

upon the world." [42] In these words the Sudanese statesman revealed one of the danger signals of our present world situation.
The less-developed states of the rural areas and deserts of the
world may be willing, in certain circumstances, to throw down
the gauntlet of world war. For they have nothing to lose any-
way.

This mood, which is one that the have-not nations tend to
reach in crises, serves to emphasize the point that peace today
is not only indivisible but must be based on the attainment by all
peoples of a certain status of justice and at least a reasonable minimum of well-being. Not that this will solve issues, but it might
promote more balance than now exists and give statesmen cause
to stop and ponder. At present the rush toward frustration goes
headlong. The failure of an organ of the United Nations to pronounce in favor of a particular step—in this case the withdrawal
of Israeli forces—is regarded as being contrary both to the
Charter and to elementary principles of justice. This view had,
in fact, been expressed by most of the members of the Assembly.
But equally present in the same situation are other injustices and
disregardings of the Charter. One such is the whole concept of
belligerency which belongs to a phase of international law that
was superseded, for Member States of the United Nations, by the
Charter. Belligerency is war, and a state of war is ruled out by
the Charter.

Three other Arab representatives explained their votes and
broadly all of them struck the same note as the Prime Minister
of Sudan. These were the representatives of Jordan, Saudi Arabia, and Syria. Moreover, most of them expressed themselves in
strong terms against the Latin Americans. Thus, Foreign Minister Ibrahim Makhos of Syria said:

The Latin American resolution comes just to deepen our wounds
and humiliation. . . . The countries of Latin America . . . have

[42] *Ibid.*

confirmed through their resolution, which is inspired by the United States, that while their hearts are on our side, their swords are brandished against us.[43]

The Syrian Foreign Minister, like the Sudanese Prime Minister, proclaimed: "This is the final funeral of this Organization." [44] In recording the similar views of the four Arab speakers on July 5, it is just as well to take note of the fact that Deputy Prime Minister Mahmud Fawzi of the United Arab Republic, when he spoke on July 4, did not indulge in either predictions of the doom of the United Nations or in acerbity in regard to the Latin Americans.

Five Latin American speakers explained their votes on July 5. Their keynote was by and large an expression of their gratification at the showing of their draft proposals in the voting by the Assembly, and a reaffirmation of their faith in their own approach. Thus, the Mexican representative, Francisco Cuevas Cancino, said: "The Latin American draft, balanced and complete . . . offered the General Assembly the best conclusion to its emergency special session." [45] This sentiment was echoed by the representatives of Colombia, Chile, Bolivia, and Costa Rica. The representative of Colombia also brought in the important point that it would in fact be impracticable to deal in isolation with the issue of Jerusalem, a point which the Assembly in its enthusiastic vote over Jerusalem had pushed aside from its field of vision. As long as Israel holds all the surrounding territory it is difficult to provide for a return to the *status quo ante bellum* only in the island of the Old City of Jerusalem. Naturally, some of the Latin Americans expressed their strong resentment of the bitter Arab remarks directed against them.

A third category of states—Sweden, Austria, Finland, and Italy—avoided both pronouncements of doom and criticism of

[43] *Ibid.,* p. 97.   [44] *Ibid.,* p. 101.   [45] *Ibid.,* pp. 73–75.

their colleagues. Their attitude was more in keeping with the final hope that had been expressed by the President of the Assembly. Ambassador Sverker Astrom of Sweden said:

We feel that the world has a right to expect some contribution by the General Assembly to the establishment of peace with justice in the Middle East. . . . A confirmation of or a reference to the relevant Articles of the Charter might be advisable, combined, perhaps with a formal decision to forward the records of this session to the Security Council.[46]

Ambassador Piero Vinci of Italy carried this thought forward.

We sincerely hope that before the session ends a further and greater effort may still be made in order to show that the United Nations can still perform a useful task in securing the conditions of peace and security in the Middle East.[47]

Ambassador Kurt Waldheim of Austria and Ambassador Jakobson of Finland were of the same view. The representative of Chile also hoped that the General Assembly would "exert an additional effort."

The remaining five speakers of July 5 did not fall into any specific category. India took a strong position in favor of withdrawal. Japan felt that either the Latin American or the nonaligned draft would have served a useful purpose. Somalia was close to the Arab point of view. South Africa took a legalistic view which, it said, had prompted it to abstain on both the main draft resolutions, and Greece did little more than announce its sympathy for the refugees.

At the end of the meeting President Pazhwak fastened on the statements which had been made in favor of a further effort by the Assembly. Indeed, behind the scenes he had already consulted with a cross section of the membership. In a formal sense the Assembly session was virtually over. The various sections of its membership had placed their proposals before their colleagues and the voting had been completed. But President Pazhwak, as a

[46] *Ibid.*, pp. 23–25.   [47] *Ibid.*, pp. 32–33.

result of his informal consultations, announced that "all delegations agreed that, with the consent of the Assembly—which I told them I would have to consult—the next meeting should be convened a week from today." [48]

The President added that during this fairly extended period he would be available for discussions with the members in order to assist in the advance toward a common objective. Ambassador Pazhwak informed the Assembly that "one delegation stated that it did not agree that any time should be given for these [further] consultations." [49] The President was referring to the delegation of Israel. Ambassador Raphael of Israel then stated to the Assembly that in a spirit of compromise he would suggest a recess of not more than forty-eight hours.[50] However, there was no support for the Israeli position and the Assembly did not object to the President's proposal. Thus it came about that the emergency session of the General Assembly gave itself a last chance to find agreement on the Middle East situation.

[48] *Ibid.*, p. 112.   [49] *Ibid.*   [50] *Ibid.*, p. 116.

CHAPTER XI

The Security Council Helps Out

WHILE THE members of the Assembly were still engaged in discussions, a degree of progress toward preserving the peace in the Middle East, at least during an interim period, was made by the Security Council.

July 8 marked a new development so far as Israel and the United Arab Republic were concerned. For the first time in the Security Council's consideration of the issue which had commenced on May 24, 1967, these two states requested that the Council convene to consider the Middle East situation. At 11 o'clock in the morning the President of the Council, Ambassador Makonnen of Ethiopia, was telephoned by the Ambassador of the United Arab Republic with a request, on instructions from his government, for a meeting of the Council. An hour later the Israeli representative made a similar request on behalf of his government. Both representatives complained that the other side had breached the cease-fire in the area of the Suez Canal. Ambassador M. A. El-Kony of the United Arab Republic set out his government's interpretation of Israeli offenses in a letter to the President of the Security Council.[1] Israel was alleged to have shelled positions on the west bank of the Suez Canal and to have bombed Egyptian habitations in that area from the air. In an immediately succeeding letter of the same date (July 8), Ambassador Raphael of Israel countered that Egyptian army units had crossed the Suez Canal and had been driven back. The complaint stated that the Egyptians had also shelled Israeli positions

[1] S/8043.

on the east bank of the Canal, causing heavy casualties, in response to which action Israeli planes had bombed Egyptian gun emplacements.[2] Both representatives said that the situation demanded urgent attention by the Security Council.

It is noteworthy that neither of them sought an urgent meeting of the emergency special session of the Assembly. When they wanted action they returned, as was more appropriate, to the Security Council. In this manner they illustrated the interesting interaction between the Security Council and the General Assembly which has occurred in this crisis more strikingly than in any other in recent years at the United Nations. We have seen that the calling of the emergency session of the Assembly for the adoption of substantive resolutions was perhaps not fully in conformity with the rules as they stood or with the provisions of the Charter of the United Nations. The Council had remained seized of the Middle East issue, and under Article 12 of the Charter the General Assembly was, in this circumstance, limited only to discussion.

Though the matter before the Security Council on July 8 was urgent, as had been asserted both by Israel and the United Arab Republic, Ambassador Fedorenko of the USSR felt that the Council should at first deliberate on its agenda. The President of the Council, on the recommendation of the Secretary-General, had placed before the Security Council its previous agenda on the Middle East, not mentioning the urgent charges now brought by both Israel and the UAR. Fedorenko contended that this was absurd. The issue before the Council now was simply the breach of the cease-fire. The United States supported the decision of the President to place the old agenda before the Council. Finally, the Indian representative ended a half-hour of procedural debate by suggesting that the issue could be settled by adding to the previous agenda the two letters which had just come in from the parties. This was accepted with a sense of relief by the

[2] S/8044.

Council. Indeed, it turned out that the whole delay could have been avoided if the Council members had been more familiar with their own rules of procedure. After half an hour of debate Ambassador Fedorenko pointed out that rule 7 in the Council's rules of procedure enjoins that in addition to items which it has previously decided to defer, and uncompleted items, those items which have been brought to the attention of the representatives of the Council can also be placed on the agenda. The Indian suggestion which resolved the situation applied this rule of procedure.

Before Egypt and Israel presented their cases to the Security Council, U Thant asked for the floor and made an important statement. He pointed out that Council resolutions 235 and 236 relating to the cease-fire between Israel and Syria had invoked the assistance of the Secretary-General and of UN machinery in obtaining compliance by the parties. However, the Council's resolutions of June 6 and 7, Nos. 233 and 234 relating to the cease-fire between Israel and the United Arab Republic, had made no provision for any United Nations assistance with regard to implementation of the cease-fire. They had merely asked the Secretary-General to keep the Council informed of the situation. U Thant went on to say that he could not discharge his reporting responsibility without some means of obtaining reliable information, and he regarded "a cease-fire without any observation or policing assistance in its implementation [to be] inevitably vulnerable." In this circumstance, he "decided on 4 July to take an initiative towards a possible alleviation of this situation." [3] He had discussed with the delegates of Israel and the UAR whether they would accept observers on both sides of the Canal to help implement the cease-fire. He was awaiting a reply from the two governments concerned.

After the Secretary-General's statement, the representatives of Egypt and Israel addressed the Council and repeated the

[3] S/PV.1365, p. 36.

charges which they had made in their letters to the President. However, neither of them referred specifically to the Secretary-General's suggestions and there was no indication that they would be accepted. The Council reconvened on Sunday, July 9, for the members to express their views on the situation. Ambassador Fedorenko, the first speaker, made two significant points. One was virtually a warning of the possibilities of a much wider conflict which could affect the whole world if the aggression was not curbed. He said that, until this was done, "The situation will remain red hot and a military explosion could grow to a size which would be dangerous to mankind." [4] Since this statement was made at a time when the Soviet Foreign Minister himself was present in New York and must be presumed to have approved it, it reminded the membership of the United Nations that the Middle East situation could not be regarded as a totally isolated "local war." It contained the ominous seeds of widespread and highly destructive conflict.

The second point of significance made by Fedorenko was that the Soviet Union was prepared to apply sanctions against Israel as an aggressor under Chapter VII of the Charter.[5] This part of Fedorenko's statement, while indicating the views of the Soviet Union in favor of stringent measures against Israel, was not immediately practicable. It was highly unlikely that the other permanent members of the Council would accept the Soviet view.

Among the members of the Council it was Lord Caradon of the United Kingdom who first supported U Thant's practical suggestion. In doing so, Caradon expressed the view that steps away from violence in the Middle East could be taken only in the United Nations. "We should at once authorize the Secretary-General to send observers to Sinai and to the Canal, and I trust that we shall do so without delay and without reservations." [6]

Ambassador Goldberg, who spoke next, also supported the

[4] S/PV.1366, p. 6.   [5] *Ibid.*, p. 17.   [6] *Ibid.*, pp. 22–25.

Secretary-General's suggestion and thus took it further toward
attainment. But Goldberg also used the occasion to reaffirm certain important positions of the United States. In his speeches in
the concluding phases of the debate in the General Assembly on
the draft resolutions before it Goldberg had twice pointed out
that the United States was in favor of Israel's withdrawal—but
in conjunction with other steps in the Middle East. On July 9,
though the question of withdrawal was not directly being de-
bated in the Council, Goldberg again said: "The withdrawal of
forces—something which we support—is of course an important and essential part of any overall peaceful solution of the
problems of the area. But . . . that withdrawal must be accompanied, at the very least, by a termination of any state of war
and of any claims to the exercise of belligerent rights." [7] This
statement of the United States position was made to dispel any
impression that the United States was in any way trying to
evade the issue of Israeli withdrawal.

The next speaker, Ambassador Keita of Mali, did not advance
the practical course which U Thant had suggested. He directed
his comments to the question of belligerency and took the view
that it was impossible to expect the Arabs to be nonbelligerent
when their enemy had occupied their territory. This is a very
natural response to the situation but it overlooks the fact that the
Charter of the United Nations substitutes United Nations action
for belligerent action in such situations as the one that exists in
the Middle East. This is all the more so when the Security Council has been seized of an issue and is engaged in taking measures
to maintain international peace and security. To insist on re-
version to the exercise of rights of belligerency is to retreat to a
pre-Charter era in which the risks are taken of the results of
belligerency, including such eventualities as the conquest and
occupation of territory. On the other hand, in order that the
Charter provision should prevail it is essential for the organs of

[7] *Ibid.*, pp. 28–30.

the United Nations to act with appropriate speed in undoing occupation of territory by conquering armies and in insisting upon strict observance of the requirements of an era of peace and nonbelligerency among the Member States of the United Nations.

Undeterred by the silence of some members regarding his suggestion, the Secretary-General informed the Council, after Ambassador Keita's statement, that General Bull had estimated that twenty-five additional observers would be required for the Suez sector if UN observation was to be instituted.[8]

At this juncture the President suggested that the meeting of the Council be suspended for a half-hour. The purpose of this suggestion obviously was to see whether U Thant's ideas could be followed up. As often happens, the suspension turned out to be for a much longer period than that agreed upon—somewhat over three hours. The Council reconvened at 10:20 P.M. Rather than the taking of steps to approve the Secretary-General's suggestion, its immediate task turned out to be to listen to a forceful statement by Ambassador Adib Daoudy of Syria on the generally bellicose nature of Israel. Ambassador Rafael made a response, but directed it largely to the previous statement of Ambassador Fedorenko. Thereupon, the representative of India proposed another brief suspension of the meeting—this time asking for a recess of only ten minutes.

During the earlier recess of three hours the President of the Council had discussed intensively with individual members the chances of reaching agreement on the Secretary-General's practical suggestions. At first the Soviet Union and some other delegations opposed these steps as being too meager a response to the Middle East situation. On the other hand, in a sense Ambassador Fedorenko had played into the hands of the Secretary-General. He had insisted, in the discussion on the agenda, that the only issue before the Council was the breakdown of the

[8] *Ibid.*, p. 38.

cease-fire. Even on July 9 in his statement on the substance of the issue, he had said:

Israel must strictly fulfill the decision of the Security Council with regard to the cease-fire. . . . The Security Council, as stressed in the request of the representative of the United Arab Republic [S/8043], must call upon Israel immediately and fully to carry out the decisions of the Council and refrain from any military operations. The Council, in that way, must prevent a further deterioration of the situation, which, as it is, is already fraught with dangers to the cause of peace in the Middle East and beyond.[9]

This strong demand amounted to an urging of decisive action by the Council to ensure maintenance of the cease-fire; and this is precisely what the Secretary-General's proposals would help to achieve. Against those proposals no member of the Council had offered any alternative constructive suggestion. Ambassador Keita's argument had amounted to a statement that breaches of the cease-fire were inevitable, but the United Arab Republic had come to the Council asking that breaches be ended. This line of approach was, therefore, no answer to the immediate situation.

Fedorenko had vaguely suggested the possibilities of enforcement action under Chapter VII of the Charter but had not reduced this suggestion to a specific proposal. He could have proposed Council action to maintain the cease-fire and that, in the first instance, the Council should strengthen UNTSO to the extent that had been recommended by the Secretary-General. In this way Fedorenko would have obtained a convergence of his own vague suggestion for the use of Chapter VII and the proposal of the Secretary-General. He could have argued that a proposal such as the one above would have been within the purview of Chapter VII. Article 42 permits the Security Council to take such action by land forces "as may be necessary to maintain or restore international peace and security." He could have argued that observation for the purposes of ensuring compliance

[9] *Ibid.*, pp. 16–17.

with the Security Council resolutions demanding that the parties cease fire is action to maintain peace and is within the terms of Article 42. However, in informal discussions behind the scenes the Soviet Union did not shape its views into a specific proposal on these lines.

The only practicable suggestion remained that of the Secretary-General, which had been supported first by Caradon and then by Goldberg. Seeing this, Ambassador Parthasarathi of India had called for a brief recess of ten minutes so as to persuade his Soviet colleague and others that the wisest course would be to raise no objection to the Secretary-General's proposal. This would not entail voting on the proposal: a consensus formula could be devised to let it go through. Meanwhile, those members of the Council who wanted stronger action would be on record and could return to the issue at an appropriate time. To fortify this view, Ambassador Parthasarathi informed his colleague that he too would go on record for stronger action, but would not object to the Secretary-General's proposal.

This behind-the-scenes negotiation took somewhat over an hour instead of the ten minutes to which the Council had agreed. When it reconvened at midnight Ambassador Parthasarathi stated that "the Council must now take the next step, which is to call upon Israel to withdraw immediately all its armed forces."[10] At the same time he expressed the view that the Secretary-General should be asked to strengthen United Nations machinery in the area so as to arrest deterioration of the situation, as well as to secure withdrawal of Israeli forces and ensure observance of the Armistice Agreement. This wide formulation included maintenance of the cease-fire but also served to maintain the position of the Indian delegation on the urgent need for withdrawal and a strict observance of the Armistice Agreements. It should be noted that the last of these proposals was conceived by the Indian delegation as being of practical

[10] *Ibid.*, p. 67.

value also to Israel. As long ago as January 24, 1957, Dag Hammarskjöld said of Article I of the Armistice Agreement between Israel and Egypt: "This Article assimilates the Armistice Agreement to a non-aggression pact, providing for mutual and full abstention from belligerent acts." [11]

Immediately following the completion of the Indian Ambassador's statement, Ambassador Makonnen of Ethiopia, the President of the Council during July, 1967, presented his colleagues with what he considered to be the consensus of the Council.

Recalling Security Council Resolutions 233, 234, 235, and 236, and emphasizing the need for all parties to observe scrupulously the provisions of these resolutions, having heard the statements made by the Secretary-General and the suggestions he has addressed to the parties concerned, I believe that I am reflecting the view of the Council that the Secretary-General should proceed, as he has suggested in his statements before the Council on 8 and 9 July 1967, to request the Chief of Staff of UNTSO, General Odd Bull, to work out with the Governments of the United Arab Republic and Israel, as speedily as possible, the necessary arrangements to station United Nations Military Observers in the Suez Canal sector under the Chief of Staff of UNTSO.[12]

The President added: "I believe that the statement which I have just read represents the consensus of the views of the Council members." He waited a few moments; no objection was raised to this statement and Ambassador Makonnen said: "Since I hear no objection, I declare the consensus accepted by the Council." [13] The President embroidered somewhat this occasion of post-midnight consensus. He said that he could not let "this moment of accord" pass without expressing the common feeling of satisfaction of all members "at the *decision* which we have just adopted." [14] In using these words the President raised the status of the consensus to the level of a formal Council decision.

[11] A/3512, January 24, 1957.
[12] S/PV.1366, p. 71. The consensus was also issued separately as Security Council Doc. S/8047, July 10, 1967.
[13] S/PV.1366, p. 71.   [14] *Ibid.* Italics added.

No objection was raised by any member to this formulation. The Council adjourned at 12:20 A.M. after the President had thanked the Secretary-General for his useful initiative.

The Fifth Emergency Special Session of the General Assembly had been unable in three strenuous weeks to develop steps toward the restoration of peace additional to those which had been taken by the Security Council from June 6 to June 15. Then, in two businesslike sessions, thanks largely to the initiative of U Thant, and arising also partly out of the inescapable sense of responsibility that most of the members of the Security Council have in relation to issues of war and peace, it had been possible to take another step. In some respects this was indeed a more substantive action by the Council than any of those contained in its resolutions Nos. 233–235 on the Middle East crisis. The strongest of those resolutions had called for a cease-fire. The decision of July 9 authorized arrangements to observe the cease-fire, including the taking of steps necessary to strengthen UN machinery for the achievement of this purpose. If anything, this was somewhat stronger than the terms of Resolution 236 relating to the cease-fire between Israel and Syria.

The additional twenty-five observers asked for by General Odd Bull to man the Suez Canal sector were rapidly drawn from the armed forces of such countries acceptable to both Israel and the United Arab Republic as Burma, Sweden, Canada, and France. Subsequently General Bull asked for another twenty-five observers and these were also provided.

CHAPTER XII

The Emergency Assembly's Last Chance

IN BEHIND-THE-SCENES discussions on July 5, Assembly President Pazhwak had obtained the consent of a large number of delegations to what amounted to a week's reprieve. Israel had thought no purpose would be served by an additional effort, but the Assembly as a whole had gone along with its President's suggestion and had agreed to reconvene on July 12 with the hope that the week's negotiations would result in a definite step toward the resolving of the crisis in the Middle East.

During the week of July 5–12, 1967, there were frequent meetings between representatives of the Afro-Asian and non-aligned groups on the one hand, and those of the Latin Americans on the other. The representatives of India, Yugoslavia, Tanzania, Pakistan, and Ghana met with those of Brazil, Mexico, and Trinidad. Progress was made. On some sensitive issues the non-aligned group had been able to sense a willingness on the part of the United Arab Republic and some of the other Arab states to move in the direction of arrangements which would be conducive to a final settlement. This was so particularly in regard to the use of the Gulf of Aqaba and to the renouncement of the use, or threat, of force in relations between states in the Middle East. However, there was no unanimity among the Arabs on these matters. Indeed, whenever they met together as a group the unbending attitudes of Algeria, Syria, and some others would quickly silence any tentative voices of accommodation with Israel. During this period informal discussions were also held by the representatives of a number of interested states with the great powers, particularly with the United States and the Soviet Union. In these talks the nonaligned representatives learned that the United States continued to regard a clear renunciation of belligerency by all the states concerned to be an essential element in any viable settlement. However, the United States representatives informally indicated that negotiations between the Arabs and the Israelis need not be conducted directly if an acceptable third party could be named for the purpose. This was a concession to the Arab point of view.

The Soviet Union, during the week of July 5–12, gave no indication of any modification of its total political support for the Arab position. However, there was an important area of ambiguity in regard to this support. Did it extend to a commitment that the Soviet Union and its allies would take military measures to push back Israel, or would they seek to do so only within the framework of the United Nations? On July 9, 1967, Chairman Kosygin, in an interview with a correspondent for the French government's radio-television system, said: "It is an error to believe that all international problems can be resolved by the two great powers. . . . We believe in the United Nations, where all countries, large and small, are represented." [1] This view seemed to indicate that the Soviet Union would strive to work through the United Nations rather than outside it. It would follow that enforcement measures against Israel could be taken only with the consent of the Security Council. To this important extent Soviet support of the Arabs was limited by the provisions of the Charter of the United Nations. Nevertheless, during the week of July 5–12 the Arab states counted on the full support of the Soviet Union and its allies. This was a factor which conduced toward the hard Arab position rejecting the interpretation of Article I of the Armistice Agreement which Hammarskjöld had offered in January, 1957.

In these circumstances, though there was an inching forward

[1] New York *Times*, July 10, 1967.

in the prolonged negotiations between the Latin Americans and the nonaligned states, no agreement was reached. However, in accordance with its decision of July 5, the Assembly reconvened on July 12. It did so not in order to consider the major substantive issues before it but to hear a statement by the representative of Pakistan with reference to Abba Eban's letter of July 10 addressed to the Secretary-General. In that letter the Israeli Foreign Minister had in effect rejected General Assembly Resolution 2253 of July 4 regarding the status of Jerusalem. Abba Eban pointed out that for the first time in nineteen years Jerusalem had been reunited, and he claimed that the Holy Places now were open to all. He said that Israel would secure the respect of universal spiritual interest in Jerusalem.[2] The Pakistani representative held that Israel was in breach of previous resolutions on Jerusalem and he proposed that the Assembly should reiterate the call in Resolution 2253 for the rescinding of the new measures relating to the status of Jerusalem. On July 14 the Assembly adopted Resolution 2254 along the lines proposed by the representative of Pakistan.

The Assembly members who were negotiating for progress on substantive issues regarded the debate on Jerusalem as mainly serving the purpose of lengthening the life of the emergency session of the Assembly and thereby adding to the opportunities for negotiation. Few of the states interested in substantive issues spoke in the Jerusalem debate. For example, no Latin American country spoke during the first two days of the debate, and only one of them (Venezuela) spoke briefly on July 14. The nonaligned states also generally eschewed this debate, only Afghanistan and Nepal making brief statements. The intervention of the United States by Ambassador Goldberg was significant in two respects. First, he stated: "One immediate, obvious and imperative step is the disengagement of all forces and the withdrawal of Israeli forces to their own territory."[3] This was an unambiguous stand

[2] A/6753.   [3] A/PV.1554, p. 46.

on the vacating of Arab territory by Israel. Maintaining the already stated position of the United States, Goldberg added: "A second and equally immediate, obvious and imperative step is the termination of any claims to a state of war or belligerency on the part of the Arab States in the area." [4] Regarding the measures taken by Israel in Jerusalem, he said: "I wish to make it clear that the United States does not accept or recognize these measures as altering the status of Jerusalem." [5]

The debate on Jerusalem was of significance mainly because it gave the Assembly a few more days for behind-the-scenes negotiations. On its concluding day, July 14, President Pazhwak again appealed "for the exertion of every effort to bring the work of this emergency special session of the Assembly to a fruitful conclusion," and he hoped that on July 17 the Assembly would be informed about the outcome of consultations. [6]

However, on July 17 there was still no word that the negotiations, mainly between the nonaligned and the Latin Americans, with a strong degree of interest on the part of the United States and the Soviet Union, had gotten anywhere. Still clinging to the hope that some results would be achieved, President Pazhwak suggested that the Assembly should consider the consultations concluded by the morning of July 20 with the clear understanding that no further time would be allowed. This was accepted by the Assembly. [7]

The Saudi Arabian representative, however, came to the podium and once again stated that "the whole creation of Israel was illegal and immoral, to say the least." [8] As to the future, he saw it written in the past: conquerors had come and gone from Alexander the Great, the Romans, and the Crusaders, to the Mandatory Powers. Eloquently Jamil Baroody said of them: "Conquerors all, but the bones of their troops have, throughout the ages, bleached our soil, and their works are mere relics for

---

[4] *Ibid.*   [5] *Ibid.*, p. 48.   [6] *Ibid.*, pp. 7–10.
[7] A/PV.1555, pp. 2–3.   [8] *Ibid.*, p. 6.

the tourists to see. They are gone—all gone—those conquerors
of yore. But the Arabs, in spite of all the vicissitudes that have
shaped their destiny, still remain—approximately a hundred million of them." [9] There was no reply from any quarter of the
Assembly to this attempt at prophecy, indicating that the general community of nations was not willing to entertain it seriously no matter how strongly one section of its members might
feel.

When the Assembly met on July 20 Ambassador Jakobson of
Finland, a spokesman selected for his widely accepted neutrality,
asked for one more day for behind-the-scenes negotiations. This
was granted without demur because exciting possibilities were
being discussed in a crescendo of activity which had started on
July 18. On that date Anatoli Dobrynin, the able Soviet Ambassador at Washington, called on Arthur Goldberg at the
United States Mission to the United Nations and showed some
interest in a Latin American draft resolution which had been
the focus of negotiations between the Latin Americans and the
nonaligned states. For several days those discussions had reached
the verge of acceptance on the basis of slight verbal modifications of the new Latin American draft. Copies of the draft were
circulated and the Latin Americans seriously considered formally
presenting it to the Assembly, but the final decision was that,
unless the draft could command wide support among the nonaligned states, mainly of Asia and Africa, it should not be introduced officially. In view of the importance of this unintro-
duced draft resolution, and of the effect it had on succeeding
phrases of the discussions, it is a document not to be lost sight
of. Its text read as follows:

The General Assembly:
Having examined the grave situation in the Middle East,
Considering that there was virtual unanimity in agreeing that the
crisis in the Middle East merits the attention of all Member States

[9] *Ibid.*, p. 12.

in every part of the world, and indeed requires the full participation of all Members to achieve results,

1. *Declares* that final peace and final solutions to this problem can be achieved within the framework of the Charter of the United Nations:

2. *Affirms* the principle that conquest of territory by war is inadmissible in our time and under our Charter and consequently that the withdrawal of Israel's forces to their original positions is expected:

3. *Affirms likewise* that the political sovereignty and territorial integrity of Member-States in the Middle East allow them a rightful freedom from threat of war and consequently the termination of a state or claim of belligerency by all such states is expected:

4. *Expects* [10] the Security Council to continue examining the situation in the Middle East with a sense of urgency, working directly with the parties and utilizing a United Nations presence in order to achieve an appropriate and just solution of all aspects of the problem, in particular bringing to an end the long-deferred one of the refugees and guaranteeing freedom of transit through international waterways.

The Latin Americans, in formulating the core provisions of their proposals, had seized upon the statement made by President Pazhwak on July 5.[11] Setting out his own interpretation of the results which had thus far been achieved by the emergency special session, he had viewed the Assembly as having laid down principles and guidelines in the statements of the vast majority of its members, even though no substantive resolutions had been adopted incorporating them. It was President Pazhwak who first used the phrase that withdrawal of forces to their original position "is expected."

Again, President Pazhwak had discerned "a broad consensus that the political sovereignty and territorial integrity of States allow them a rightful freedom from threat of belligerency." [12] This formulation was closely followed in the third operative paragraph of the Latin American text. The final paragraph of

[10] Some versions read "Requests."   [11] A/PV.1549, pp. 2–15.
[12] *Ibid.*, p. 11.

that text retained the concepts and largely the wording of the
Latin American draft resolution in Document A/L.523, on
which the Assembly had voted on July 4. By taking two of the
important formulations made by the President of the Assembly,
the Latins had made a move toward a compromise. However,
as had been the case in the earlier negotiations before the voting
on July 4, the Latin position remained one of principle. There
was no compromising on the issues of renunciation of belligerency or full withdrawal by the Israeli forces. The text was in
no sense one-sided, however. Full withdrawal by Israel had been
demanded by the Arabs and by the nonaligned states. It had
never been clearly conceded by Israel itself. Equally, the renunciation of belligerency had been demanded by Israel but had
not been conceded by the Arabs. By July 17 it had become clear
that the nonaligned were unable, though many of them had
made an effort in this direction, to convince the Arab states that
the new Latin American proposal offered a just basis for a
Middle East settlement.

   It was in these circumstances that Ambassador Dobrynin
visited Arthur Goldberg on July 18 to discuss possible modifications of the Latin American text. The main problem that
faced the two negotiators was what to do about "belligerency."
This word had become totally repugnant to one side, while the
concept contained in it continued to be jealously guarded by
the other side as a national right. The essential point was whether
peaceful relations and the renunciation of warlike acts of all
kinds in the Middle East could be secured without maintaining
this word in a draft resolution. On July 18 it proved impossible
to find precise words to meet these requirements. The interest
of both the United States and the Soviet Union in a viable
peace was not superficial, even though the Soviets had acted in
the Assembly as strong supporters of the extreme Arab position
while the United States had insisted on the termination of all
claims by the Arabs to the exercise of any form of belligerency.

Though the talks on July 18 had not produced a final convergence of views, or of verbal formulations, they had gone well, and on July 19 Arthur Goldberg saw Andrei Gromyko. It became clear that the two super powers were interested in the substance of peace and the renunciation of all acts of war rather than in the inviolability of any single verbal formulation of a draft resolution. On this basis, Gromyko and Goldberg were able to reach agreement on the precise wording of a draft proposal which they could both support in the Assembly. The text of that agreement was never made public but Ambassador Goldberg came very near to an exact statement of its operative content in his address before the International Platform Association at Washington, D.C., on July 27, 1967. He said about the text tentatively agreed upon between himself and Gromyko: "It provided that the withdrawal of Israel's troops would be linked with the acknowledgement by every member of the U.N. in the area that each enjoys the right to maintain an independent national state of its own and to live in peace and security and with a renunciation of all claims and acts inconsistent therewith —meaning particularly all claims or acts flowing from an asserted state of belligerency." [13]

There were, in fact, two operative clauses in the agreed draft: one on withdrawal and the other immediately following —and linked as Arthur Goldberg has said—on the full enjoyment of the right to statehood and the renunciation of all claims and acts inconsistent with that right. The word "belligerency," as Arthur Goldberg indicated in his address of July 27, was not used in the text. Its exclusion was a verbal concession to Arab sentiment. At the same time the meaning was clear enough and the wording fully did away with claims to any right of warlike activities or the threat of force in the Middle East. This agreement between the United States and the Soviet Union was not

[13] Department of State, *Bulletin*, LVII, No. 1470 (August 28, 1967), 263. For the operative paragraphs of the text of this agreement, see Appendix 25.

only the peak of success in negotiations in and around the emergency special session. It represented something even more significant and fundamental: a meeting of the minds of the super powers on one of the most dangerous and deeply entrenched international problems of the era. This gives it a memorable character and makes it an indication of the possibilities that happily exist for peace in our world.

Disappointingly, however, the agreement was too dramatic and too sudden to stimulate an alteration of intransigency among some of the Arabs. When Gromyko put the proposal to Foreign Minister Abdelaziz Bouteflika of Algeria, the latter rejected it. Gromyko urged acceptance. The new text gave back to the Arabs all the territory they had lost. It also gave them peace and security in those territories by a United Nations affirmation of their rights in this regard. Naturally, however, those rights would be enjoyed on a reciprocal basis which would cover the case of Israel. The Arab delegations agreed to consider the matter in a caucus. They did so on the night of July 20 and again on the morning of July 21, only to reject firmly the magnificent opportunity for peace created by the agreement reached between the United States and the Soviet Union. There was profound and even bitter disappointment among members of the Assembly. Little of this was expressed publicly by the nonaligned, or even privately by the East Europeans. One of the senior diplomats of the latter group stated regretfully in private: "The elements of a solution, all the elements, were present, but the timing has been fantastic—always out of step. Always something was missing at a given time."

Many of the nonaligned spoke privately in strong terms, deeply dismayed at the uncompromising position of the Arabs. Of course, the nonaligned fully realized and supported to the hilt the Arab demand for withdrawal of Israeli forces, but every diplomat knows that no negotiation can possibly succeed on terms of satisfying the demands of only one party to an international conflict or dispute. Indeed, on this basis no negotiation can even begin. What is even more serious is that on this basis no international relations of a peaceful character are possible. And it must soon become obvious to all states that the era has passed when the world community can agree to leave the development of events to this attitude, no matter how powerful may be the emotions underlying it.

At the same time it must be admitted that the movement toward agreement between the United States and the Soviet Union was at once unexpected, belated, and swift. These characteristics tended to divorce the agreement from any probability of acceptance by the Arabs, and the Assembly demanded an immediate conclusion. Hitherto Soviet support of the Arab case had appeared to be so total that the Arab states had had no incentive to rethink and revise their own approach toward belligerency in their dealings with Israel. Is it not conceivable that the situation on July 21 would have been different if early in the crisis the Soviet Union had made it clear to the Arab states that, while it would firmly support their right to absolute security against any further territorial inroads by Israel, it could not countenance the use of force or any other methods inconsistent with the UN Charter in dealings with that state? Had this attitude been put to the Arabs by the Soviet Union and the non-aligned states even by mid-June, the Arab position toward the end of July might have changed somewhat. Many of the major characteristics of the Middle East situation are not unique. There have been refugees in numbers many times greater than those in the Arab world. There are divided states and ancient geographical entities which have been truncated. In each case deep emotions and long histories have been involved, and yet in each case there has been some recognition of the fact that ultimately it is better to permit a modicum of mutual accommodation and tolerance to influence relations rather than to insist on total victory for one side and total defeat for the other.

The Assembly reconvened on July 21, 1967, in a state of profound disappointment. The main negotiators—the super powers, the Latin Americans, and the nonaligned states—were dismayed and silenced. In these circumstances little could be salvaged, and any action to accomplish even this would have to come from states on the periphery of the problem. Understandably, then, it was Austria, Finland, and Sweden that sounded out a number of other Member States on adjourning the emergency special session. Sverker Astrom of Sweden opened the proceedings on July 21, introducing a draft resolution with three brief operative paragraphs recommending that the Security Council resume consideration of the Middle East situation as a matter of urgency and that the Assembly be temporarily adjourned with authorization for its President to reconvene it if necessary.

The resolution was simple enough, so simple that it might have even been regarded as redundant. The Middle East crisis had not been removed from the agenda of the Security Council. It was open for consideration by that body at any time. A direction to this effect was certainly permissible but not essential. The decision to adjourn the Assembly temporarily could simply have been announced by the President and required no formal resolution. However, there was no reason to suppose that the formal step of a resolution would be opposed. President Pazhwak accordingly suggested, immediately after Ambassador Astrom's brief statement, that the Assembly proceed to vote on the draft resolution. But the representatives of Iraq, Tanzania, Saudi Arabia, and Mali raised objections and apprehensions.

The major apprehension was that, if the Assembly was unable to undo the consequences of aggression in this case, any member of the "third world" could find itself in a like position at any time, and could not come with confidence to the organs of the United Nations. To this, the Foreign Minister of Algeria added a new dimension of concern. He thought it was "urgent that a more just distribution of responsibilities should be established between the Security Council and the General Assembly of the United Nations." [14] The Foreign Minister was acutely aware of the persuasions of Gromyko that he should endorse the United States–Soviet agreement. He was now clearly apprehensive that if the issue returned to the Security Council a unanimous resolution might be adopted there on the basis of the new agreement between the two super powers. In the Council the Arabs would not be able to frustrate the constructive conclusion which had evaded the Assembly. This led the Algerian Foreign Minister to raise the basic question of the responsibilities of the principal organs of the United Nations, a question which related to the contents of the Charter of the United Nations and could not be resolved without amendment of the Charter. Most of the Arab states made statements strongly resisting the return of the issue to the Security Council.

The Nordic draft resolution was slightly amended by its sponsors but its sense remained unaltered. When it came to a vote the Soviet Union, for the first time in the whole consideration of the 1967 Middle East crisis, parted company with the Arabs. It voted for the resolution, as did the other Eastern European states, the Western states, the Latin Americans, and some of the nonaligned, such as India, making a total of 63 states. Opposing the resolution were 26 states—exactly half of them Arabs and the other half consisting of eleven Afro-Asian states [15] together with Cuba and Albania. Thus, the hard-core supporters of the most extreme position of the Arabs consisted of just over 10 per cent of the membership of the United Nations, only one of these states being currently a member of the Security Council.

Immediately after the vote Foreign Minister Gromyko justi-

[14] A/PV.1558, pp. 58–60.
[15] Afghanistan, Burundi, Congo (Democratic Republic), Guinea, Malaysia, Mali, Mauritania, Pakistan, Somalia, Tanzania, and Zambia.

fied the initiative of the Soviet Union to call the now adjourning emergency special session. He claimed that a large number of states had voted for the nonaligned proposals and that a significant number had voted for the Soviet proposals. He blamed Israel and the United States for the Assembly's failure to deal with the major issues and he asserted that the Latin Americans had given in to the pressures of Washington. Arthur Goldberg, following Gromyko to the podium, resisted the temptation of answering in detail the charges of the Soviet Foreign Minister. However, he stoutly rejected the charge of pressure on the Latin Americans and pointed out that those states had voted on many of the draft proposals differently from the United States. The Israeli Foreign Minister maintained the position of his government with such characteristic eloquence that Mahmud Fawzi of the United Arab Republic referred to "wordologist Eban" in his statement. Fawzi lauded the Assembly's resolutions on Jerusalem and the refugees and on the whole felt buoyed by some aspects of the Assembly's work.

France had been the only permanent member of the Security Council not to vote in favor of the Nordic resolution. It had abstained, and French Ambassador Roger Seydoux explained that it was unnecessary to adopt a resolution turning the issue over to the Security Council when the issue was already on its agenda.[16]

The Ambassador of Trinidad and Tobago replied with vigor and emphasis to Gromyko's charges. The Assembly brought its proceedings to a close on a note of dissonance, with only the President still urging it forward, exhorting members to continue their search for a solution when they dispersed at almost 11 P.M. on July 21.

Potentially the emergency special session still lived. The President had been authorized to reconvene it. But would there be any point in doing so? The Security Council, though asked by

16 A/PV.1558, p. 142.

the Assembly to resume its task as a matter of urgency, did not reconvene, even at the end of August when all sections of the UN membership felt that a Security Council meeting might be in the offing. Equally, the General Assembly remained in suspension. There was simply no evidence of any development of positions which would help forward the work of any organ of the United Nations. The Arab heads of state convened at Khartoum at the end of August. They took action to meet the economic disabilities of the United Arab Republic and Jordan arising out of the conflict. But they resolved also against negotiation with Israel as well as recognition of that country. Egypt had been reported to be more moderate than some of the other states.[17] But the Arabs, as a whole, retained their previous posture, which did not augur well for any new attempt at the United Nations to resolve the crisis.

When the Fifth Emergency Special Session of the General Assembly reconvened for the 35th time on September 18, 1967, it did so simply to extinguish itself. This it did briefly. Again Austria, Finland, and Sweden presented a draft resolution, a brief text transferring the Middle East issue to the 22d regular session of the General Assembly (A/L.530). This draft resolution was adopted with no negative votes but with Israel, Portugal, and South Africa abstaining. Adnan Pachachi, a leading Arab spokesman at the United Nations, again expressed the Arab view of the crisis: it stemmed not from the events of May, 1967, "but from the day the Zionist movement challenged the people of Palestine with the avowed intention of taking over their country, liquidating their national existence in their homeland and dispossessing them." [18] In the light of this view the 22d session of the General Assembly too would face virtually an insoluble problem. The Iraqi delegate accused Israel of refusing to join in the universal concern of the international community

[17] *Le Monde*, September 2, 1967, and New York *Times*, September 7, 1967.
[18] A/PV.1559, pp. 6–7.

by abstaining in the vote on the Nordic resolution. The Israeli delegate explained that there had been a technical error and that his delegation had intended to vote for the resolution. He asked that this be recorded in the Assembly's proceedings.

Ambassador Fedorenko's statement revealed that the attitude of the Soviet Union on the crisis would be governed primarily by the effect of the prevailing situation on the balance of power. At the very commencement of his statement he said:

This was a carefully prepared provocation designed to ensure political changes in the Middle East favorable to the imperialists, to subvert the national liberation movements of the Arab peoples, and to weaken the progressive regimes in the United Arab Republic, Syria and the other countries of the Arab East.[19]

He added that Israel and the imperialist forces "strive in all parts of the world to stop by means of armed force the historic movement of peoples on the road towards national independence, democracy and socialism." [20] The main concern of the Soviet Union was that its view of the development of history and the maintenance of a balance between pro-Socialist and anti-Socialist forces in the Middle East had become tenuous. Its endeavor to attain peace in the area would, at the least, be related to maintaining that balance.

Fedorenko went on to make two other significant points. First, he associated himself with the efforts of the Arab states and the nonaligned states, "as well as many Latin American countries . . . in their statements and draft resolutions." [21] This was a different tone from that used by Foreign Minister Gromyko on July 21 and seemed to be an attempt to restate a more friendly approach toward the Latin Americans and perhaps even to indicate openly an interest in their draft resolution for resolving the crisis. Here was at least some glimmer of a possible basis for constructive action at the 22d session of the Assembly. Another important point was that in his summation of the ur-

19 *Ibid.*, p. 17.   20 *Ibid.*   21 *Ibid.*, pp. 18–20.

gent steps now required Fedorenko did not mention condemnation of Israel.

Though the Iraqi delegate had already laid down with firmness the basic Arab position, Ambassador Mahmoud Mestiri of Tunisia injected two sentences into his statement which could have some significance for the future: "The Arab countries have heard many appeals for moderation and realism. Those appeals, especially those coming from friendly countries, have had profound repercussions throughout the Arab world." [22]

Ambassador Goldberg did not enter into the substance of the matter. He promised a full statement of the United States case in the general debate at the 22d regular session of the Assembly. Ambassador Raphael of Israel stated that the emergency special session had not taken the parties a single step nearer the goal of peace in the Middle East. He reiterated Israeli insistence on direct talks with the Arabs when he said: "Peace will not be secured by foreign guarantees or by outside and unsolicited diplomatic initiatives." [23] This was a not entirely realistic statement because this complex situation certainly demands some form of international engagement through guarantees, whether in a treaty or in Security Council resolutions. Furthermore, the brusque rejection of outside diplomatic initiatives is also unrealistic because when a situation is an emotionally overwrought as is that of the Middle East third-party endeavors become meaningful. This is a general rule of negotiation. However, Ambassador Raphael ended on a constructive note. He hoped that the new session of the Assembly would bring about reconciliation between Israel and the Arab states. By expressing this hope he was in a measure showing awareness of the role that the world community, as a third party, could play.

At 12:15 P.M. on September 18 President Pazhwak stated: "I declare closed the fifth emergency special session of the General Assembly." [24]

22 *Ibid.*, p. 31.   23 *Ibid.*, p. 42.   24 *Ibid.*, p. 47.

CHAPTER XIII

The Elusive Solution

BETWEEN June 6 and June 15, 1967, the Security Council had adopted unanimously four resolutions on a cease-fire [1] and on July 9 and 10 it had arrived at a consensus on the placing of UN military observers in the Suez Canal sector.[2] The major issues that had convulsed the Middle East, however, remained unresolved. By stretching the law and existing procedures the United Nations convened the Fifth Emergency Special Session of the General Assembly. The Assembly too failed to resolve any of the major issues. It passed the problem back to the Security Council "as a matter of urgency." [3] Notwithstanding the urgency of the General Assembly's demand, the Security Council did not meet for over three months to reopen consideration of the crisis, in spite of the fact that the Security Council had throughout remained seized of the problem of the Middle East: it had taken no action to remove the issue from its own agenda when the Fifth Emergency Special Session of the Assembly convened. The last act of the emergency session was to supplement its recommendation to the Security Council by placing the Middle East issue on the agenda of the Assembly's 22d regular session "as a matter of high priority." [4]

There has never been in the history of the United Nations such swift passage of an item from the Security Council to the General Assembly, back to the Security Council, again to the

1 Resolutions 233, 234, 235, and 236.   2 S/8047.
3 A/Res./2256 (ES-V), July 21, 1967.
4 A/Res./2257 (ES-V) September 18, 1967.

General Assembly, and then remittals to both the Security Council and a new session of the Assembly, all within four months. This is a brave and dazzling procedural effort to resolve an international problem.

Both sides in the Middle East conflict have an extended and sustaining historical memory. This fact might, in certain circumstances, conduce to a spirit of mutual accommodation between the parties. But in this case each side swells with the memory of those pages of history that glow with its own tales of heroism or endurance, a condition that promotes intransigence. Each side tends to imagine that it can afford to wait for decades if necessary to gain its own exclusive ends. After the failure of the emergency session of the Assembly this mood was more prevalent among the Arabs than among the Israelis.

The faith in historical precedents that in the long run the situation will work out exclusively to the interests of one side is, however, almost certainly bound to be disappointing. The present and the future are likely to be significantly different from the historic past. The world has shrunk. Issues of peace and war today inevitably involve much or the whole of the world community, if only because the prospect of escalation of local conflicts to much larger and frighteningly destructive wars is an ever present one. It follows that there is no precedent in any historical age to which a party to a conflict can turn for support for the attainment of its own exclusive ends. Today the world community of necessity steadily presses for the application of certain emerging norms of conduct to any situation of wide international concern. True, it is still possible to point to situations in which these norms do not operate, but all the situations which fall into this category have occurred in regions where some of the parties are not members of the United Nations. Thus we have had Korea and Vietnam, and one might interpolate that the unruliness of situations to which the law of

the United Nations is not fully applicable is an unanswerable
pragmatic reason for universality of membership in the Organization.

The states directly involved in the Middle East crisis are all
members of the United Nations. The international community
will tend to insist that among those states there is at least a working implementation of the norms of the United Nations Charter.
Even if any of the Middle East states should contemplate withdrawal from the UN, still the Charter norms would continue to
be applicable, because this has become the general will of the
international community, and no technical manipulation will be
acceptable as valid ground for escape from the operation of this
will.

At the same time, the international community prefers to
secure a willing acceptance of its norms by states rather than
their imposition, though Article 25 and Chapter VII of the
United Nations Charter remain available to be invoked in extreme circumstances. It is because persuasion is preferable to
imposition that the arts of diplomacy become, as a vehicle of
progress in the relations of states, more important than the ultimate prescriptions of the law. This is why in any situation,
and in particular in the Middle East crisis, the modalities both of
the international community as a whole and of the states directly
involved are of prime importance.

Such were some of the thoughts with which concerned states
wrestled while the crisis simmered and the UN forums remained untended. It was relatively easy to identify the necessary
elements of a settlement. Though the Soviet Union made its
point of departure immediate and full withdrawal of Israeli
forces to the positions of June 4, 1967, we have seen how it
reached agreement with the United States on July 19, 1967, on
the terms of a major step in the resolving of fundamental issues.
Though the United States approaches the problem on a much

broader front than does the Soviet Union,[5] it too was able to acquiesce in the more restrictive agreement reached with Foreign Minister Gromyko in July. This was a significant success of the art of diplomacy which took into account the necessity of filtering the process of implementation of the norms of the Charter through internationally constructed sieves.

Israel continued to insist that the Arab states negotiate directly with it on the terms of a settlement. In the last analysis there almost invariably has to be a certain degree of directness in negotiation. The resolving of issues must involve at least a final mutual acceptance of the terms of a settlement. Herein lay one of the greatest obstacles to precise steps forward in the Middle East. One side—Israel—insisted on direct negotiation. The other side—the Arabs—rejected direct negotiation. The United States, in the resolution which it introduced at the Fifth Emergency Special Session, envisaged direct negotiation but injected also the possibility of third-party assistance. Its formulation read: "Considers that this objective should be achieved through negotiated arrangements with appropriate third-party assistance." [6] However, on September 21, 1967, Ambassador Goldberg's statement to the General Assembly was more flexible regarding the methods to be used. He said: "Both sides must have the will to work out a political solution; both must be committed to peace; and no appropriate method, such as good offices or mediation, should be excluded." [7] The draft proposals of the Latin Americans and of the nonaligned states which received the largest numbers of votes at the Fifth Emergency Special Session moved even further away from direct negotiation. The Latin American proposals requested the parties to use the procedures for peaceful settlement set out in Article 33 of the Charter of the United

[5] See the eight principles proposed by Arthur Goldberg in his statement in the general debate of the 22d General Assembly session on September 21, 1967; A/PV.1562, September 21, 1967.

[6] A/L.520, June 20, 1967.   [7] A/PV.1562, p. 23.

Nations, several of which involve the use of third parties. Furthermore, the Latin American proposals placed a major part of
the negotiations in the hands of the Security Council, although
the Council was, of course, to work directly with the parties.[8]
The nonaligned states leaned heavily on third-party participation
in negotiation. They requested the Secretary-General to designate a personal representative who would be in contact with the
parties, and again a major role in the negotiations was given to
the Security Council.[9] The implication of the text agreed upon
by the United States and the Soviet Union on July 19, 1967,
was that negotiations would be largely, if not entirely, in the
hands of the organs of the United Nations or would be assisted
by persons named by them. However, there was no direct mention of modalities, thus indicating that there was to be flexibility
in the diplomatic methods to be used.

The foregoing comments on a number of the proposals which
were considered during the months of June and July indicate
that the proposals which gained the widest support did not stress
direct negotiation between the parties. Also, the crucial proposal
on which the United States and the Soviet Union reached informal agreement pointed in the direction of United Nations
modalities and allowed for the widest possible measure of flexibility as regards procedure. It thus became clear that there was
a wide and perhaps increasing measure of agreement that direct
negotiation alone—which one party still demanded—was not
the course most likely to lead to the implementation of the
norms of the Charter in the Middle East. If a solution is to be
less elusive than it has been in the past it would be wise not to
retreat to rigid and exclusive positions demanding the use of
only one of the many possible procedures of pacific settlement.[10]

Another procedural problem which had to be considered was

[8] A/L.523, June 30, 1967.   [9] A/L.522/Rev.3, July 3, 1967.
[10] For categories of issues which tend to be amenable to third-party assistance in negotiation, see chapters 7 and 12 of the author's *Modern International
Negotiation: Principles and Practice* (New York, 1966).

whether methods which involved the organs of the United Nations, particularly the Security Council, would, in fact, effectively achieve the objective of peaceful relations between the states of the Middle East. As we have observed, there has been a Security Council resolution calling for the termination of all restrictions on the passage of international commercial shipping through the Suez Canal.[11] Article 25 of the UN Charter makes it a solemn obligation that Member States shall carry out the decisions of the Council. This clear obligation notwithstanding, the terms of the resolution have remained inoperative. If the United Nations is to obtain a solution of the crisis it must insist that there be no trifling with any of its obligatory decisions. However, the question would still arise whether it would not be well to supplement resolutions of the Security Council with other international processes.

Such were the considerations regarding the Middle East crisis in the minds of delegations to the United Nations when the General Assembly convened its 22d regular session on September 19, 1967. In the general debate, which opened on September 21, all the speakers addressed themselves, among other matters, to the crisis. However, since for the most part the same speakers had recently enunciated their positions at the Fifth Emergency Special Session, there was no outpouring of new wisdom which could dissipate the knotty problems that underlay the crisis. At the same time, these statements stimulated the members of the Security Council, particularly the great powers, to attend once again to the Middle East issue which, in spite of its inherent dangers and urgings by the emergency special session, they had been evading for over two months. It was not until early in October, goaded on by manifestations of renewed interest in the Assembly and prompted also by their determination not to let the issue return again to the Assembly, that the Security Council members started actively to discuss the situation.

[11] Resolution 95 (1951) of September 1, 1951.

Though he had come almost each year to the Assembly, the arrival of V. V. Kuznetsov, First Deputy Foreign Minister of the Soviet Union—upon Gromyko's return to Moscow after spending two weeks or so in New York—was regarded in some quarters as indicating renewed Soviet interest in moves to obtain a settlement which would encompass the withdrawal of Israel and the general cessation of belligerency in the Middle East.

Lord Caradon of the United Kingdom was especially active among the representatives of the great powers. The strength of his position lay in his resolute adherence to the two main principles which in his view would have to govern the whole process of pacification in the Middle East: complete withdrawal by Israel and the unambiguous right of all states in the Middle East to co-exist in full and equal sovereignty. Moreover, he was optimistic that these two principles would be acceptable to the parties mainly concerned. Lord Caradon's optimism was based upon several factors. First, there was some credible indication that the Arab states directly involved were more willing to settle than they had been in the closing stages of the Fifth Emergency Special Session. King Hussein of Jordan indicated that there was a serious desire on the part of these states to consider the possibilities of an equitable settlement. Though it was to be assumed that there was still a gulf between Arab and Israeli concepts of equity, there was, in the view of most governments, a perceptible movement from previous total or near total Arab unwillingness to make any concessions at all in regard to Israel. Second, the general principles which Lord Caradon had in mind were in substance the same as the principles that had been contained in the abortive United States–Soviet agreement of July 19. Third, Caradon proposed that there should be added to the two principles the practical step of dispatch to the area of a representative of the Secretary-General who would encourage the parties to implement the agreed principles. If any party wished to go beyond the principles or refused to carry out its share of responsibilities inherent in them, the Secretary-General's representative would point out that he was there squarely to facilitate implementation of the Security Council's resolution, no more and no less.

By mid-October, however, no widely acceptable formula had emerged. Some of the Arabs concerned were still reluctant to make a clean break with past practices and theories of belligerency; and the Israelis seemed increasingly reluctant to accept a formula which would require their complete withdrawal from territories occupied in the war, even if their objectives of secure frontiers, nonbelligerency, and freedom of navigation were conceded.

The focus of effort shifted somewhat from the great powers to the nonpermanent members of the Security Council. The representatives of these ten states met on October 19 and 20 and felt that they were making some progress. In particular they were all agreed that the Council should ask the Secretary-General to send a special representative to the area. There was also wide agreement that both withdrawal and nonbelligerency, including such practical matters as freedom of navigation, would have to be established, but there was no agreement on how these requirements would be defined in a Council resolution. Meanwhile the great powers were continuing their efforts. On October 19 Ambassador Dobrynin of the Soviet Union called on U.S. Secretary of State Dean Rusk to discuss possibilities, and on the same day Kuznetsov continued his intensive negotiations with the Arabs, the nonaligned, and several Western states. He felt that the Arabs would now accept the July 19 formula but that Israel would not do so.

It was still not clear that the two sides were willing to accept the major principles which most Member States regarded as the essential basis of a fair settlement. This meant, in the final analysis, that the super powers were reluctant to insist that the Arabs and the Israelis should implement to the full the Caradon formula or the formula of July 19. The real issue became the extent to which the super powers themselves could accept those formulas. If they could do so, on the ground that the interests of both Israel and the Arab states would thereby be sufficiently and effectively safeguarded, then the parties to the conflict would not be able to resist the implementation of the agreed formula. True, they would be reluctant. They would multiply excuses and delays. But the joint pressure of the great powers together with all the other members of the Security Council, and the basic fairness of the formula in the eyes of an overwhelming majority of the members of the UN, would finally prevail. However, the super powers had not yet made up their minds to join in a consensus to apply these pressures to the two sides.

This was the situation when, on October 21, the Israeli destroyer *Eilat* was sunk by missiles launched from Egyptian boats. Three days later, on October 24, the Israelis destroyed major oil installations and other facilities at the Egyptian port town of Suez. Each side had its own reason for these actions. The government of the United Arab Republic claimed that the *Eilat* had been in Egyptian territorial waters.[12] So far as the attack on the Suez area was concerned, it was not announced by Israel as retaliation but as an outcome of firing in that area which the Israelis alleged had been started by the Egyptians.[13] The actions of October 21 and 24 constituted the gravest breaches of the Middle East cease-fire to that date. Both the United Arab Republic and Israel asked for Security Council action.[14] This was the second time that the demand for Security Council action had come from the parties themselves, the first having occurred on July 8 when there had been some fighting in the area of the Suez Canal.

[12] S/PV.1369, p. 13.
[13] S/8208, October 24, 1967, Israeli letter to President of Security Council.
[14] S/8207, October 24, 1967, and S/8208, October 24, 1967.

The hitherto tentative probings of the issue by the members of the Security Council now had to take into account new and conclusive evidence of the gravity of the situation, as well as the united will of both the major parties concerned for further action by the Council. These two factors pushed the efforts of the members of the Council into high gear, and opened a new phase in the handling of the crisis by the United Nations.

CHAPTER XIV

The Security Council in High Gear

ON THE SECOND DAY of the Council's renewed sessions—October 25, 1967—Ambassador S. O. Adebo of Nigeria said:

Action began to be taken by members of the Security Council as long as two or three weeks ago. I mention this in order to reassure the general public of all the world that what has now happened is not a result of any lethargy on the part of the members of the Security Council. . . . In the last few days meetings have been held every day under the guidance of our distinguished and very experienced President in order to try to work out something that will enable us to put a stop to this kind of development. Two days ago it seemed to many of us that there might be an opening. . . . Everybody began to work harder than ever to try to see what we could make of that opening.[1]

Chief Adebo thus lifted the curtain a little and revealed in outline the nature of the efforts which had been in train when the latest Middle East clash occurred. Later in his statement he referred to the fact that about a week earlier the permanent members of the Security Council had "let it be known to the President that they would welcome any initiative which the non-permanent members of the Council might take to help to resolve the whole of the Middle East situation." [2] This was a reference to the meetings of the nonpermanent members which, as we have noted, had begun on the morning of October 19 after the permanent members had failed to agree on the formula on which Caradon had been working. Though Ambassador Adebo quite rightly drew attention to these efforts, there can

[1] S/PV.1370, p. 6.   [2] Ibid., p. 11.

be no gainsaying the fact that the fresh outbreak of hostilities in the last ten days of October led to redoubled efforts in search of a long-term solution of the problems of the Middle East.

While the parties to the conflict addressed the Council at the opening of its new series of meetings on October 24 almost exclusively in terms of charges and countercharges relating to the breakdown of the cease-fire,[3] strong emphasis was placed by virtually all members of the Council on the urgent need to develop a long-term solution which would bring peace to the area. On October 24 and 25 all the members of the Council made speeches and all of them, with the exception of the representatives of Mali and China, spoke of the need for a long-term settlement. As might have been expected, the first speaker to voice this necessity was Lord Caradon, who called attention to the tragic breakdown of the cease-fire: "Surely no one now can claim that we should hesitate any longer." [4] The Council had to go forward to a secure peace. In a spirited effort to lead the Council forward by infusing a mood of urgency, he concluded: "I cannot remember a greater sense of common purpose, common impatience and general agreement amongst us." [5] His general sentiments were quickly echoed by the representatives of Canada, the United States, India, Denmark, and Ethiopia. And the representatives of Bulgaria, France, and the Soviet Union also spoke of the need for a settlement. Ambassador Fedorenko said: "The latest events compel the Security Council to be mindful of its responsibilities, to understand that it is necessary to bring about a political settlement in the Near East." [6]

---

[3] Gideon Raphael of Israel, however, did go further when in his statement of October 24 he said: "Israel again declares that it is ready right here and now, tonight, under this very roof, to meet representatives of the U.A.R. and of any other Arab State and to discuss with them all measures designed to ensure security for all and to lay the basis for a peaceful future." S/PV.1369, p. 22.

[4] S/PV.1369, pp. 23–25.   [5] *Ibid.*, p. 27.   [6] *Ibid.*, pp. 37–40.

Of course, political alignments and differing approaches to peace influenced the members of the Council. Consistently with his past endeavors, Fedorenko introduced a draft resolution comdemning Israel, demanding compensation for the United Arab Republic, and calling upon Israel alone to observe the cease-fire.[7] Arthur Goldberg, on the other hand, moved a more evenhanded proposal condemning all violations of the cease-fire and calling for its strict observance by all concerned.[8]

On the morning of October 25 Chief Adebo concluded his statement by proposing a brief recess in order that the Council members should try to reach agreement on a resolution to deal with the immediate situation of a breakdown of the cease-fire. The suspension of the meeting proved to be a wise step. The Council was able to reconvene in the afternoon and adopt unanimously a text which was not strikingly different from the proposal of the United States delegation. It condemned violations of the cease-fire, regretted loss of life and property, reaffirmed the need to observe the cease-fire strictly, and demanded that this be done.[9]

Immediately after the adoption of the resolution Secretary-General U Thant stated that it was necessary to strengthen the UN observation arrangement in the Suez Canal sector. The number of observers would have to be increased from 43 to 90, they would be stationed at 18 posts instead of nine, and small patrol craft and helicopters would have to be made available to them.[10] This proposal followed logically from the initiative that U Thant had taken in July to institute UN observation in the Suez Canal area. On that occasion the Council had not laid down the number of observers. The Secretary-General, who was far more clearly aware than Council members could be of the needs in men and equipment for observation to be effective, was now

[7] S/8212. See Appendix 17.   [8] S/8213. See Appendix 18.
[9] S/RES/240, October 25, 1967. See Appendix 19.
[10] S/PV.1371, pp. 6–7.

reporting to the Council the further elaboration of observation arrangement which he proposed to undertake. He was not seeking the sanction of the Council but he wished it to be aware of his next step, including its financial implications. He said: "The estimated financial implications will be submitted to the Council as soon as the necessary calculations are completed." [11]

Fedorenko was the first delegate to respond to the Secretary-General's statement. He noted the Secretary-General's intention to give more information on his proposals, including the financial effects thereof. Fedorenko added: "We also consider it necessary to underline that the question of the increase in the number of observers must be examined by the Security Council in accordance with its competence under the Charter." [12]

Arthur Goldberg, immediately following his Soviet colleague, took a different view of the executive necessities of the situation: "We regard the steps he [U Thant] has announced that he will take to be fully in accord with his responsibilities to strengthen UNTSO and in full keeping with his established authority under the Charter and established practices of the United Nations." [13]

The two views of Fedorenko and Goldberg reflect the continuing differences between the Soviet Union and the United States in regard to peacekeeping. These differences, however, should not be overemphasized because they do not in fact prevent agreement being reached on the institution and development of specific UN peacekeeping operations. In practice the Security Council and the Secretary-General have managed to cooperate in order to get the necessary results. This tends to establish the encouraging conclusion that the opposing views of the two super powers need not inevitably create conflicts of jurisdiction. Neither the Security Council nor the Secretary-General can have exclusive and full jurisdiction in regard to UN peacekeeping operations. Both have an essential role to

[11] *Ibid.*, pp. 7–10. [12] *Ibid.*, p. 26. [13] *Ibid.*, pp. 27–28.

play. We should add that, in this case, the operation was part of the functions of UNTSO for which the guidelines had been prescribed by the Council.

The adoption of Council Resolution 240 on October 25 did not mean that Council members had turned aside from the urgent need for a peace settlement. Six members spoke after the adoption of the resolution—Canada, China, India, Japan, the USSR, and the United States—and all of them reiterated the need for a long-term settlement. Fedorenko, who was the second speaker (the first had been the representative of China), said: "There is an almost unanimous feeling that consultations must be speeded up to work out a decision leading to a political settlement in the Near East, to the ensuring of peace and the lawful rights of peoples." [14] Goldberg, the next speaker, said: "What the Near East needs is not just a cease-fire, essential though it is, but new steps towards a durable, permanent and just peace. We . . . again express the conviction that this Council must begin promptly to help move towards a just settlement of all the outstanding questions between the parties." [15] Ambassador Senjin Tsuruoka of Japan declared that "the clear duty of the Security Council at this juncture is to measure up to its solemn responsibilities by finding that formula which, acceptable to the parties concerned, will establish a durable and just peace in the Middle East." [16]

Ambassador Parthasarathi of India called for an intensification of the consultations on a settlement and Ambassador Ignatieff of Canada associated himself with the remarks made by the representatives of Japan and India.

These were not just words. Daily consultation had in fact been going on since the middle of October, and immediately after the sessions of the Council on October 24–25 those consultations were intensified. The nonpermanent members formed the negotiating caucus, keeping in touch with the permanent members

14 *Ibid.*, p. 26.   15 *Ibid.*, p. 27.   16 *Ibid.*, p. 37.

and, through individual representatives in their caucus, with the parties. On general principles the nonpermanent members made considerable progress, but their formulation in the specific case of the Middle East raised difficulties. The Latin American states (Argentina and Brazil) advanced the formula that the Israelis should withdraw to their positions prior to the outbreak of hostilities. The delegate of India and the African delegates wanted the further precision of withdrawal to the positions of June 4, 1967. Canada and Denmark had yet another formula for withdrawal. This was, in effect, that no state should occupy territory of another state against its wishes. Similarly, though the principles of refugee resettlement and free navigation were widely acceptable, there was no agreement on the language which would convey these essential elements of a settlement. The prospects for agreement among the ten nonpermanent members did not look good on October 30. However, on that date India withdrew its previous insistence on withdrawal to the positions of June 4 and came into line with the Latin American formula on this aspect of the matter. But there remained a considerable gap between this formulation and that of Canada and Denmark. Long meetings were held on October 31 and November 1 but the ten nonpermanent members failed to reach agreement. They gave themselves another chance on November 2 but made no significant progress and so reported to the permanent members of the Council on the morning of November 3.

While the admission of failure by the ten stimulated a new round of activity among the great powers, particularly on the part of the United States, it did not end the effort of some of the nonpermanent members to find a satisfactory formula. For a brief period Canada and Denmark considered submitting their own draft resolution based on their withdrawal formula. This proposal, however, had no chance of obtaining the requisite nine votes. It would have failed to secure the votes of the two African states, the two Latin American members, France, India, the

USSR, Bulgaria, and Japan. Thus it would have been favored by, at most, six members of the Council.

Behind the scenes the United Arab Republic was urging its friends to accelerate their efforts to find a solution. The UAR had had to displace 300,000 civilians in the Suez area and resettle them elsewhere because the hazards of life in their ancestral homeland had become very great. The economy had been further hit by the destruction of the important industrial complex at Suez. It was becoming urgently necessary to convince the people that effective measures could be taken to push the Israelis back from the Suez Canal area and the Sinai so that normal living conditions could be reestablished. Besides, discredited though the army was because of the results of the war in June, the younger officers were to be reckoned with as a possible center for a movement toward army reform and even toward bringing in a new administration. This possibility also underscored the urgent need to counteract some of the sharp discontents and to do so, if possible, by methods that could not be claimed by the army as its creation.

King Hussein's visit to the United States strengthened the conviction in some quarters that the Western powers could settle the broad terms of a peace agreement with Jordan and the United Arab Republic. Moreover, it was thought that these terms would be acceptable to all the other Arab states except Syria and Algeria. These two exceptions would not invalidate the settlement: at most they would create complications on a relatively small sector of the Arab-Israeli border. It was natural that the United States should now assume the leadership in making the effort on the Western side, not only because of its inherent capacity, but because the French position was considered to be pro-Arab and British efforts had so far not succeeded in arousing great enthusiasm at Washington. The United States also had the advantage of special opportunities to understand the Arab position as expounded by King Hussein.

It became known that the United States was preparing its own draft resolution for consideration by the Council. It was also known that though the United States had not pressed to a vote the draft resolution it had presented on June 20 at the Fifth Emergency Special Session of the General Assembly, it felt that the time had now come for a final effort in which it could, because of a number of circumstances, play a vital role.

Meanwhile, the nonpermanent members, less the representatives of Canada and Denmark, had been jointly responsive to the urgency of the situation. An Indian draft resolution was considered by the Latin American representatives and the Asian and African delegates. These members came very near reaching full agreement. The Indian position had now come to approach very closely the Latin American proposal that had almost succeeded in obtaining a two-thirds majority at the emergency special session. This being so, the revised Indian proposals were acceptable to the Latin American members of the Council, particularly to Argentina. Moreover, since the United States and the other Western powers (except France) had voted for the Latin American proposal at the emergency session, a new proposal on those lines would logically stand a good chance of gaining very wide acceptance in the Security Council. With these considerations in mind, and in view of the private urgings of the UAR, on November 7 a joint draft resolution, in the names of India, Mali, and Nigeria, was submitted to the President of the Council.[17]

Simultaneously the United Arab Republic asked for an urgent meeting of the Security Council,[18] requesting consideration of "the dangerous situation prevailing in the Middle East as a result of the persistence of Israel not to withdraw its armed forces."

These moves took the Western powers somewhat by surprise. They had hoped that a Council session could be delayed until the United States proposals had been cleared with the interested

17 S/8227. See Appendix 20.   18 S/8226.

states. They let it be known that King Hussein had termed these
proposals acceptable to him. Now the Western powers were
faced with the dilemma of what to do about an Asian-African
proposal along the lines of the earlier Latin American proposal
they had supported. It could be argued that nothing remains
fixed in international life and that the circumstances in November, 1967, called for a somewhat different approach. Also to be
considered was the support of King Hussein, as well as the fact
that although the Asian-African proposal was known to have the
backing of some of the Arab states it did not have the support of
Israel. Indeed, few of the Asian-African states had conferred
directly with Israeli representatives. Their counterargument had
been twofold: first, the Latin American members of the Council
had been in close touch with the Israelis, whose views had
therefore been taken into account. Second, the new draft proposal was based on those principles which had been almost unanimously acceptable at the emergency session of the Assembly.

Immediately following the submission of the Asian-African
proposal, the United States tabled its own draft resolution.[19] The
new U.S. proposal differed from the American proposal before
the emergency session in two main respects. First, the Assembly
proposal had called for negotiations based, *inter alia*, on "disengagement and withdrawal of forces." The new proposal was
much firmer in regard to withdrawal. The Council would affirm
that "withdrawal of armed forces from occupied territories" was
required. While it could theoretically be argued that Gaza had
been occupied by the United Arab Republic and that the west
bank of the Jordan had been occupied by the state of Jordan,
the new American formulation was more clearly directed to
the withdrawal of Israeli forces that had been the United States
proposal to the Assembly. The second major difference between
the two formulations was that, whereas the earlier proposal had
averred that the objectives "should be achieved through nego-

[19] S/8229. See Appendix 21.

tiated arrangements with appropriate third party assistance," there was much less stress in the new proposals on direct negotiation between the Arabs and Israelis. The United States now accepted the suggestion originally made by India and espoused by the United Kingdom and others that the Secretary-General should designate a special representative who would assist the parties in the working out of solutions. Both these major changes could be described as movements in the direction of meeting Arab demands. At the same time, these movements were known to be within the limits of Israeli acceptance. The new formulation on the withdrawal of forces did not specifically mention Israeli forces and it did not say that withdrawal was to be from all the territories occupied by Israel. Again, the formulation regarding the special representative did not rule out direct negotiation.

The Asian-African text, on the other hand, specifically called for the withdrawal of Israel's armed forces "from all the territories occupied as a result of the recent conflict." This was more than would be acceptable to Israel, at any rate immediately. The formulation regarding the representative of the Secretary-General, "who would contact the States concerned in order to coordinate efforts to achieve the purposes of this resolution," was not substantially different from the American text. It too did not rule out direct negotiation. A real difference between the two proposals was that while the American text affirmed the necessity of freedom of navigation through international waterways the Asian-African text interpolated the words "in accordance with international law" after the words "freedom of navigation." This meant that the right of passage through the Suez Canal and through the Gulf of Aqaba could and would become the subject of protracted international litigation with a view to establishing the applicable jurisprudence.

However, Ambassador Parthasarathi informed the Western powers that he would be glad to discuss the Asian-African pro-

posals with the U.S. delegation in order to try to reach agreement on a single text. No such direct behind-the-scenes talks
took place from the 8th to the 12th of November. Meanwhile,
though the United Arab Republic had called for an urgent convening of the Security Council, no meeting was in fact held
until two days later, the Council finally convening at 3:30 P.M.
on November 9, with no wide consensus in view on either of the
proposals now before it (those of the Asian-African states and
the United States). The first four hours of the meeting were lost
in a procedural dispute in regard to the appropriate order of
speeches. In requesting the meeting the UAR had asked to speak
first. Thereafter another five speakers had sent in their names.
Then Israel asked to speak and the question in dispute became
whether Israel should not speak immediately after the UAR so
that the Council could hear the two sides at the outset of its
session. The Soviet delegation contended that it was not necessary to hear the two sides in unbroken sequence because the
issues involved were not new and had been before the Council
for several months. The United States asked for a vote on a
proposal to give Israel the second place on the roster of speakers.
Eight instead of the requisite nine members of the Council voted
in favor of this proposal. Consequently Israel remained seventh
on the list.

The Council proceeded to listen first to the United Arab
Republic representative, Foreign Minister Mahmoud Riad. His
statement emphasized the need for immediate and unconditional
withdrawal of Israeli forces to the positions they had occupied
prior to June 5. At the same time, he described the decision of
the Arab summit meeting in late August as "a decision for a
political solution of the crisis." [20] Moreover, he said that "the
peoples of our part of the world can in no way benefit from
a state of war, belligerency and tension." [21] These pronouncements were new elements in the Arab position and counter-

[20] S/PV.1373, p. 47.   [21] *Ibid.*, p. 51.

balanced to some extent indications in the same speech to the effect that the United Arab Republic still demanded self-determination for the people of Palestine—by which was clearly meant the Arab people of Palestine. The Foreign Minister urged enforcement action under Chapter VII of the Charter if Israeli forces refused to withdraw. In crucial international situations intransigency in statements of position is to be expected. It is, however, on the flexibilities of such statements that attention should be focused. In the statement of the Foreign Minister of the United Arab Republic there were some indications of flexibility which could give hope for the future.

Immediately after Foreign Minister Riad had spoken, G. Parthasarathi of India introduced the proposal which bore the names of India, Mali, and Nigeria, the main characteristics of which have been noted. The Indian delegate brought out three significant points. First, he asked for circulation to members of the Security Council of General Assembly Document A/L.523/Rev. 1—the text of the Latin American draft resolution which, though not adopted, had received the highest vote at the Fifth Emergency Special Session. The Indian delegate said: "In finalizing the 3-Power draft we had the Latin American draft as the basic document of reference." [22] The second point of significance was an indication of flexibility in regard to the wording in the text relating to freedom of navigation. Parthasarathi said: "We are prepared to examine very carefully any arguments that might be advanced in the Council in respect of the words 'in accordance with international law.' " [23] This was one way of saying that these words were dispensable. The third important point was that the draft proposal did not rule out direct negotiations between the parties if at some stage this procedure proved feasible. The Indian delegate said: "The draft resolution provides for the adoption of all peaceful means to settle the dispute." [24]

We have noted some of the characteristics of the U.S. pro-

[22] *Ibid.*, p. 68.　　[23] *Ibid.*, p. 72.　　[24] *Ibid.*, pp. 73-75.

posal. Arthur Goldberg's statement on November 9 threw further light on the American position. First, Goldberg made the point that the Council's meeting was perhaps somewhat premature: "We should have preferred to have this meeting take place only after the intensive diplomatic consultations of recent weeks had led to advance agreement." [25] In this connection he claimed that both Israel and the Arab states concerned had accepted President Johnson's five principles enunciated on June 19, 1967: "It is of the greatest significance that the principal parties on both sides have stated their acceptance of these principles as the framework for a just and lasting peace." [26]

The most significant point made by Goldberg was the re-iteration that the United States proposal sought to accommodate the positions of both parties:

Our draft resolution contains a meaningful mandate which should be acceptable within the Council and which is sufficiently comprehensive for all the States directly concerned. . . . We have attempted to state it in terms that set forth guidelines . . . in language which, in our opinion, takes into account and in no way prejudices the positions or the vital interests of the States concerned.[27]

This insistence on meeting the requirements and the positions of the parties contained several implications. First, it meant that the United States—and this point had been stressed by other members of the Council—conceived that the Security Council was, at that stage, functioning strictly within the terms of Chapter VI of the Charter on the pacific settlement of disputes. There could, indeed, be no doubt that this was the appropriate part of the Charter on which to base the type of Council action envisaged. However, it is not to be lost sight of that even under Chapter VI, while the main emphasis is on getting the parties to seek a solution by negotiation, enquiry, mediation, conciliation, arbitration, or other peaceful means of their own choice, the Security Council has the right if it considers that a dispute "is

25 *Ibid.*, p. 126.   26 *Ibid.*, p. 127.   27 *Ibid.*, pp. 128–30.

in fact likely to endanger the maintenance of international peace and security . . . to recommend such terms of settlement as it may consider appropriate." [28] This gives the Council an over-riding responsibility to come to its own conclusions, if necessary, as to the kind of settlement to be attempted. It need hardly be added that in doing so the Council would obviously take into full account the positions of the parties and do its utmost to move those positions forward so that they were no longer completely incompatible, and to bear in mind such movements in making its own recommendations.

Another implication of Arthur Goldberg's statement was that the United States felt that the vital interests of the parties could be accommodated by application of the affirmations of principle set out in the United States proposal. This was at once an assessment, a hope, and an exhortation to the parties.

However, Lord Caradon, speaking immediately before Arthur Goldberg and with the United States draft proposal before him, made it clear that he did not consider that either the American proposal or that of the three powers met the needs of the case. He ended his statement by saying: "Consequently, I would earnestly put to the Council the suggestion that when we have heard the opening statements in this debate, we should allow a short period for further urgent consultations among ourselves." [29]

The Japanese Ambassador, who had worked closely with the permanent members, particularly the United States, and with the nonpermanent members in his capacity as President of the Council during the month of October, made this point with even greater precision. Of the two draft proposals he said: "I find merit, if not complete satisfaction in both of them. But it does appear that neither of those draft texts adequately reflects a consensus of the Council. . . . My delegation is still hopeful that further consultations might very well lead to compromise and a consensus that all members of the Council could support.

[28] Article 37 of the Charter. [29] S/PV.1373, p. 126.

We attach great importance to that objective." [30] Several other members of the Council attached importance to finding a proposal which would be supported by all Council members. Ambassador Otto Borch of Denmark, for example, called for "a solution which can command the support of all members of this Council." [31] The representative of Ethiopia, while praising the three-power draft and supporting it, said that the representative of the United Nations whom both draft proposals would send to the Middle East should begin his work "with the unreserved blessing and united support of all members of the Council and, more particularly, of the permanent major Powers." [32] And the delegate of Canada stated: "Our aim, however, is not—and I agree in this with the representative of Ethiopia—to enter into competition and contention but to seek agreement among us." [33]

Thus there was a strong current in the Council in favor of further efforts to reach agreement. At the same time, and this too was fortunate, some members said that the Council had to remain conscious of its own responsibilities toward the Middle East situation. Ambassador Adebo of Nigeria said: "We cannot continue to labor in the hope that irreconcilable views will be reconciled. We have to muster enough courage to tell both parties that unless they move they cannot have peace in the Middle East." [34] In the same vein the delegate of Canada said: "I do not mean by this that the parties must approve what we do. Clearly the members of the Council have to accept their responsibilities under the Charter to take practical steps leading to a just solution." [35]

What these last-mentioned statements were doing was to remind the parties that in the last analysis the Council could and should act on its own initiative. However, it remained broadly true that in November, 1967, the Council addressed itself to the possibilities of an agreed solution. This was no ad-

---

[30] *Ibid.,* pp. 153–55.   [31] *Ibid.,* p. 147.   [32] *Ibid.,* p. 136.
[33] *Ibid.,* p. 141.   [34] *Ibid.,* p. 91.   [35] *Ibid.,* pp. 139–40.

mission of weakness. On the contrary, the Council's approach was both wise and appropriate.

Deputy Foreign Minister V. V. Kuznetsov of the Soviet Union made it clear that he did not like the United States draft. He stressed the need for clarity on withdrawal. He read the U.S. draft as not calling for complete withdrawal and added:

If that is not so, we devoutly hope that we shall hear from the United States representative a clear-cut and unambiguous statement to the effect that the United States is in favor of the withdrawal of Israeli troops from all occupied territories to the positions occupied by them on 5 June this year.[36]

Regarding the heart of the problem, Kuznetsov stated:

The Soviet Union is prepared categorically to support a decision which would provide for the immediate withdrawal of Israeli forces from all occupied Arab territories as a result of the recent conflict, together with a recognition of the principle of the independent national existence of every State in that area, and their right to live in peace and security.[37]

To the three-power draft resolution the Soviet Union gave only qualified support: "Although the Soviet delegation would have preferred a more radical solution, it will be ready to support the draft resolution of India, Mali and Nigeria, if the Arab countries, the victims of aggression, do not oppose it." [38]

The remaining speaker on November 9 was Ambassador José Maria Ruda of Argentina. He maintained the Latin American position enshrined in the draft resolution which had been submitted to the emergency session of the Assembly, and added a note of perplexity regarding the shift in positions of certain powers:

Now we are in the month of November, and in the course of the present debate we note the strange paradox whereby some of those members of the Council who supported the Argentine formula seem today to prefer to overlook that act when they define and speak of

---

[36] *Ibid.,* p. 112.   [37] *Ibid.,* p. 107.   [38] *Ibid.,* pp. 108–10.

the present picture in the Middle East. On the other hand, others, who saw fit to criticize, today find themselves supporting us.[39]

This telling remark embraced the current positions on the one hand of Canada, Denmark, and the United States, which had voted in the Assembly for the Latin American draft resolution, and, on the other hand, of India, Mali, and Nigeria, which had not voted for the Latin American proposal but had now adopted it as their own. Further and ripened consideration had moved some states toward the Latin American position and others away from it. Such are the hazards of international relations and negotiation.

The Council reconvened on the Middle East issue on November 13. Foreign Minister Abba Eban again presented the Israeli position with brilliance. Expectedly he reminded the Council, quoting from statements of President Nasser and Radio Cairo, that the Arabs had been out to destroy Israel and had said so clearly at the end of May, 1967. This was inevitably the background of the Israeli approach to the problem. Said Eban: "After the cease-fire lines a permanent and mutually recognized territorial boundary is our only possible destination." [40] Contrasting the Arab and Israeli policies, Eban said: "Against the Khartoum policy of no recognition, no negotiation and no peace, Israel presents its policy: Recognition, negotiation, peace." [41] He traced the retreat of the Security Council from its early position of demanding negotiation in the Middle East to its present silence on this subject:

Just as it is paradoxically necessary to labor hard to persuade international organs of the necessity to advocate peace treaties, so is it necessary to prove that the advocacy of negotiation is not an extravagant and somewhat immoderate pursuit. This is the most extraordinary of all recent developments. The United Nations jurisprudence on the problem of negotiation has been in constant retreat for many years.[42]

[39] *Ibid.*, pp. 162–63.   [40] S/PV.1375, p. 16.   [41] *Ibid.*, p. 17.
[42] *Ibid.*, pp. 23–25.

This telling criticism was not without foundation and Eban rightly carried the attack forward against the detractors of negotiation. He quoted a negative view about the possibilities of negotiation in the Middle East expressed by the Foreign Minister of France at the emergency session of the Assembly and commented:

One of the factors which make negotiations difficult is the proclamation by eminent statesmen of their impracticality. The prediction helps to create the conditions which it predicts. And when the representative of France tells us on 9 November that it would be "unrealistic" to have negotiations without withdrawal, I only invite the Council to believe that it is unrealistic to believe that there can be withdrawal without negotiation.[43]

While never revealing a precise geographical position on withdrawal, Eban argued the case for flexibility by pointing to the fact that most areas of Palestine were, in fact, conquered territories:

If territorial dispositions based on military considerations are "inadmissible" then the inadmissibility applies to territories occupied by Egypt and Jordan in defiance of cease-fire and truce resolutions in May 1948. Indeed, it applies to the whole of the territory—to the whole of the territory—of the previous Palestine mandate. It would be discriminatory to apply the principle in one direction alone.[44]

Immediately after the closely argued Israeli statement came the statement of Monim El-Rifai, the Foreign Minister of Jordan. He said that the issue before the Council was "one of principle." This principle was whether the "occupation or acquisition of territory by military conquest [was] admissible under the Charter of the United Nations and international order." [45] Accusing Israel of systematic aggression over the last twenty years (but not commenting on Eban's charge of military conquest by Jordan), Rifai said that "the most fundamental requirement in the present crisis . . . is undoubtedly the removal of Israel's

[43] *Ibid.*, p. 26.   [44] *Ibid.*, p. 28.   [45] *Ibid.*, p. 37.

military occupation." [46] The stress was entirely on the subject
of withdrawal. However, it could be argued that this statement
implied that there were other fundamental requirements which
would have to be given attention. More information about them
was available behind the scenes where the following position had
developed. First, the Arab states were willing to live with the
three-power draft resolution which guaranteed full rights of
statehood to Israel and the complete termination of any form of
belligerency. This draft resolution also guaranteed freedom of
navigation, and its sponsors had indicated that the troublesome
clause "in accordance with international law" could be dropped.
In agreeing behind the scenes to go along with this resolution
the Arab states had certainly moved very considerably from
their prior adamant refusal to entertain the notion of equal statehood for Israel. The three-power resolution, however, was firm
on the need to effect a full withdrawal of Israeli forces as part
of the total process of settlement. This was the *quid pro quo* for
Arab acceptance of Israel's rights.

Second, it was not absolutely clear that the Arabs were totally
unwilling to parley with Israel through a third party even on the
basis of some frontier rectifications. The U.S. delegation was insistent that its formulation which would permit such flexibility
was acceptable to some of the Arab states.

In view of the aforementioned factors the Arab statements
in the Security Council were more for the record than accurate
revelations of the basis on which those states were willing to
envisage the establishment of peaceful conditions in the Middle
East. That they were, on balance, willing to envisage such a
state of affairs seemed clear. It was the representative of the
UAR who had insisted that the Council be convened urgently.
It was known that Cairo felt the urgent necessity for steps to be
taken by the United Nations to undo the results of the war, and
it was also known that the United Arab Republic was ready to

[46] *Ibid.*, p. 42.

make adjustments of its own political position so as to enable the United Nations to achieve those steps.

The period immediately preceding the meeting on November 13 at which Eban and Rifai had spoken, as well as the day or two thereafter, brought in several new elements in behind-the-scenes negotiation. Lord Caradon saw the Indian representative on Sunday, November 12, and discussed the possibility of a compromise position between the draft resolutions of the United States and the three powers. He pointed out that the two texts were very similar and that what was required was only the bridging of one or two differences in nuance. The Indian delegate reiterated his willingness to discuss compromises and pointed out that the "rectification" of frontiers was not ruled out by the Indian formula.

At this stage the Latin American representatives produced their own draft text for private circulation. Some members of the Council felt that this draft might offer a way out, particularly as the United States, according to the Indian delegation, seemed uninterested in the possibilities of a joint U.S.–three-power compromise draft resolution. On the day when Eban and Rifai spoke in the Council, the Latin draft was privately circulated. However, it was as firm on withdrawal as the three-power draft. The main difference was that in regard to navigation it guaranteed freedom to all ships without reservations. The United States did not consider this draft to be a likely key to a solution. Its delegates privately said that it was not a helpful move. The United States was against it and Israel would not implement it.

In these circumstances the Council met again on Wednesday, November 15. It looked as though the prospects of a settlement had, if anything, diminished. The gloomy outlook was further darkened by the opening statement of the delegate of Syria, who said that "the only draft resolution which is in harmony with the Charter is the one submitted by the USSR at the Fifth Special Session of the General Assembly, which asks for, first, condemnation of Israeli aggression; second, withdrawal of Israeli troops to the positions occupied by them on 4 June; and third, compensation to the Arabs for damages sustained by them." [47] This position was entirely different from that contained in the three-power resolution, which was still known to be acceptable to most Arab states. Though the statement of the Syrian delegate again could not be regarded as a final revelation of the Arab position, it did show how easy it was for some states atavistically to return to positions which were incompatible with any movement toward a Middle East settlement.

The redoubtable Lord Caradon was undeterred by the Syrian speech. Following the Syrian delegate to the podium, he was so sanguine that he said: "This week we hope to see the work of finding a way to permanent peace transferred from this Council to the Middle East." [48] He stated the position of the two sides as follows:

The Arab countries insist that we must direct our special attention to the recovery and restoration of their territory. The issue of withdrawal is to them of top priority. The Arabs want not charity but justice. They seek a just settlement to end the long and bitter suffering of the refugees. . . . The Israelis tell us that withdrawal must never be to the old precarious truce; that it must be to a permanent peace, to secure boundaries, to a new era of freedom from the use or the threat or the fear of hostility and force.[49]

Immediately after this statement of the two cases, Caradon commented: "Both are right. The aims of the two sides do not conflict. They converge. . . . They are of equal validity and equal necessity." [50]

This was statesmanship of a very high order. It showed both the capacity to state frankly the two positions without partisanship and the courage to weld them together. Lord Caradon did not support either of the two draft resolutions before the Council and he asked for "a short time to conclude our consultations."

[47] S/PV.1377, p. 21.   [48] *Ibid.*, p. 22.   [49] *Ibid.*, pp. 23–25.
[50] *Ibid.*

It was known that he was again busily engaged in formulating and reformulating concepts that could be expressed in language acceptable to both sides.

Arthur Goldberg spoke immediately after Caradon; though by now a large number of Council members, including close friends and allies of the United States, had indicated that they were not wholly satisfied with the United States draft, he said:

Our draft resolution, in our view, is the only resolution now before the Council which conforms to the axioms set forth [the reference was to three fundamental bases of settlement contained in Goldberg's speech] both in content and in the procedures used in drawing it up.[51]

However, Goldberg recognized that the search "for the right formula for Council action" was still going on and he made it clear that it was not in the interest of the United States to insist on "an American label on the successful formula."[52]

The essential purpose served by the statements of both Caradon and Goldberg and the subsequent statement by Ignatieff of Canada was to counterbalance the seeming retreat from possibilities of a solution by a strong manifestation of the will to persevere.

The statement of Soviet Deputy Foreign Minister Kuznetsov did something to strengthen this mood even though he was critical about the United States draft resolution. He reiterated that he still hoped to hear a clear-cut and unambiguous statement from the United States to the effect that it favored full withdrawal of Israeli forces. He was not against the suggestion for further consultations but he wanted it to be clear that under the guise of consultations there must be no unnecessary delay in arriving at a solution. "We want these consultations to be held and to yield positive results, but we do not wish to see them unduly prolonged because the problem is urgent and it has to be settled."[53] This statement was taken to imply that the United

[51] *Ibid.*, pp. 33–35.   [52] *Ibid.*   [53] *Ibid.*, p. 62.

Arab Republic continued to be restive and to demand urgent Council action. The Soviet position reflected this urgency, just as it had reflected Arab opposition to action at the end of May, 1967.

That evening (November 15) and the following morning Caradon went from the Arabs to the Israelis and back again several times and completed the drafting of a new formula. The next Council meeting was postponed until late in the afternoon of November 16. The Council met at 4 P.M. and Caradon introduced his draft resolution. It differed from the United States draft in calling specifically for the withdrawal of Israeli armed forces instead of just the withdrawal of armed forces. Moreover, it specified more clearly the territories from which withdrawal was to take place. The United States draft had called for withdrawal from "occupied territories." The United Kingdom draft called for withdrawal "of Israeli armed forces from territories occupied in the recent conflict." [54] This formulation, together with another provision in the resolution which read, "emphasizing the inadmissibility of the acquisition of territory by war," amounted to undoing Israeli gains by force of arms. In this respect, then, the British resolution was nearer the three-power resolution than it was to the United States proposal. In the matter of freedom of navigation it took out the contentious words in the former and repeated, in fact, the formulation in the latter. On the refugee problem, territorial inviolability, and political independence it again repeated the U.S. text. Unfortunately it left out the U.S. reference to limitation of the arms race in the area.

The effect of the introduction of the Caradon text was profound. The representatives of the UAR and Israel made their shortest substantive statements before the Council. They realized that the time for polemics and partisanship had passed. There

[54] S/8247. This was later adopted by the Security Council; for text, see Appendix 23.

was much content in the following remarks of Foreign Minister Riad of the United Arab Republic:

During the private consultations which have taken place, we have willingly discussed all fomulas and all drafts. We have never refused to discuss in these endeavors any idea which was presented to us, but we made our position very clear on the question of the withdrawal of Israeli forces. The withdrawal of those forces from the territories occupied by them is a matter prescribed by every essential rule of the Charter.[55]

This statement did not endorse the new draft resolution but it seemed to say that as long as full withdrawal was provided for its other formulations could also be entertained and even accepted.

Immediately following Riad, Eban reiterated the Israeli position in favor of peace treaties, secure and recognized boundaries, and direct negotiation.[56]

The Council adjourned for another full day to give itself time to consider the new situation. A peak of negotiation had been reached. It was necessary to test out prudently and finally whether that peak was firm and could be the take-off point for the actual work of pacification in the Middle East.

V. V. Kuznetsov at once met with the Arab delegates, who told him that the formulation on the withdrawal of Israeli forces in the first operative paragraph of the British draft was not acceptable to them. They insisted that the wording read either that Israeli forces would be withdrawn from "all the territories," instead of "territories" occupied by Israel, or that Israel would "withdraw to the positions of 4 June 1967." In addition, the Arabs were unwilling to accept the phrase "recognized boundaries" also occurring in the first operative paragraph.

On the evening of November 16 some Arab diplomats were skeptical about the possibilities of a meeting of minds on the basis of the British draft resolution. On the other hand, the

[55] S/PV.1379, pp. 13–15.　　[56] *Ibid.*, p. 16.

major Arab delegates, including Foreign Minister Riad and Adnan Pachachi of Iraq, were reserving judgment.

The Arab states met on the morning of November 17 and took a dramatic decision. The United Kingdom resolution, though not perfect, was adjudged better than the United States draft resolution. Their preference was still for the three-power draft resolution, but against them was the fact that this proposal could not obtain the votes of the United States, the United Kingdom, and several other members of the Council. The Arabs concluded that it was better to get a resolution backed by all fifteen votes in the Council than to insist on a resolution which might not be adopted or which might obtain the bare minimum of nine votes. Several of them discussed matters with Caradon. Could he not use the formulation "all the territories" instead of "territories" in relation to the clause requiring Israel's withdrawal? Caradon's response was that his draft represented a delicate balance which would be upset by any changes. Besides, he had gone as much beyond the U.S. draft as practicable. Any attempt at further movement would mean no Council resolution. Most of the Arab delegates realized that they had obtained as much as was feasible. Besides, the clause on withdrawal, taken together with the clause on the inadmissibility of acquiring territory by war, meant that in principle their point had been conceded. Privately, representatives of the United Arab Republic, Jordan, and even Iraq, as well as additional Arab states, indicated to other diplomats their willingness to go along with the United Kingdom resolution.

However, when the Council met again in the afternoon of November 17 it became known that the Soviet Union had not yet received instructions from Moscow. Though it had heard directly from the Arab delegates at New York that the British resolution was acceptable to them, the Soviet delegation had undoubtedly desired to check this out with the Arab capitals through its government. Milko Tarabanov of Bulgaria asked for postponement until Monday, November 20. There was trepidation over his request even among some the the Arab states. Most Council members felt that postponement could be dangerous because unforeseen obstacles might again arise. However, there was no point in contesting the move and the Council agreed to meet again on that date. During the early part of the weekend there was a strong if quiet current of optimism among the members of the Security Council regarding the British draft resolution.

On Sunday, November 19, an unforeseen development intervened: V. V. Kuznetsov received from Moscow a new draft resolution for submission to the Council. He was informed that Chairman Kosygin had sent the draft to President Johnson with a special message expressing the hope that the United States would vote for it because it contained basically the provisions which had been agreed upon by the Soviet Foreign Minister and Ambassador Arthur Goldberg on July 19—exactly four months previously. President Johnson is said to have replied that he considered it too late to open negotiations on another draft resolution inasmuch as the Security Council was on the verge of voting on the British proposal, which appeared to be widely acceptable and which had been endorsed by the parties to the conflict. This exchange between President Johnson and Chairman Kosygin was facilitated by the Glassboro meeting between the two heads of government in June. There had thus been a small but useful dividend from Kosygin's visit to New York in connection with the Fifth Emergency Special Session of the General Assembly. Kuznetsov saw Arthur Goldberg, G. Parthasarathi of India, and the Arab delegates on Sunday, giving each of them an advance copy of the Soviet proposals. He saw Caradon and some other delegates on Monday morning, November 20. He urged all delegations to study carefully the Soviet text, stressing the point that it not only contained the essence of the agreement reached between the United States and the Soviet Union in July but also incorporated all the major concepts on which wide agreement had been expressed by delegations.

When the Council convened in the afternoon of November 20 Kuznetsov presented the new Soviet proposal. His brief introduction to the reading of the text focused on three points. First, there could be unforeseen and dangerous consequences if Israel continued to occupy Arab territory. These consequences might ensue "on the international level," which in the context implied that there could be a widened military confrontation of unforeseeable dimensions. Kuznetsov's second point was that the Arab states had clearly manifested their "interest in a political settlement" and their "readiness to seek ways and means for the establishment of a lasting peace in the Middle East." [57]

Kuznetsov's third point was in some ways the most interesting of the three: "As far as the Soviet Union is concerned, it has a vital interest in seeing a lasting peace established in the area of the Middle East." [58] Later in his statement Kuznetsov spelled out the Soviet position: "The Soviet Government . . . is in favor of recognition of the inalienable right of all the States of the Middle East, including Israel, to an independent national existence." [59] This strongly phrased statement put the Soviet Union on record as being firmly opposed to any scheme to eliminate Israel. The Soviet proposal [60] was certainly remarkably different from the proposal introduced by Kosygin at the special session of the Assembly on June 19. That earlier proposal contained only three points: condemnation of Israel; its unconditional and total withdrawal; and compensation by Israel for damage inflicted on the Arab states. The new proposal, sent from Moscow and approved by Kosygin, entirely dropped condemnation and compensation. Instead it broadened its concepts to include immediate recognition of all states in the area, the renunciation of the use or threat of force, an end to the state

[57] S/PV.1381, p. 6.   [58] *Ibid.*, pp. 7–10.   [59] *Ibid.*, p. 13.
[60] S/8253. See Appendix 22.

of belligerency, limitation of the "useless and destructive arms race," a settlement of the refugee problem, and innocent passage through international waterways.

What precisely was the nature of the change in the Soviet position and what caused it? First, we should note that the earlier text of Chairman Kosygin in the Assembly had not specifically questioned Israel's right to exist and had not pronounced itself on such questions as the refugees, belligerency, and navigation. It could therefore be argued that the new proposals spelled out positions which were not necessarily contradictory to the earlier Soviet text. On the other hand, it is probably truer to say that the Soviets, in June, 1967, were not dealing with issues of principle because they knew that at that stage the Arab states would be unwilling to consider any long-term settlement with Israel. Such appeared to be the considered opinion of the Soviet government. A second reason why the Soviets were able to make the change was indicated in another sentence in the Soviet Deputy Foreign Minister's statement: "The draft resolution presented by the Soviet Union contains all the key elements of a political settlement on the need of which the views of the overwhelming majority of Member States of the United Nations converge." [61] Where the security of the Soviet Union itself is not directly involved it tends to take into account the wide expression of views of the world community. This attitude stems from the importance which Marxism assigns to world opinion. In the latest Middle East crisis this factor was a contributory one, the primary ones being the shift in the Arab position and the Soviet Union's own desire for peaceful conditions in the Middle East.

The Soviet text was in substance different from the United Kingdom text in five respects. First, it clearly called for withdrawal of all forces to positions held before June 5, 1967, whereas the British text only implied full-scale withdrawal.

[61] *Ibid.*, p. 13.

Second, the clause about navigation read that there was to be innocent passage "in accordance with international agreements." This was not so restrictive as the corresponding formulation in the three-power draft which read "in accordance with international law." At the same time it could have raised problems which the United Kingdom formulation avoided. Third, the Soviet draft was more forward-looking than the British draft in that it included an attempt to end the arms race in the Middle East. In this respect it was similar to the U.S. draft. Fourth, it did not specifically ask for the appointment of a UN representative in the Middle East. However, it seemed to leave the door open for such a possibility by the phrase "making use of the presence of the United Nations." Fifth, it was more forthright than the British proposal on the question of the recognition of Israel: "All States Members of the UN in the area should immediately recognize that each of them has the right to exist as an independent national State." This was not just a statement of principle to be applied in due course through and with the help of a United Nations representative. It was an imperative injunction to be given immediate effect.

Kuznetsov ended his presentation by stating that undoubtedly the members of the Council would require some time to study the Soviet proposal. This remark inevitably gave rise to the speculation that the Soviet Union meant to urge the most serious consideration of its proposal and if necessary to delay a decision by the Council for some time to come. Caradon spoke immediately after Kuznetsov and deliberately suppressed any such apprehension. Instead he stressed Kuznetsov's remark that a decison should be reached "without delay," adding that if there had to be a postponement it should be only a short one.[62] Goldberg then announced that he would vote for the United Kingdom draft resolution because it was "entirely consistent with the policy of my Government." [63] Indeed, his whole statement

[62] *Ibid.*, pp. 23–25.   [63] *Ibid.*, p. 26.

read as though it were meant immediately to precede a vote on
the British resolution. It had apparently been written on the basis
that the British resolution would come to a vote on November
20. Tactically, a strong statement at this juncture in favor of the
British proposal was risky. It would tend to dub that proposal
as purely "Western," and could therefore raise Arab suspicions
about its real meaning, especially now that the Soviets had introduced a new proposal. Goldberg did not comment in any
detail on the Soviet proposal. Devoting three sentences to it, he
stated that it

is not an even-handed non-prejudicial draft resolution. It does not
meet the test of exact balance, acquiescence by the parties and work-
ability. Its belated introduction should not and must not impede the
consensus which has developed in support of the U.K. draft resolution.[64]

The last of the above sentences was a useful injunction to the
Council. Indeed, perhaps the primary demerit of the Soviet proposal was its timing.

Foreign Minister Eban made a brief statement rejecting the
Russian proposal and characterizing it as backward-looking. "It
seeks to restore the juridical ambiguity and the territorial vul-
nerability of the shattered armistice regime." [65] It is difficult to
see on what basis Eban made these charges. The Soviet draft
read: "Every State must respect the political independence and
territorial integrity of all other States in the area." Moreover,
it asked for immediate recognition of the right of each state to
exist as a national independent state, and called for the renunciation of all claims and acts inconsistent with such a right.

Again it was Ambassador Tarabanov of Bulgaria who asked
for a two-day adjournment to permit further consultations "and
to enable us to reach a final decision then." This was agreed to
by the Council.

Consultations during the next two days showed that the

[64] *Ibid.*, pp. 28–30.   [65] *Ibid.*, p. 31.

Soviet draft was unable to displace the British draft as the focus of attention. Though in some respects the Arab states preferred the Soviet text, they did not regard it as significantly different, on the basic issues of principle, from the British proposal. In those circumstances their efforts were directed mainly to probing the possibilities of slight changes in the text of the latter proposal. But Caradon stood firmly by his text and all efforts to move him failed. The strength of his position remained that his proposals had gained decidedly wider support among Council members and the parties concerned than any other proposal. Moreover numerous other members of the United Nations had privately voiced their support for the British proposal.

One recourse remained to those who hoped for some change. This was to interpret the United Kingdom proposal at the Council table in a manner that would give it further precision in certain respects. The Indian delegate decided to state that his understanding was that the British draft resolution meant full withdrawal of Israel's forces and that India would vote for it on this understanding. During the two days of intensive consultation there was no clear indication of what the British position would be if such a statement were to be made by India. However, on the afternoon of Wednesday, November 22, a most dramatic and critical negotiation on this issue took place behind the scenes. Caradon informed the Indian delegate that if he made the suggested interpretation regarding withdrawal he (Caradon) would respond by saying that each delegate was entitled to his own interpretation but the Indian interpretation was not binding on the Council. Thereupon Kuznetsov, who was among those with whom the Indian delegate conferred, said that if the United Kingdom were to repudiate expressly the idea of complete withdrawal the Soviet Union would veto the British proposal.

A crucial meeting took place at 3 P.M. between the Arabs and Caradon. He was able to reassure them that their position on the question of withdrawal remained unprejudiced. Further negotiations followed between Parthasarathi and Caradon which involved also the French and Nigerian delegates. As a result of these late exchanges Caradon agreed to delete from his proposed response to the Indian delegate's projected statement the words "But the Indian interpretation is not binding on the Council." On this basis Parthasarathi decided to vote for the resolution and so informed the Soviet Union. The time fixed for the Council meeting (3:30 P.M.) passed. At 3:40 Parthasarathi informed Caradon that on the basis agreed upon with him the Soviets would be able to go along with the British resolution. This also meant that behind the scenes the three powers (India, Nigeria, Mali), the United States, and the Soviet Union agreed not to press their draft proposals to a vote, thus leaving only the British proposal for decision by the Council. By 4 o'clock these crucial and delicate negotiations were successfully concluded and the Council opened its session.

The Syrian delegate rejected the British draft resolution. The next speaker was the delegate of Ethiopia who did not indicate explicitly whether the resolution had won his approval. However he equally did not indicate that it was unacceptable.

The Indian delegate (Parthasarathi) again spoke in favor of the three-power draft. He did not mention the Soviet text. Turning to the United Kingdom draft, he first drew attention to statements by British Foreign Minister George Brown at the Special Assembly Session on June 21, 1967, and at the 22d regular session of the Assembly on September 26, 1967, both of which unequivocally and without qualification called for complete withdrawal of Israeli forces. Proceeding from these statements, Parthasarathi said:

It is our understanding that the draft resolution, if approved by the Council, will commit it to the application of the principle of total withdrawal of Israeli forces from all the territories—I repeat, all the territories—occupied by Israel as a result of the conflict which began on 5 June 1967.[66]

Parthasarathi added:

[66] S/PV.1382, p. 28.

Of course, mutual territorial adjustments are not ruled out, as indeed they are not in the 3-Power draft resolution co-sponsored by India. This is our clear understanding of the United Kingdom draft resolution. Our vote on the draft will be determined accordingly.[67]

Caradon's response was carefully worded. "We stand by our declarations," he said. This covered Parthasarathi's citations of what George Brown had authoritatively stated. Without referring to the Indian statement, on matters of interpretation on his draft proposal he said:

I am sure that it will be recognized by us all that it is only the resolution that will bind us, and we regard its wording as clear. All of us, no doubt, have our own views and interpretations and understandings. I explained my own when I spoke on Monday last. On these matters each delegation rightly speaks only for itself.[68]

This statement did not repudiate the Indian interpretation but equally it did not impute the interpretation to the Council or indeed to any delegation other than that of India.

Arthur Goldberg, in a very brief statement for the United States, added: "The voting of course takes place not on the individual or discrete views and policies of various members but on the draft resolution." [69] He concluded that the United States would vote for the resolution because he believed it to be consistent with the policy expressed by President Johnson on June 19.

At this stage the Soviet Union made no statement. The President then pointed out that there were five draft resolutions before the Council: the three-power text (S/8227), which the co-sponsors had said they would not press to a vote; the U.S. text (S/8229), which the United States had said it would not press to a vote; the Soviet draft resolution on UN observers (S/8236), on which the Soviet delegate would not ask for a vote "at this time"; the British proposal (S/8247); and the new Soviet proposal (S/8253). Since the British proposal had been introduced before the Soviet proposal, it was the first to be put to a vote.

[67] *Ibid.*   [68] *Ibid.*, p. 32.   [69] *Ibid.*

If it were adopted the Soviet proposal would automatically lapse because it sought to cover the same ground as the British text.

The President of the Council called for a vote on the British draft. A tense moment of silence followed. Then all fifteen representatives at the Council table raised their hands to signify approval. The British text had been adopted unanimously.[70] Thus ended the long, precarious, and hitherto uncertain search for a widely based consensus on the Middle East crisis. After months of hard work and the most delicate negotiation in which the Council was fortunate to have available the services of so highly skilled a negotiator as Caradon, the goal had been attained.

Foreign Minister Eban's statement after the vote contained two noteworthy points. The first related to the arms race.

I also note that the Soviet text, like that of the United States, included a reference to the need for curbing the destructive and wasteful arms race. I hope that the absence of this provision in the text on which the Council has voted does not mean that that objective will be lost from sight.[71]

Thus Israel indicated its readiness to join in the highly desirable objective of limiting the arms race in the Middle East.

Eban's other point of importance related to the Indian interpretation. "For us, the resolution says what it says. It does not say that which it has specifically and consciously avoided saying." [72] The battle of interpretation was one that would obviously go on.

The statement of Foreign Minister Mahmoud Riad of the United Arab Republic was much more ambivalent. Indeed, he did not so much as mention the resolution that had been adopted by the Council. He reaffirmed the UAR's position "that the first step towards peace lies in the full withdrawal of the Israeli forces." [73] His next point related to the peoples of Palestine:

[70] For text, see Appendix 23.   [71] *Ibid.*, p. 51.   [72] *Ibid.*
[73] *Ibid.*, pp. 73–75.

The inalienable rights of the people of Palestine, recognized and continually reaffirmed by the United Nations, belong to the highest and most essential category of the norms and rules of our present international order. . . . This organization is inescapably committed to the rights of the people of Palestine.

Immediately after making these two points the UAR Foreign Minister added: "In conclusion, the U.A.R. will be guided by these considerations in its continuous search for a peaceful and just solution of the present crisis in the Middle East." [74] This statement did not add up to any indication whatsoever of acceptance of the Council's unanimous resolution. Ignoring that resolution, it seemed to revert to positions which had long been held by most of the Arab states.

The Foreign Minister of Jordan too stressed full withdrawal of Israeli forces, but there was a nuance in his statement which perhaps differed slightly from anything contained in the words of his Egyptian colleague: "We, for our part, share with the members the genuine desire to establish conditions in our area conducive to peace, based on justice and on the fulfillment of the legitimate rights of our people." [75]

The remaining Arab state directly concerned was Syria. The Syrian representative at least referred directly to the resolution adopted by the Council. "The test of the success or failure of any major resolution can be measured only by its results. The future will prove whether or not the resolution adopted today will secure the cause of peace in the Middle East." [76] This challenge to the resolution is to be read in the light of the earlier rejection of the British text by the Syrian representative.

Eban made the last remark on behalf of the parties to the conflict. He said he would send to his government the text of the resolution: "My Government will determine its attitude to the Security Council's resolution in the light of its own policy, which is as I have stated it." [77]

[74] *Ibid.*   [75] *Ibid.*, p. 76.   [76] *Ibid.*, p. 69.
[77] *Ibid.*, p. 96.

This meant that, while Israel was prima facie being more cooperative than the Arab states, it too felt under no obligation to commit itself to carry out the provisions of the Security Council resolution.

Arthur Goldberg set out the final position of the United States. As was to be expected, that country took a much more positive view of what the Council had achieved than did the parties concerned. At the same time it seemed to characterize that achievement in a manner which fell somewhat short of its full scope. Goldberg said that the Security Council took its first step in creating a framework of peace in the Middle East in June by helping to bring about a cease-fire. Then he added:

Today we have taken a second step—the appointment of a special representative to go to the area in order to promote agreement and assist efforts to achieve a peaceful settlement. . . . We know realistically from the nature of this complex problem that those two steps are very far from the goal we have set, a just and durable peace, and we must recognize that although we have begun we shall not achieve that goal easily or without many difficulties.[78]

Whereas Goldberg was correct in identifying the appointment of a representative as a new step, just as he was also right to allude to the difficulties that lay ahead, it is difficult to understand why he omitted reference to the agreement reached by all the Security Council members after patient and difficult negotiation on important principles to govern the new regime of peace in the Middle East. The negotiation on these matters had been far more difficult and crucial than that on the appointment of a special representative, and if peace is to come to the Middle East it will come by perseverance in applying the principles set out in the new resolution. This agreement on a basis for peace is the real nature of the achievement of the Council.

The comments of V. V. Kuznetsov dwelt mainly though not entirely on the issue of withdrawal. He said that the USSR had voted in favor of the resolution, interpreting it in the same way

[78] *Ibid.,* pp. 56–57.

as the representative of India. He strengthened the argument on withdrawal by pointing out that the British text itself emphasized the "inadmissibility of the acquisition of territory by war." [79] His general approach to the resolution was more positive than that of many other representatives: "The main thing now is the immediate implementation of the decision taken by the Security Council." [80] He went on to say that implementation called first of all for the withdrawal of Israeli troops. This was again a reiteration of the basic Soviet position but it did not detract from the fact that the Soviets appeared to be looking forward to full implementation of the text, which of course goes far beyond the issue of withdrawal.

While stressing the need for unanimity and for a common mandate to the special representative—both of which had been achieved—the Security Council was still of many views in regard to the possibilities of implementing the important principles which it had evolved and adopted. It had achieved an important objective but now, in a philosophical vein of caution, was meditating on the difficulties ahead. The process of tangible achievement in the Middle East is still in the future, but it is interesting that those who had set it in train in so notable an example of common assertion of fundamental objectives should dwell so much on the difficulties ahead as to denigrate to some extent their own achievement.

One of the issues brought up at the October–November meetings of the Council remained to be decided. This was the difference of opinion between the United States and other states on the one hand and the Soviet Union and a few states on the other regarding the procedures for expanding the UNTSO observer corps in the Suez area. As we have seen, the Secretary-General had informed the Council that he would need ninety observers, together with equipment, to assist the corps in carrying out its duties. The Soviet Union took the view that the

---

[79] *Ibid.,* p. 62.   [80] *Ibid.,* pp. 63–65.

Secretary-General should obtain the formal sanction of the Council for expansion of the corps and for making available to it the requisite equipment. On November 10 the Soviets introduced a draft resolution by which the Council would authorize the Secretary-General to take these steps.[81] On November 22 the President of the Council announced that "the representative of the Soviet Union will not insist that his draft resolution, contained in document S/8236, be put to the vote at this time." [82] It was, of course, extremely doubtful that the Soviet text would have received more than a few votes. Whatever sympathy there may have been for the Soviet position that it is for the Security Council to take decisions on matters involving the use of force —a position broadly shared by France, India, and possibly some other members of the Council—the Council in its early decisions on UNTSO had charged the Secretary-General with the task of ensuring adequate observation. The forerunner of UNTSO was the Truce Commission for Palestine, for which Resolution 48 of the Council, dated April 23, 1948, laid down specifically this stipulation: "The Secretary-General shall furnish the Commission with such personnel and assistance as it may require, taking into account the special urgency of the situation with regard to Palestine." Later, when a mediator was in charge of the UN's functions in the area, Resolution 54 of July 15, 1948, requested "the Secretary-General to provide the Mediator with the necessary staff and facilities." [83] This decision covered observation in the area. Growing out of these provisions, on August 11, 1949, the Security Council resolution regarding the continuance of observation stated:

Requests the Secretary-General to arrange for the continued service of such of the personnel of the present Truce Supervision Organization as may be required in observing and maintaining the cease-fire, and as may be necessary in assisting the Parties to the Armistice

---

[81] S/8236.   [82] S/PV.1382, pp. 33–35.
[83] The Soviet Union abstained in the vote on both these resolutions.

Agreements in the supervision of the application and observance of the terms of those Agreements.

In view of these clear delegations to the Secretary-General, debate on the Soviet proposal would have amounted to reconsideration of a series of previous decisions of the Council. Obviously this course was not likely to receive wide support. At the same time, the spirit of unanimity which had resulted in all fifteen members of the Council voting for the British draft resolution on November 22, 1967, was not disposed toward staging a meeting of the Council at which the Soviet proposal would have been brought to the vote and shown a division among the membership. A way out had to be found, and the Security Council members devised a novel procedure for dealing with the situation. The President of the Council, Chief S. O. Adebo of Nigeria, consulted with all members and issued the following statement, which did not mention the Soviet draft proposal:

As regards document S/8053/Add. 3, brought to the attention of the Security Council, the members, recalling the consensus reached at its 1366th meeting on 9 July 1967, recognize the necessity of the enlargement by the Secretary-General of the number of observers in the Suez Canal zone and the provision of additional technical material and means of transportation.[84]

Consensuses, as a less formal method of decision than resolutions, there had been in the past, but all of them had been reached at sessions of the Council. This was the first time in the Council's history that a substantive decision was taken by a consensus arrived at without a formal meeting being called. By doing without a meeting the Council both avoided contention and saved face for certain of its members. Thus, a conclusion in conformity with past practice was arrived at in regard to the expansion of the UNTSO observer corps.

The nature of the participation of Council members in the

---

[84] S/8289, December 8, 1967 (see Appendix 24). Doc. S/8053/Add. 3 contained a report by the Secretary-General on the observation of the cease-fire in the Suez Canal area.

series of ten meetings held between October 24 and November 22, 1967, was in striking contrast to the participation of the members in the fifteen meetings held from June 5 to June 14, during and immediately after the fighting in the Middle East. In the earlier phase polemics ran much higher than in the later phase, during which the members were in a more constructive mood. At the second of the later meetings they adopted Resolution 240 reaffirming the previous cease-fire resolutions. The Council proceeded to consider four alternative draft proposals on the basic issues between Israel and the Arab states. In doing so, the United States and the Soviet Union made six interventions each on matters of substance, while the United Kingdom made five interventions. As against these rather modest figures, at the fifteen meetings from June 5 to June 14 the USSR made 47 interventions, the United States 30, and Bulgaria as many as 27. In the last series of meetings Bulgaria spoke only four times on matters of substance.

Though in an over-all sense there were far fewer speeches—because interventions were directed toward a serious and responsible consideration of the possibilities of agreement—those Member States that had taken a purely marginal interest in the situation in June were now relatively more active. In the earlier series of fifteen meetings Denmark spoke only once, whereas in the last series its representative spoke thrice. Argentina spoke thrice at these ten meetings as against three interventions in fifteen meetings in June. In the case of Nigeria the number of interventions at the two sets of meetings was precisely the same. Latin American participation was relatively greater in October and November because in the intervening General Assembly meetings the Latins had emerged with a well-thought-out position on the basic issues involved. This gave their representatives on the Council added confidence. True, they did not present a draft proposal to the Council, but they came very near doing so, desisting only because at a certain stage it became clear that general support could be marshaled for the British proposal. The most striking contrast occurred in the case of the Soviet Union. The decrease in the number of interventions at the later meetings did not indicate a lack of interest on the part of the USSR. On the contrary, the Soviet Union introduced two draft resolutions at these meetings and voted for both the resolutions (Nos. 240 and 242) that were adopted by the Council.

CHAPTER XV

The Task Ahead

THE Secretary-General acted with all speed to appoint a special representative in accordance with paragraph 3 of the Security Council's Resolution 242 of November 22, 1967. On the very next day, November 23, he informed the governments of Israel, Jordan, Lebanon, Syria, and the United Arab Republic that he had designated Ambassador Gunnar Jarring of Sweden as his Special Representative, and he circulated this information to all members of the Security Council.[1] Indeed, it had been known for some time that, anticipating the need to designate a special representative, U Thant had informally obtained the agreement of the states concerned and of the great powers to the selection of Gunnar Jarring, who had had several years of experience at the United Nations as permanent representative of his country and had also for some years previously been a member of Sweden's delegation to the General Assembly. Moreover, in 1957 he had visited India and Pakistan in pursuance of Security Council Resolution 123 in order to assist those states in resolving the Kashmir dispute. On that occasion he had written a helpful report (S/3821). However, there had been no clear mandate from the Security Council spelling out the basic principles by which a settlement was to be governed. In short, Jarring's assignment in 1957 was of a loose good-office nature rather than one to fulfill a carefully negotiated and fairly detailed Security Council mandate. There were other points of difference between

[1] S/8259, November 23, 1967.

Jarring's mission of 1957 and his new Middle East assignment. A significant difference was that on the earlier occasion the Council had not arrived at a consensus. The Soviet Union did not vote in favor of his visit to the subcontinent. Also, the characteristics of the dispute were vastly different from those in the Middle East. India and Pakistan recognize each other, and they have well-defined frontiers. The cease-fire line in Kashmir had been in existence for ten years and had not been violated by two large-scale wars, such as those of the Middle East in 1956 and 1967. There were none of the complications relating to rights of navigation that plague the Middle East situation. The refugee problem in India and Pakistan, though involving many times the number of people concerned in the Middle East, had been more or less settled. Finally, the two states involved (India and Pakistan) are very much larger than the Arab states and Israel. Between large states armed conflict is more hazardous than between small states. Though there has been one outbreak of conflict (1965), there is some evidence to indicate that the attitudes of both India and Pakistan are far less truculent than those in the Middle East.

The main asset that Jarring has in dealing with the Middle East situation is the closely negotiated unanimous resolution of the Security Council which constitutes his mandate. True, some Council members, as we have seen, pointed to the need to secure the agreement of the parties to the steps which remain to be taken toward peace in the Middle East. On the other hand, the great powers and indeed the generality of Council members had voted for Resolution 242 on November 22 on the ground that the parties concerned had, in various ways, indicated their willingness to go along with the resolution. In their statements immediately after the resolution the parties had fallen back to positions in line with their maximum requirements. Such statements are consistent with a normal negotiating tactic: the parties to a dispute, especially when approaching negotiation—whether direct or indirect—remind each other of their maximum claims. But all states also have minimum requirements in regard to disputes in which they are concerned.

What Resolution 242 did was to set out principles and make provisions based on the minimum essential expectations of the disputants, and it did this with the concurrence of all the members of the Council. In this last respect the resolution carried the resolving of the substantive issues of the Middle East much further forward than any previous efforts of the Council. For example, in 1951 when the Security Council adopted Resolution 95 on September 1 calling upon Egypt to terminate restrictions on the passage of international shipping through the Suez Canal there was no unanimity among the Council members. As many as three of the eleven members (China, India, and the USSR) did not vote for the resolution. That fact put the Council's injunction of 1951 on a very different footing from its resolution of November 22, 1967.

While the Council had acted under Chapter VI of the Charter, the unanimity that had emerged through protracted and meticulous negotiation meant that the Council was firmly committed to the view that the principles it had adopted were to be implemented. This being the case, the capacity of the parties to resist implementation had, in the last analysis, been seriously eroded. This prospect, however, is subject to one hazard. There is the possibility that some members of the Council might not be willing to maximize their diplomatic pressures on the parties to implement Resolution 242. However, there has not yet been any indication that such a lack of resoluteness exists.

Both the United States and the Soviet proposals before the Security Council contained provisions regarding the arresting of the arms race. Since these two states are the main purveyors of arms to the area, their mutual will to restrict the arms race gives Gunnar Jarring an extra-mandatory possibility on which to work. Indeed, this sector of the Middle East horizon may turn out to be one of the brightest both because of its potential locally and because of its possible repercussions on international affairs. The maximum possibility in regard to armaments in the Middle East is a regional arms control and limitation agreement under which United Nations personnel would inspect armaments in the Arab states in the area and in Israel so as to ensure that the level of such equipment remains within the agreed limitations.

Indeed, having regard to the dangers of conflict escalation and to the nature of modern weaponry, it should become a standard procedure of conflict management by the United Nations that regional arms control agreements are brought into being as part of the terms of settlement, or as a preliminary step toward settlement. For example, nothing would be so salutary for the welfare of the Indo-Pakistani subcontinent as a UN-supervised arms limitation agreement between the two countries. The 1965 conflict and its aftermath of unanimous resolutions by the Security Council offered an opportunity to institute such arrangements. Unfortunately no advantage was taken of that opportunity. It would be very much in the interests of the Middle East if the opportunity now offered there for such arrangements is grasped. It is not enough for the great powers to enter into ill-defined informal arrangements restricting the supply of weapons. The manufacturing potential of the states in the area, the possibilities of supplies from states other than the great powers, and the possibilities of the acquisition through intermediaries of weaponry manufactures in the United States and the Soviet Union should be taken into account.

Israel has no fear of the non-Arab states and it should be willing to agree to some rational arms limitation arrangement provided the Arab states are also agreeable. Indeed, Abba Eban stated before the Council on November 22:

I also note that the Soviet text, like that of the United States, included a reference to the need for curbing the destructive and wasteful arms race. I hope that the absence of this provision in the text on which the Council has voted does not mean that that objective will be lost from sight.[2]

The Arab states made no clear statement in favor of arms limitation. However, if they can implement the political aspects of Resolution 242, they might well be disposed to consider the institution of arrangements to limit armaments provided that they were fully assured of similar arrangements in Israel. Such arrangements would assist greatly in realizing ambitions which Foreign Minister Mahmoud Riad of the United Arab Republic mentioned to the Security Council on November 9, 1967: "The Arab people are in the process of fulfillment of their national aspirations. These aspirations are for peace, justice, freedom and progress with a deep commitment and a determination to share in the universal task of meeting the great human challenges of our age." [3]

An arms control agreement in the Middle East would obviously permit the Arabs to devote more of their resources to social, economic, and cultural needs. And since there is evidence that the fulfillment of these needs is more and more widely demanded by the Arab peoples the states concerned should be disposed to accept the kind of arms limitation agreement which is here suggested.

If arms limitation agreements could be instituted in the Middle East, in the subcontinent of South Asia, and in other trouble spots, valuable experience in dealing with problems of disarmament control and inspection would be acquired. That experience could be of some relevance to the present suspicions and hesitations of the great powers in regard to the adoption and implementation of inspection and other regulatory arrangements relating to arms control and disarmament among themselves.

The Arab states and even Israel might, however, balk at the prospect of being made a test case in regard to disarmament

[2] S/PV.1382, p. 51.   [3] S/PV.1373, p. 62.

matters. The negotiations on a treaty prohibiting the proliferation of nuclear weapons show that many states are strongly inimical to discriminatory action; and a regional arms control arrangement would almost certainly be regarded as discriminatory. This reaction could be counterbalanced by limiting the arms control provisions to a five-year period during which it would be stipulated that the great powers must make a beginning in universalizing such arrangements. Desirable though arms limitations are in certain parts of the world, it is not practicable to expect such arrangements to exist indefinitely without being supplemented by universal steps toward disarmament. The negotiation of any arrangements in the Middle East would have to take this point fully into account. In short, a responsible attitude toward arms control and limitation in any region of the world must necessarily be supplemented by an equally responsible attitude toward the same matter on the part of the great powers. There must be no suspicion that the leading states are complacently laying down desirable arrangements for the rest of the world without bestirring themselves and adjusting their own international policies.

In this regard, and indeed in other significant respects, the Middle East question is closely linked with the policies of the leading states. Those states must maintain an unswerving adherence to the need to eliminate the outworn and anti-Charter notion of belligerence in the area. Similarly, they must unswervingly stand for the implementation of the principle contained in Resolution 242 that the acquisition of territory by war is inadmissible. Third, they must offer realistic assistance to resettle the Arab refugees. In human terms this is by no means an insoluble problem. As we have observed, the number of refugees involved is nowhere nearly as large as those in other parts of the world. Moreover, there are underpopulated areas in the Middle East. Fourth, the great powers must equally maintain their adherence to the principles of freedom of navigation through the Suez Canal and the Gulf of Aqaba. Finally, their adherence to these principles must necessarily be backed by parallel performance in their own relations within the international community, particularly in regard to their Charter commitment to renounce the use of force or the threat of force.

None of these are commitments beyond the will or capacity of the great powers. In some parts of the world the use of force between states is practically unthinkable, e.g., between Norway and Denmark, between Ceylon and India or India and Burma, between Mexico and the United States, or between the Soviet Union and Afghanistan. There are many other countries in similarly peaceful relationships. And there are increasing and well-known reasons for the great powers to follow similar codes of behavior in their relations *inter se* and with all other states. As to international waterways, there are working arrangements for the Bosporus, the Straits of Gibraltar, the Panama Canal, and even for the Suez Canal. In regard to the last-named waterway, the great powers must join with all other states in insisting that the provisions of the Constantinople Convention of 1888 are fully and impartially observed.

Acceptable and appropriate modalities for establishing peace in the Middle East are as difficult to find as the substantive elements of a peaceful settlement; indeed, perhaps more difficult. On the one hand, there is a large body of United Nations opinion which favors at least a degree of direct negotiation between the Arabs and Israelis leading to a treaty or treaties which all the contesting parties would sign and ratify. This spectrum of views would permit varying degrees of third-party assistance in the negotiations, and at one end might go so far as to envisage third-party activity substantially working out the substantive terms of the final settlement. Those terms would then be included in a treaty or treaties for signature and ratification by the parties.

It might, however, be desirable to explore the appropriateness

of an alternative system to govern peaceful relations between
the states of the Middle East, and therefore of a somewhat different procedure for its development. The basis of this system
would be not a treaty or treaties between the parties but two
parallel treaties or two sets of parallel treaties governing all the
issues to be included in a settlement. On the substance of each
issue the contents of the parallel treaties would be precisely
similar. For example, the wording in regard to nonbelligerence
between all Member States of the UN in the area would be the
same, and similarly in regard to the clauses on freedom of navigation, territorial integrity, and other matters. One set of the
parallel treaties thus composed would be signed and ratified by
the Arab states and other members of the United Nations, including the great powers. The corresponding set of parallel
treaties would be signed and ratified by Israel and other members
of the United Nations. All the treaties would of course be regis-
tered in accordance with Article 102 of the United Nations
Charter. In this way the Arab states and Israel would both be
bound by treaties involving themselves and the great powers
and other members of the United Nations and yet direct treaty
relations between the contestants would be deferred to a future
date. This device would not, in fact, be less definitive than direct
treaty relations in the Middle East and would have the advantage
of not pushing the contestants beyond the limits of their present
capacities for mutual relationships. At a later stage it should be
possible for Israel to sign and adhere to the treaty or set of
treaties engaging in the first instance the Arab states and other
members of the UN and thus all the parties would achieve a
direct treaty relationship. The suggestions here made would
render it possible to arrive at this ultimate result in two stages,
and would do so on the basis of firm treaty commitments in both
stages.

The working out of an arrangement on these lines would give
the Secretary-General's representative—and, indeed, the back-

stage efforts of friendly and interested powers—a wider role
than at present envisaged. Such activity by intermediaries would,
in the circumstances of the Middle East, assist the process of
assuagement and pacification.

Resolution 242 of the Security Council marks the opening of
a new level of achievement in international diplomacy in regard
to the Middle East. Such an achievement generates its own
momentum. There is no reason to expect that this momentum
will immediately falter. There is probably available a time span
of a year or two during which the new phase can be consolidated by tangible steps in the Middle East compatible with
the resolution. Undoubtedly Gunnar Jarring's task, or that of
whomever else might also be impressed into service in the Middle East, will be arduous and delicate in the extreme. There will
be rebuffs and retractions of position. These will not undo the
chances of success so long as the Security Council remains firm
in its position. The fact that for 1968–69 Algeria will be a
member of the Council and might dissociate itself from resolutions reaffirming the provisions of Resolution 242 will not
significantly or seriously detract from the Security Council's
stand. In an extended sense Algeria is a party to the dispute. The
Algerian Foreign Minister has certainly talked of the dispute
as one which concerns the Arab states as a whole. In the spirit
of Article 27 of the Charter, whatever positions Algeria might
take up in the Security Council on proposals relative to the
peaceful settlement of the Arab-Israeli issue, its vote should for
practical purposes be regarded as an abstention.

Never was the prospect of peace in the Middle East brighter
than at the beginning of 1968. The chances of moving forward
from the armistice regime instituted nineteen years previously
were good and solid. Only grave errors on the part of the international community could fail to convert this opportunity into a
reality.

APPENDIX 1

Joint Draft Resolution of Canada and Denmark

S/7905, May 24, 1967

The Security Council,
Having been seized of the current situation in the Middle East,
1. *Expresses* full support for the efforts of the Secretary-General to pacify the situation;
2. *Requests* all Member States to refrain from any steps which might worsen the situation, and
3. *Invites* the Secretary-General to report to the Security Council upon his return to enable the Council to continue its consideration of the matter.

APPENDIX 2

Draft Resolution of the United States

S/7916/Rev. 1, June 1, 1967

The Security Council,
Having considered the report of the Secretary-General in document S/7906,
Having heard the statements of the parties,
Concerned at the gravity of the situation in the Middle East,
Noting that the Secretary-General has in his report expressed the view that "a peaceful outcome to the present crisis will depend upon a breathing spell which will allow tension to subside from its present explosive level," and that he therefore urged "all the parties concerned to exercise special restraint, to forego belligerence and to avoid all other actions which could increase tension, to allow the Council to deal with the underlying causes of the present crisis and to seek solutions,"

1. *Calls on* all the parties concerned as a first step to comply with the Secretary-General's appeal,

2. *Encourages* the immediate pursuit of international diplomacy in the interests of pacifying the situation and seeking reasonable, peaceful and just solutions,

3. *Decides* to keep this issue under urgent and continuous review so that the Council may determine what further steps it might take in the exercise of its responsibilities for the maintenance of international peace and security.

Resolution 233 (1967)

Adopted by the Security Council at Its 1348th Meeting on June 6, 1967

The Security Council,
Noting the oral report of the Secretary-General in this situation,
Having heard the statements made in the Council,
Concerned at the outbreak of fighting and with the menacing situation in the Near East,

1. *Calls upon* the Governments concerned as a first step to take forthwith all measures for an immediate cease-fire and for a cessation of all military activities in the area;

2. *Requests* the Secretary-General to keep the Council promptly and currently informed on the situation.

Resolution 234 (1967)

Adopted by the Security Council at Its 1350th Meeting on June 7, 1967

The Security Council,

Noting that, in spite of its appeal to the Governments concerned to take forthwith as a first step all measures for an immediate cease-fire and for a cessation of all military activities in the Near East (resolution 233 [1967]), military activities in the area are continuing,

Concerned that the continuation of military activities may create an even more menacing situation in the area,

1. *Demands* that the Governments concerned should as a first step cease fire and discontinue all military activities at 2000 hours GMT on 7 June 1967;

2. *Requests* the Secretary-General to keep the Council promptly and currently informed on the situation.

Draft Resolution of the United States

S/7952/Rev. 2, June 9, 1967

The Security Council,

Recalling its resolutions 233 and 234,

Recalling that in the latter resolution the Council demanded that the Governments concerned should as a first step cease fire and discontinue military operations at 2000 hours GMT on 7 June 1967,

Noting that Israel, Jordan, Syria and the United Arab Republic have indicated their acceptance of the Council's demand for a cease-fire,

Noting further with deep concern reports of continued fighting between Israel and Syria,

1. *Insists* on an immediate scrupulous implementation by all the parties concerned of the Council's repeated demands for a cease-fire and cessation of all military activity as a first urgent step toward the establishment of a stable peace in the Middle East;

2. *Calls for* discussions promptly thereafter among the parties concerned, using such third party or United Nations assistance as they may wish, looking toward the establishment of viable arrangements encompassing the withdrawal and disengagement of armed personnel, the renunciation of force regardless of its nature, the maintenance of vital international rights and the establishment of a stable and durable peace in the Middle East;

3. *Requests* the President of the Security Council and the Secretary-General to take immediate steps to seek to assure compliance with the cease-fire and to report to the Council thereon within twenty-four hours;

4. *Also requests* the Secretary-General to provide such assistance as may be required in facilitating the discussions called for in paragraph 2.

Resolution 235 (1967)

Adopted by the Security Council at Its 1352d Meeting on June 9, 1967

The Security Council,
Recalling its resolutions 233 (1967) and 234 (1967),
Noting that the Governments of Israel and Syria have announced their mutual acceptance of the Council's demand for a cease-fire,
Noting the statements made by the representatives of Syria and Israel,

1. *Confirms* its previous resolutions about immediate cease-fire and cessation of military action;

2. *Demands* that hostilities should cease forthwith;

3. *Requests* the Secretary-General to make immediate contacts with the Governments of Israel and Syria to arrange immediate compliance with the above-mentioned resolutions, and to report to the Security Council not later than two hours from now.

Draft Resolution of the United States

S/7971, June 10, 1967

The Security Council,

Having heard the reports of the Secretary-General on the current situation,

Gravely concerned at reports and complaints it has received of air attacks, shellings, ground activities and other violations of the cease-fire between Israel and Syria,

1. *Condemns* any and all violations of the cease-fire;

2. *Requests* the Secretary-General to order a full investigation of all reports of violations and to report to the Security Council as soon as possible;

3. *Demands* that the parties scrupulously respect its cease-fire appeals contained in resolutions 233, 234 and 235;

4. *Calls on* the Governments concerned to issue categoric instructions to all military forces to cease all firing and military activities as required by these resolutions.

APPENDIX 8

Resolution 236 (1967)

Adopted by the Security Council at Its 1357th Meeting on June 12, 1967

The Security Council,

Taking note of the oral reports of the Secretary-General on the situation between Israel and Syria, made at the 1354th, 1355th, 1356th and 1357th meetings and the supplemental information supplied in documents S/7930 and Add.1-3,

1. *Condemns* any and all violations of the cease-fire;

2. *Requests* the Secretary-General to continue his investigations and to report to the Council as soon as possible;

3. *Affirms* that its demand for a cease-fire and discontinuance of all military activities includes a prohibition of any forward military movements subsequent to the cease-fire;

4. *Calls for* the prompt return to the cease-fire positions of any troops which may have moved forward subsequent to 1630 GMT on 10 June 1967;

5. *Calls for* full co-operation with the Chief of Staff of the United Nations Truce Supervision Organization in Palestine and the observers in implementing the cease-fire, including freedom of movement and adequate communications facilities.

Revised Draft Resolution of the Union of Soviet Socialist Republics

S/7951/Rev. 2, June 13, 1967

The Security Council,

Noting that Israel, in defiance of the Security Council's resolutions on the cessation of military activities and a cease-fire (S/RES/233 of 6 June 1967, S/RES/234 of 7 June 1967 and S/RES/235 of 9 June 1967), has seized additional territory of the United Arab Republic, Jordan and Syria,

Noting that although military activities have now ceased, Israel is still occupying the territory of those countries, thus failing to halt its aggression and defying the United Nations and all peace-loving States,

Considering unacceptable and unlawful Israel's territorial claims on Arab States,

1. *Vigorously condemns* Israel's aggressive activities and continued occupation of part of the territory of the United Arab Republic, Syria and Jordan, regarding this as an act of aggression and the grossest violation of the United Nations Charter and generally recognized principles of international law;

2. *Demands* that Israel should immediately and unconditionally remove all its troops from the territory of those States and withdraw them behind the armistice lines and should respect the status of the demilitarized zones, as prescribed in the General Armistice Agreements.

APPENDIX 10

Resolution 237 (1967)

Adopted by the Security Council at Its 1361st Meeting on
June 14, 1967

The Security Council,
Considering the urgent need to spare the civil populations and the
prisoners of the war in the area of conflict in the Middle East
additional sufferings,
Considering that essential and inalienable human rights should be
respected even during the vicissitudes of war,
Considering that all the obligations of the Geneva Convention
relative to the Treatment of Prisoners of War of 12 August 1949 [1]
should be complied with by the parties involved in the conflict,
  1. *Calls upon* the Government of Israel to ensure the safety, welfare and security of the inhabitants of the areas where military operations have taken place and to facilitate the return of those inhabitants who have fled the areas since the outbreak of hostilities;
  2. *Recommends* to the Governments concerned the scrupulous
respect of the humanitarian principles governing the treatment of
prisoners of war and the protection of civilian persons in time of
war, contained in the Geneva Convention of 12 August 1949; [2]
  3. *Requests* the Secretary-General to follow the effective implementation of this resolution and to report to the Security Council.

[1] United Nations, *Treaty Series,* Vol. 75 (1950), No. 972.
[2] United Nations, *Treaty Series,* Vol. 75 (1950), Nos. 970–73.

Draft Resolution of the Union of Soviet Socialist Republics

A/L.519, June 19, 1967

The General Assembly,

Noting that Israel, in gross violation of the Charter of the United Nations and the universally accepted principles of international law, has committed a premeditated and previously prepared aggression against the United Arab Republic, Syria and Jordan, and has occupied parts of their territory and inflicted great material damage upon them,

Noting that, in contravention of Security Council resolutions 233 (1967), 234 (1967) and 235 (1967) of 6, 7 and 9 June 1967 on the immediate cessation of all hostilities and a cease-fire, Israel continued to conduct offensive military operations against the above-mentioned States and seized additional territory,

Noting further that, although military activities have now ceased, Israel continues its occupation of the territory of the United Arab Republic, Syria and Jordan, thus failing to halt its aggression and defying the United Nations and all peace-loving States,

Regarding as unacceptable and unlawful Israel's territorial claims on the Arab States, which prevent the restoration of peace in the area,

1. *Vigorously condemns* Israel's aggressive activities and the continuing occupation by Israel of part of the territory of the United Arab Republic, Syria and Jordan, which constitutes an act of recognized aggression;

2. *Demands* that Israel should immediately and unconditionally withdraw all its forces from the territory of those States to positions behind the armistice demarcation lines, as stipulated in the general

armistice agreements, and should respect the status of the demilitarized zones, as prescribed in the armistice agreements;

3. *Demands also* that Israel should make good in full and within the shortest possible period of time all the damage inflicted by its aggression on the United Arab Republic, Syria and Jordan and on their nationals, and should return to them all seized property and other material assets;

4. *Appeals* to the Security Council to take for its part immediate effective measures in order to eliminate all consequences of the aggression committed by Israel.

Draft Resolution of the United States

A Stable and Durable Peace in the Middle East

A/L.520, June 20, 1967

The General Assembly,
Bearing in mind the achievement of a cease-fire in the Middle East, as called for by the Security Council in its resolutions 233 (1967), 234 (1967), 235 (1967) and 236 (1967) of 6, 7, 9 and 12 June 1967,
Having regard to the purpose of the United Nations to be a centre for harmonizing the actions of nations,
1. *Endorses* the cease-fire achieved pursuant to the resolutions of the Security Council and calls for its scrupulous respect by the parties concerned;
2. *Decides* that its objective must be a stable and durable peace in the Middle East;
3. *Considers* that this objective should be achieved through negotiated arrangements with appropriate third-party assistance based on:
(a) Mutual recognition of the political independence and territorial integrity of all countries in the area, encompassing recognized boundaries and other arrangements, including disengagement and withdrawal of forces, that will give them security against terror, destruction and war;
(b) Freedom of innocent maritime passage;
(c) A just and equitable solution of the refugee problem;
(d) Registration and limitation of arms shipments into the area;
(e) Recognition of the right of all sovereign nations to exist in peace and security;
4. *Requests* the Security Council to keep the situation under careful review.

APPENDIX 13

Draft Resolution of Argentina, Bolivia, Brazil, Chile, Colombia, Costa Rica, Ecuador, El Salvador, Guatemala, Guyana, Honduras, Jamaica, Mexico, Nicaragua, Panama, Paraguay, Trinidad and Tobago, and Venezuela

A/L.523, June 30, 1967

The General Assembly,

Considering that all Member States have an inescapable obligation to preserve peace and, consequently, to avoid the use of force in the international sphere,

Considering further that the cease-fire ordered by the Security Council and accepted by the State of Israel and the States of Jordan, Syria and the United Arab Republic is a first step towards the achievement of a just peace in the Middle East, a step which must be reinforced by other measures to be adopted by the Organization and complied with by the parties,

1. *Urgently requests:*

(a) Israel to withdraw all its forces from all the territories occupied by it as a result of the recent conflict;

(b) The parties in conflict to end the state of belligerency, to endeavour to establish conditions of coexistence based on good neighbourliness and to have recourse in all cases to the procedures for peaceful settlement indicated in the Charter of the United Nations;

2. *Reaffirms its conviction* that no stable international order can be based on the threat or use of force, and declares that the validity

of the occupation or acquisition of territories brought about by such means should not be recognized;

3. *Requests* the Security Council to continue examining the situation in the Middle East with a sense of urgency, working directly with the parties and relying on the presence of the United Nations to:

(a) Carry out the provisions of operative paragraph 1 (a) above;

(b) Guarantee freedom of transit on the international waterways in the region;

(c) Achieve an appropriate and full solution of the problem of the refugees and guarantee the territorial inviolability and political independence of the States of the region, through measures including the establishment of demilitarized zones;

4. *Reaffirms,* as in earlier, recommendations, the desirability of establishing an international régime for the city of Jerusalem, to be considered by the General Assembly at its twenty-second session.

Revised Draft Resolution of Afghanistan, Burundi, Cambodia, Ceylon, Congo (Brazzaville), Cyprus, Guinea, India, Indonesia, Kenya, Malaysia, Mali, Pakistan, Senegal, Somalia, United Republic of Tanzania, Yugoslavia, and Zambia

> *Immediate Withdrawal of the Armed Forces of Israel from Territories Belonging to Jordan, Syria, and the United Arab Republic*
>
> A/L.522/Rev. 3, July 3, 1967

The General Assembly,

Having discussed the grave situation in the Middle East,

Noting that the armed forces of Israel occupy areas including territories belonging to Jordan, Syria and the United Arab Republic,

1. *Calls upon* Israel to withdraw immediately all its forces to the positions they held prior to 5 June 1967;

2. *Requests* the Secretary-General to ensure compliance with the present resolution and to secure, with the assistance of the United Nations Truce Supervision Organization established by the Security Council, strict observance by all parties of the provisions of the General Armistice Agreements between Israel and the Arab countries;

3. *Requests further* the Secretary-General to designate a personal representative who will assist him in securing compliance with the present resolution and be in contact with the parties concerned;

4. *Calls upon* all States to render every assistance to the Secretary-

General in the implementation of the present resolution in accordance with the Charter of the United Nations;

5. *Requests* the Secretary-General to report urgently to the General Assembly and to the Security Council on compliance with the the terms of the present resolution;

6. *Requests* that the Security Council consider all aspects of the situation in the Middle East and seek peaceful ways and means for the solution of all problems—legal, political and humanitarian— through appropriate channels, guided by the principles of the Charter of the United Nations, in particular those contained in Articles 2 and 33.

Resolution 2253 (ES-V), July 4, 1967

Measures Taken by Israel to Change the Status of the City of Jerusalem

The General Assembly,

Deeply concerned at the situation prevailing in Jerusalem as a result of the measures taken by Israel to change the status of the City,

1. *Considers* that these measures are invalid;

2. *Calls upon* Israel to rescind all measures already taken and to desist forthwith from taking any action which would alter the status of Jerusalem;

3. *Requests* the Secretary-General to report to the General Assembly and the Security Council on the situation and on the implementation of the present resolution not later than one week from its adoption.

APPENDIX 16

Consensus Expressed by the President and Approved by the Security Council at the 1366th Meeting on July 9–10, 1967

S/8047

Recalling Security Council resolutions 233, 234, 235 and 236 (1967), and emphasizing the need for all parties to observe scrupulously the provisions of these resolutions, having heard the statements made by the Secretary-General and the suggestions he has addressed to the parties concerned, I believe that I am reflecting the view of the Council that the Secretary-General should proceed, as he has suggested in his statements before the Council on 8 and 9 July 1967, to request the Chief of Staff of the United Nations Truce Supervision Organization in Palestine, General Odd Bull, to work out with the Governments of the United Arab Republic and Israel, as speedily as possible, the necessary arrangements to station United Nations Military Observers in the Suez Canal sector under the Chief of Staff of UNTSO.

Draft Resolution of the Union of Soviet Socialist Republics

S/8212, October 24, 1967

The Security Council,

Having considered the communication of the representative of the United Arab Republic concerning a new act of aggression by Israel in the area of the city of Suez,

Having considered also the information provided by the Secretary-General in document S/7930/Add.44 that the Israel forces began and continued an artillery barrage, ignoring the proposal by the Chief of Staff of the United Nations Truce Supervision Organization in Palestine for an immediate cease-fire,

Expressing grave concern that the said act of aggression has resulted in heavy losses among the peaceful population and in serious physical damage,

Considering that the actions of the Israel armed forces in the area of the city of Suez constitute a gross violation of the Security Council resolutions of 6 June 1967 (S/RES/233) and of 7 June 1967 (S/RES/234) calling for a cease-fire and the cessation of military activities, as well as of other Security Council resolutions on that question,

1. *Strongly condemns* Israel for the act of aggression committed by it in the area of the city of Suez;

2. *Demands* that Israel compensate the United Arab Republic for the damage caused by that act;

3. *Urgently calls upon* Israel strictly to observe the aforementioned resolutions of the Security Council concerning the cease-fire and the cessation of military activities.

Draft Resolution of the United States

S/8213, October 24, 1967

The Security Council,

Gravely concerned at the reports and complaints it has received of military hostilities in violation of the cease-fire between Israel and the United Arab Republic,

Convinced that progress toward the establishment of a just and durable peace in the area requires mutual respect for the cease-fire, in accordance with resolutions of the Security Council and the agreements of the parties,

1. *Condemns* any and all violations of the cease-fire;

2. *Insists* that the Member States concerned scrupulously respect the cease-fire as contained in resolutions 233, 234, 235 and 236 and the consensus of 10 July and co-operate fully with the Chief of Staff of the United Nations Truce Supervision Organization and the United Nations Military Observers in their tasks in connexion therewith;

3. *Calls on* the Governments concerned to issue categoric instructions to all military forces to refrain from all firing, as required by these resolutions.

Resolution 240 (1967)

Adopted by the Security Council at Its 1371st Meeting on October 25, 1967

The Security Council,

Gravely concerned over recent military activities in the Middle East carried out in spite of the Security Council resolutions ordering a cease-fire,

Having heard and considered the statements made by the parties concerned,

Taking into consideration the information on the above-mentioned activities provided by the Secretary-General in documents S/7930/Add.43-49,

1. *Condemns* the violations of the cease-fire;

2. *Regrets* the casualties and loss of property resulting from the violations;

3. *Reaffirms* the necessity of the strict observance of the cease-fire resolutions;

4. *Demands* of the Member States concerned that they cease immediately all prohibited military activities in the area and that they co-operate fully and promptly with the United Nations Truce Supervision Organization in Palestine.

APPENDIX 20

Joint Draft Resolution of India, Mali, Nigeria

S/8227, November 7, 1967

The Security Council,

Expressing its continuing concern with the grave situation in the Middle East,

Recalling its resolution 233 (1967) of 6 June 1967 on the outbreak of fighting which called for, as a first step, an immediate ceasefire and for a cessation of all military activities in the area,

Recalling further General Assembly resolution 2256 (ES-V),

Emphasizing the urgency of reducing tensions, restoring peace and bringing about normalcy in the area,

1. *Affirms* that a just and lasting peace in the Middle East must be achieved within the framework of the Charter of the United Nations and more particularly of the following principles:

   (i) Occupation or acquisition of territory by military conquest is inadmissible under the Charter of the United Nations and consequently Israel's armed forces should withdraw from all the territories occupied as a result of the recent conflict;

   (ii) Likewise, every State has the right to live in peace and complete security free from threats or acts of war and consequently all States in the area should terminate the state or claim of belligerency and settle their international disputes by peaceful means;

   (iii) Likewise, every State of the area has the right to be secure within its borders and it is obligatory on all Member States of the area to respect the sovereignty, territorial integrity and political independence of one another;

2. *Affirms further:*

   (i) There should be a just settlement of the question of Palestine refugees;

(ii) There should be guarantee of freedom of navigation in accordance with international law through international waterways in the area;

3. *Requests* the Secretary-General to dispatch a special representative to the area who would contact the States concerned in
order to co-ordinate efforts to achieve the purposes of this resolution
and to submit a report to the Council within thirty days.

Draft Resolution of the United States

S/8229, November 7, 1967

The Security Council,

Expressing its continuing concern with the grave situation in the Middle East,

Recalling its resolution 233 (1967) on the outbreak of fighting which called, as a first step, for an immediate cease-fire and for a cessation of all military activities in the area,

Recalling further General Assembly resolution 2256 (ES-V),

Emphasizing the urgency of reducing tensions and bringing about a just and lasting peace in which every State in the area can live in security,

Emphasizing further that all Member States in their acceptance of the Charter of the United Nations have undertaken a commitment to act in accordance with Article 2 of the Charter,

1. *Affirms* that the fulfilment of the above Charter principles requires the achievement of a state of just and lasting peace in the Middle East embracing withdrawal of armed forces from occupied territories, termination of claims or states of belligerence, and mutual recognition and respect for the right of every State in the area to sovereign existence, territorial integrity, political independence, secure and recognized boundaries, and freedom from the threat or use of force;

2. *Affirms further* the necessity:

(a) For guaranteeing freedom of navigation through international waterways in the area;

(b) For achieving a just settlement of the refugee problem;

(c) For guaranteeing the territorial inviolability and political independence of every State in the area, through measures including the establishment of demilitarized zones;

(d) For achieving a limitation of the wasteful and destructive arms race in the area;

3. *Requests* the Secretary-General to designate a Special Representative to proceed to the Middle East to establish and maintain contacts with the States concerned with a view to assisting them in the working out of solutions in accordance with the purposes of this resolution and in creating a just and lasting peace in the area;

4. *Requests* the Secretary-General to report to the Security Council on the progress of the efforts of the Special Representative as soon as possible.

Draft Resolution of the Union of Soviet Socialist Republics

S/8253, November 20, 1967

The Security Council,

Expressing concern at the lack of progress towards a political settlement in the Middle East and at the increased tension in the area,

Noting that there have even been violations of the cease-fire called for by the Security Council in its resolutions 233 of 6 June, 234 of 7 June, 235 of 9 June and 236 of 12 June 1967, a cease-fire which was regarded as a first step towards the achievement of a just peace in the area and which was to have been strengthened by other appropriate measures,

Recalling General Assembly resolutions 2252 (ES-V), 2253 (ES-V), 2254 (ES-V) and 2256 (ES-V),

Emphasizing the urgent necessity of restoring peace and establishing normal conditions in the Middle East,

1. *Declares* that peace and final solutions to this problem can be achieved within the framework of the Charter of the United Nations;

2. *Urges* that the following steps should be taken:

(a) The parties to the conflict should immediately withdraw their forces to the positions they held before 5 June 1967 in accordance with the principle that the seizure of territories as a result of war is inadmissible;

(b) All States Members of the United Nations in the area should immediately recognize that each of them has the right to exist as an independent national State and to live in peace and security, and should renounce all claims and desist from all acts inconsistent with the foregoing;

3. *Deems it necessary* in this connexion to continue its consideration of the situation in the Middle East, collaborating directly with the parties concerned and making use of the presence of the United Nations, with a view to achieving an appropriate and just solution of all aspects of the problem on the basis of the following principles:

(a) The use or threat of force in relations between States is incompatible with the Charter of the United Nations;

(b) Every State must respect the political independence and territorial integrity of all other States in the area;

(c) There must be a just settlement of the question of the Palestine refugees;

(d) Innocent passage through international waterways in the area in accordance with international agreements;

4. *Considers* that, in harmony with the steps to be taken along the lines indicated above, all States in the area should put an end to the state of belligerency, take measures to limit the useless and destructive arms race, and discharge the obligations assumed by them under the Charter of the United Nations and international agreements.

Resolution 242 (1967)

Adopted by the Security Council at Its 1382d Meeting on
November 22, 1967

The Security Council,

Expressing its continuing concern with the grave situation in the
Middle East,

Emphasizing the inadmissibility of the acquisition of territory by
war and the need to work for a just and lasting peace in which every
State in the area can live in security,

Emphasizing further that all Member States in their acceptance of
the Charter of the United Nations have undertaken a commitment
to act in accordance with Article 2 of the Charter,

1. *Affirms* that the fulfilment of Charter principles requires the
establishment of a just and lasting peace in the Middle East which
should include the application of both the following principles:

(i) Withdrawal of Israeli armed forces from territories occupied
in the recent conflict;

(ii) Termination of all claims or states of belligerency and respect
for and acknowledgement of the sovereignty, territorial integrity and political independence of every State in the area
and their right to live in peace within secure and recognized
boundaries free from threats or acts of force;

2. *Affirms further* the necessity

(a) For guaranteeing freedom of navigation through international waterways in the area;

(b) For achieving a just settlement of the refugee problem;

(c) For guaranteeing the territorial inviolability and political independence of every State in the area, through measures including
the establishment of demilitarized zones;

3. *Requests* the Secretary-General to designate a Special Repre-

sentative to proceed to the Middle East to establish and maintain contacts with the States concerned in order to promote agreement and assist efforts to achieve a peaceful and accepted settlement in accordance with the provisions and principles in this resolution;

4. *Requests* the Secretary-General to report to the Security Council on the progress of the efforts of the Special Representative as soon as possible.

APPENDIX 24

Statement by the President of the Security Council

S/8289, December 8, 1967

The following statement is circulated in connexion with the report by the Secretary-General on the observation of the cease-fire in the Suez Canal sector (S/8053/Add.3). After consultations I have had with the representatives, I understand there is no objection to my transmittal of this statement as reflecting the view of the members of the Council:

As regards document S/8053/Add.3, brought to the attention of the Security Council, the members, recalling the consensus reached at its 1366th meeting on 9 July 1967, recognize the necessity of the enlargement by the Secretary-General of the number of observers in the Suez Canal zone and the provision of additional technical material and means of transportation.

APPENDIX 25

Operative Paragraphs of the Tentative U.S.-Soviet Draft Resolution, July 19, 1967

[Not Introduced]

Affirms the principle that conquest of territory by war is inadmissible under the UN Charter and calls upon all parties to the conflict to withdraw without delay their forces from the territories occupied by them after June 4, 1967;

Affirms likewise the principle of acknowledgement without delay by all Member States in the area that each of them enjoys the right to maintain an independent national state of its own and live in peace and security, as well as the renunciation of all claims and acts inconsistent therewith are expected.

Index

Abbreviations

GA   General Assembly
SC   Security Council
SG   Secretary-General
UAR   United Arab Republic
U.K.   United Kingdom
UNEF   United Nations Emergency Force
UNTSO   United Nations Truce Supervision Organization
U.S.   United States

Adebo, Chief S. O. (Nigeria): as SC President, 230-31, 232, 263, 267; quoted, 230, 244, 268, 311 (*text*)

Afghanistan: in GA, 144, 186, 206, 298; *see also* Pazhwak, Abdul Rahman

Aiken, Frank (Ireland), 151-52; quoted, 151, 152

Albania: in GA, 150, 169, 170, 182, 215; GA draft resolution on condemnation of Israel and blockade, 169, 185, 186

Algeria: in GA, 181, 204, 212, 214-15

Al-Rachach, Ghassan (Saudi Arabia): quoted, 44

Aqaba, Gulf of, 15, 51; blockade of Israeli ships and ships destined for Israel in, 26, 31, 32, 33-34, 35, 37, 39, 49, 107, 204; *see also* Tiran, Strait of

Arab-Israeli War: background of, 1-10; outbreak (April 7), 2, 7; SC consideration, May 24-June 14, 28-115; first armed clash, 37, 46-48; events in, 50, 59, 62, 72, 77, 194-95, 228-29; SC resolution (233) on cease-fire, 52-53, 55, 56, 66, 283 (*text*); second SC resolution on cease-fire, 58-63, 59-60 (*text*), 284 (*text*); SC resolution (235) on ces-
sation of hostilities, 72-73 (*text*), 286 (*text*); continuation of fighting after SC resolutions, 77, 78, 82, 84, 91; SC resolution (236) on violations of cease-fire, 93-94, 288 (*text*); SC resolution (237) on refugees and prisoners of war, 105, 290 (*text*); GA, 5th Emergency Special Session consideration, 116-93, 206-19; SC consideration, July 8-10, 195-203; GA, 22d session consideration, 223, 225-29; SC consideration, October 25-November 22, 230-70; SC resolution (240) on cease-fire and cooperation with UNTSO, 232-34, 302 (*text*); SC resolution (242) on designation of Special Representative of SG, 252, 254, 260-66, 271, 273, 275, 276, 279, 309-10 (*text*); summary of problems, 273-79; *see also* Cease-fire (1967); *for actions and draft resolutions, see under* GA and SC

Arab states: support of Eastern European governments, 78-79; statements of positions in GA, 128-32; and GA Latin American resolution, 180-81, 187; and U.S.–Soviet Union draft resolution, 212

Argentina: in SC, 38, 52-53, 56, 93, 101, 105, 108, 111, 112, 153, 235, 237, 245-46; in GA, 154-56, 164; statement of position, 154-56

Armistice Agreements: Israeli-Syrian (1949), 2, 3; Egyptian-Israeli (1949), 11, 18-19, 22-24, 27, 34, 36, 39, 69, 98, 138, 202, 205

Armistice Commission, *see* Israeli-Syrian Mixed Armistice Commission

Armistices: and continuation of state of war, 22-24

Astrom, Sverker (Sweden), 214; quoted, 192

Atassi, Noureddin (Syria), 128-29; quoted, 128-29

Australia: in GA, 187

Austria: in GA, 191, 192, 214; GA draft resolution (with Finland and Sweden) *re* referral of problem to SC and adjournment of GA, 214-17; GA resolution transferring problem to GA, 22d session, 217

Barbados: in GA, 164

Baroody, Jamil (Saudi Arabia), 128, 129, 207-8; quoted, 128, 207-8

Belgium: in GA, 136-37, 143, 145

Benites, Leopoldo (Ecuador), 157-59; quoted, 158

Bolivia: in GA, 164, 191

Bourguiba, Habib, Jr. (Tunisia), 180-81; quoted, 181

Bouteflika, Abdelaziz (Algeria), 181, 212; quoted, 181

Brazil: in SC, 38, 53, 54, 56, 57-58, 59, 101, 105, 108, 111, 112, 153, 235; in GA, 159-60, 164; statement of position, 159-60

Brown, George (U.K.), 135-36, 143; quoted, 135-36, 175

Bulgaria: in SC, 42, 50, 53, 60, 62, 71, 88, 90, 93, 99, 103, 106, 107, 111, 231, 236, 254-55, 259, 269 (*see also* Tarabanov, Milko)

Bull, General Odd, 2-3, 9, 46, 81, 84, 87, 89, 90, 93, 199

Burundi: in GA, 186, 296

Cambodia: in GA, 296

Canada: in SC, 8, 29, 38, 53, 56, 60, 62, 68, 84, 86-87, 93, 105-6, 107, 111, 112, 114, 231, 234, 235, 244, 246 (*see also* Ignatieff, George); SC draft resolution (with Denmark) *re* support to SG, 29, 107, 281 (*text*); in GA, 143, 145-46, 177, 187; statement of position, 145-46

Caradon, Lord (U.K.): in SC, 43, 68-71, 92-93, 99-100, 115, 197, 243, 249, 250-51, 252, 255, 260; quoted in SC, 52, 68, 69, 70, 81, 85-86, 92, 100, 101, 106, 197, 231, 243, 250, 251, 252, 254, 262; quoted in GA, 177; in GA, 22d session, 226-27

Cease-fire (1967): SC discussions on call for, 51; SC resolution (233) on, 52-53 (*text*), 55, 56, 66, 112, 283 (*text*); acceptance by Jordan, 57, 61, 67; second resolution (234) on, 58-63, 59-60 (*text*), 112, 284 (*text*); nonacceptance by Kuwait, 67; acceptance by Israel, 67, 73, 88; acceptance by Syria, 72, 73, 88; SC resolution (235) on cessation of hostilities, 72-73 (*text*), 112, 286 (*text*); SC consideration of implementation of three resolutions, 73-75 (*text*), 77-88; SC consideration on firming, 77-106; reported violations of, 78, 79, 80, 83-85, 86, 87, 88, 91; draft resolution (U.S.) *re* violations, 88-89, 287 (*text*); SC consideration of strengthening, 89-93, 95-105; SC resolution (236) on violations, 93-94, 112, 288 (*text*); demand (Soviet Union) for enforcement, 200; draft resolution (Soviet Union) *re* observation of, 232, 300 (*text*); draft resolution (U.S.) *re* violations, 232, 301 (*text*)

Ceylon: in GA, 296

Chagla, M. C. (India), 133-34; quoted, 133-34

Charter, United Nations: Article *99*, 3; Articles *24* and *28*, 4-5, 10, 41, 47, 48, 111; Article *51*, 19, 47, 130; and armistice agreements, 24; acts of aggression under, 48; conciliation *vs.* condemnation in, 65; Article *25*, 67; Article *20*, 116, 120; Articles *11* and *12*, 119, 122, 195; Article *2*, 135, 175, 177, 184; Article *33*, 175, 177, 184, 223; Article *18*, 186; Article *42*,

200-1; Article 37, 243; Article *102*, 278; Article 27, 279

Chile: in GA, 164, 191, 192

China (Taiwan): in SC, 6, 39, 53, 101, 109, 111, 231, 234; in GA, 187

China-India dispute (1962), 171

Colombia: in GA, 156-58, 164, 191; statement of position, 156-58

Congo (Brazzaville): in GA, 296

Costa Rica: in GA, 162-63, 164, 191; statement of position, 162-63

Coste Mendez, Nicanor (Argentina), 154-56; quoted, 155-56

Couve de Murville, Maurice (France), 141-44; quoted, 141, 142

Cuba: in GA, 144, 150, 170, 185, 186, 187, 215

Cuevas Cancino, Francisco (Mexico), 164; quoted, 191

Cyprus: in GA, 296

Damascus, 79, 83, 85, 87, 88

Daoudy, Adib (Syria), 199

Dara, 92

Dayan, General Moshe, 86, 87; quoted, 91-92

de Gaulle, Charles: statement on Middle East question, 42-43

Demetrio Tinoco, Luis (Costa Rica), 162-63; quoted, 162, 163

Demilitarized Zone: cultivation rights in, 1-2, 10; outbreaks in, 2-4, 7

Denmark, in SC, 29, 39, 53, 56, 107, 231, 235, 246, 269 (*see also* Tabor, Hans); SC draft resolution (with Canada) *re* support to SG, 29, 107, 281 (*text*); in GA, 134-45, 140-41; statement of position, 134-35

Dobrynin, Anatoli (Soviet Union), 208, 210-11, 227

Dominican Republic: in GA, 164

Dulles, John Foster: quoted, 12

Eban, Abba (Israel): in SC, 15, 71, 126, 206, 246-47, 253, 259, 263; quoted in SC, 61, 246, 259, 263, 264, 274-75; in GA, 139-41, 216; quoted in GA, 139-40, 180

Ecuador: in GA, 157-59, 164; statement of position, 157-59

Egypt: and Israeli-Syrian clashes, 7-8; and Soviet Union, 8, 17, 51; and Egyptian-Israeli General Armistice

Agreement (1949), 11, 18-19, 22-24, 27, 34, 36, 39, 69, 98, 202, 205; and creation of UNEF, 15-17, 19; *see also* United Arab Republic

Eisenhower, Dwight D., 123

Elath, 35, 37

El Fateh organization, 3, 36

El-Kony, Mohamed A. (UAR), 30, 35, 39, 40, 60-61, 65, 99, 194; quoted, 35-36, 40, 47, 77

El-Rifai, Monim (Jordan): in SC, 247-48

El Salvador: in GA, 164

Eshkol, Levi (Israel), 7, 27, 33, 35, 44

Ethiopia: in SC, 38, 40, 43, 53-54, 101, 103, 105, 108, 112, 231 (*see also* Makonnen, Lij); in GA, 178-79

Fawzi, Mahmud (UAR), 129, 191, 216

Fawzy, General M.: quoted, 19

Fedorenko, Nikolai (Soviet Union): in SC, 43, 56-57, 59, 64-65, 78, 80, 82, 87, 89-90, 95-97, 110, 126, 195, 196, 197, 199-201, 232, 233; quoted in SC, 31, 38, 53, 54, 64, 65, 74-75, 76, 85, 104, 105, 200, 231, 233, 234; in GA, 218-19

Finland: in GA, 150-51, 191, 192, 208, 214; statement of position, 150-51; GA draft resolution (with Austria and Sweden) *re* referral of problem to SC and adjournment of GA, 214-17; GA draft resolution transferring problem to 22d session of GA, 217

France: in SC, 6, 41, 42-43, 49, 50, 54, 81, 89, 93, 102, 111, 231, 235, 261; in GA, 141-44, 177-78, 181, 186, 216; statement of position, 141-44

Garcia Sayan, Enrique (Peru), 160-62; quoted, 161

General Assembly: ultimate authority on UNEF, 13-14, 18, 20; Suez crisis in (1956), 17, 171; previous emergency sessions, 116-18, 123

General Assembly, 5th Emergency Special Session, 122-93, 204-19; Soviet Union call for, 116-22; convening of, 121, 123; U.S. objection to calling, 121-22; President, 123 (*see also* Pazhwak, Abdul Rahman); draft resolution (Soviet Union) *re*

General Assembly (*Continued*)
condemnation, withdrawal, and restitution, 126, 169, 176-77, 185-86, 291-92 (*text*); resolution (Pakistan) on status of Jerusalem, 132, 185, 187, 191, 206, 298 (*text*); draft resolution (U.S.) *re* stable and durable peace, 138-39, 185, 293 (*text*); draft resolution (Yugoslavia and fourteen states) *re* removal of Israeli armed forces, 160, 162, 172, 182, 296-97 (*text*); draft resolution (Latin American states) *re* troop withdrawal and establishment of coexistence and continued SC action, 164-68, 165-66 (*text*), 170, 172-85, 186-87, 208-12, 208-9 (*text*), 294-95 (*text*); failure to act, 169-73; draft resolution *re* refugees and prisoners of war, 185, 187-88; meetings, July *12*-September *18*, 206-19; draft resolution (Austria, Finland, Sweden) *re* referral of problem to SC and adjournment, 214-17; resolution transferring problem to 22d session of GA, 217, 220; summary of work, 220-25; *see also heading* "in GA" *under names of countries*
—— position statements, 123-68; Soviet Union, 123-28; Arab states, 128-32; Yugoslavia, 132-33; India, 133-34; Denmark, 134-35; U.K., 135-36; U.S., 137-39; Israel, 139-41; France, 141-44; Canada, 145-46; Rumania, 146-47; Jordan, 148-50; Finland, 150-51; Ireland, 151-52; Latin American states, 153-68; Argentina, 154-56; Colombia, 156-58; Ecuador, 157-58; Brazil, 159-60; Peru, 160-62, 168; Costa Rica, 162-63; Uruguay, 163; Honduras, 166-68; Venezuela, 168
General Assembly, 22d session, 223, 225-29; *see also heading* "in GA, 22d session" *under names of countries*
Geneva Convention on the Territorial Sea and Contiguous Zone (1958), 34
Ghana: in GA, 187, 204
Goldberg, Arthur (U.S.), 208, 210-12, 223; in SC, 32-35, 39, 40, 58-59, 63, 73-74, 79-80, 82, 88-89, 97-99, 102-3, 197-98, 232, 233, 242, 251, 255, 265;

quoted in SC, 33-34, 43, 52, 63, 71, 74, 79, 83, 102-3, 104, 121-22, 198, 233, 234, 242-43, 251, 259, 262, 265; in GA, 5th Emergency Special Session, 127, 137-39, 206-7, 216, 219; quoted, 137-38, 176, 179, 206, 207, 211; in GA, 22d session, quoted, 223
Greece: in GA, 186, 192
Gromyko, Andrei (Soviet Union): in GA, 119, 176-77, 211-12, 215-16, 218-19, 223
Guatemala: in GA, 164
Guinea: in GA, 144, 179, 186, 266
Guyana: in GA, 164

Hague Regulations on the Laws and Customs of War on Land (1907), 23, 24
Hammarskjöld, Dag, 5; quoted, 14, 202; and creation of UNEF, 14-15, 18, 20
Harmel, Pierre (Belgium), 136-37, 143
Honduras: in GA, 164, 166-68 (*see also* Lopez Villamil, Humberto); statement of position, 166-68
Hungary: in GA, 144
Hussein, King of Jordan, 51; in GA, 148-50; quoted in GA, 148-49; in GA, 22d session, 226; in SC, 236, 238

Ignatieff, George (Canada), 62, 86; quoted, 8, 60; as SC President, 8-9
India: in SC, 38, 40, 47, 49, 50, 53, 55, 56, 76, 84, 87, 88, 93, 99, 103, 108, 112, 113, 195, 196, 199, 201, 231, 234, 235, 237, 241, 266 (*see also* Parthasarathi, Gopalaswami); in GA, 133-34, 179, 182-83, 186, 192, 204, 215, 296 (*see also* Chagla, M.C.; Parthasarathi, Gopalaswami); statement of position, 133-34; SC draft resolution (with Mali and Nigeria) *re* Special Representative of SG, 237, 238-40, 241, 245, 246, 261, 262, 303-4 (*text*)
India-China dispute (1962), 171
Indonesia: in GA, 144, 296
Iran: in GA, 131
Iraq: in GA, 148, 214, 217
Ireland: in GA, 151-52, 177; statement of position, 151-52
Israel: Israeli-Syrian General Armis-

tice Agreement (1949), 2, 3; Egyptian-Israeli General Armistice Agreement (1949), 11, 18-19, 22-24, 27, 34, 36, 39, 69, 98, 202, 205; and creation of UNEF, 15; in SC, 28, 44, 47, 48, 49, 61, 71, 77, 79, 83, 91, 99, 196-97, 199, 240, 246, 253, 259, 263, 264 (*see also* Eban, Abba; Kidron, Reginald; Rafael, Gideon); question of condemnation as aggressor (SC), 47, 50, 55, 65-66, 74, 92, 96, 110, 112-13; question of demanding troop withdrawal (SC), 49, 50, 51, 53, 54-55, 56, 65-66, 69, 76, 88-92, 96; acceptance of cease-fire, 67, 73, 88; acceptance of cessation of hostilities resolution, 73; Soviet Union demands for condemnation, 78, 82, 88, 89, 92, 96, 103-4; in GA, 139-41, 180, 187, 193, 216, 217, 219 (*see also* Eban, Abba; Rafael, Gideon); statement of position, 139-41; rejection of GA resolution on status of Jerusalem, 206

Israeli-Syrian Mixed Armistice Commission (ISMAC): reconvening of, 2; activities, 83, 85

Israeli-Syrian relations: border incidents, 1-10

Italy: in GA, 136, 145, 181, 191, 192

Jakobson, Max (Finland), 150-51, 208; quoted, 150-51, 192

Jamaica: in GA, 164

Japan: in SC, 39-40, 53, 101, 108, 111, 234, 236, 243-44; in GA, 187, 192

Jarring, Gunnar, 271-72

Jerusalem: Government House, 51, 80, 81, 87, 93; GA resolution (Pakistan) on status, 132, 185, 187, 191, 206, 298 (*text*)

Johnson, Lyndon B., 34, 137, 138, 184, 242, 255, 262

Jordan: and Arab-Israeli War, 51; acceptance of cease-fire, 57, 61, 67; in GA, 5th Emergency Special Session, 148-50, 190; statement of position, 148-50; in GA, 22d session, 226; in SC, 236, 247-48, 264; *see also* Hussein, King of Jordan

Keita, Moussa Léon (Mali), 42, 198-99; quoted, 54

Kenya: in GA, 187, 296

Kidron, Reginald (Israel), 99

Kosygin, Alexei (Soviet Union): in GA, 5th Emergency Special Session, 123-28, 185; quoted, 124, 125, 126-27; in GA, 22d session, 255; quoted, 205

Krag, Jens Otto (Denmark), 134-35; quoted, 134-35, 140-41

Kuneitra, 82, 87, 88, 89, 91

Kuwait: nonacceptance of cease-fire, 67

Kuznetsov, V. V. (Soviet Union): in SC, 245, 251-52, 253, 255, 259, 265-66; quoted in SC, 17, 245, 251, 266; in GA, 22d session, 226, 227

Laos: in GA, 187

Latin American states: statements of positions in GA, 153-68; GA resolution on troop withdrawal and establishment of coexistence and continued SC action, 164-68, 165-66 (*text*), 170, 172-85, 186-87, 208-9 (*text*), 208-12, 294-95 (*text*); draft text on solution, 249; in SC sessions, 269-70

Lebanon: in GA, 185, 186

Lekic, Danilo (Yugoslavia), 160, 173

Lesotho: in GA, 187

Liberia: in GA, 187

Libya: in GA, 185, 186

Liu Chieh: as President of SC, 6

Lopez Villamil, Humberto (Honduras), 166-68, 175; quoted, 166, 167

Luisi, Hector (Uruguay), 163

Madagascar: in GA, 187

Magalhaes Pinto, José de (Brazil), 159-60

Mahgoub, M. A. (Sudan), 129-31, 189-90; quoted, 129-30, 189

Makhos, Ibrahim (Syria), 190-91; quoted, 190-91

Makonnen, Lij Endalkachew (Ethiopia), 42; quoted, 53, 54, 202; as SC President, 194, 199, 202-3

Malawi: in GA, 187

Malaysia: in GA, 186, 296

Mali: in SC, 42, 50, 53-54, 93, 99, 102, 103, 108, 198-99, 231; in GA, 186, 214, 296; SC draft resolution (with India and Nigeria) *re* Special Rep-

Mali (*Continued*)
  resentative of SG, 237, 238-40, 241, 245, 246, 261, 262, 303-4 (*text*)
Martin, Paul (Canada), 145-46; quoted, 143, 145
Matsui, Akira (Japan), 40, 243-44
Maurer, Ion Gheorghe (Rumania), 145, 146-47; quoted, 146, 148
Mauritania: in GA, 144
Mestiri, Mahmoud (Tunisia), 219
Mexico: in GA, 164, 191, 204
Mongolia: in GA, 144
Moro, Aldo (Italy), 136
Morocco: in GA, 148, 185
Murtagi, General: quoted, 48

Nase, Nesti (Albania), 150
Nasser, Gamal Abdel, 37; quoted, 7-8, 26, 27, 30, 246; talks with U Thant, 28, 30, 32
Nepal: in GA, 145, 187, 206
Newsweek: quoted, 44
New York *Times:* quoted, 48, 205
New Zealand: in GA, 187
Nicaragua: in GA, 164
Niger: in GA, 187
Nigeria: in SC, 39, 99, 101, 103, 108, 111, 230-31, 261, 269 (*see also* Adebo, Chief S.O.); in GA, 145; SC draft resolution (with India and Mali) *re* Special Representative of SG, 237, 238-40, 241, 245, 246, 261, 262, 303-4 (*text*)
Nonaligned states: in GA, 170-79, 206, 212-13

Pachachi, Adnan (Iraq), 217
Pakistan: in GA, 131-32, 185, 187, 204, 206, 296; GA resolution on status of Jerusalem, 132, 185, 187, 191, 206, 298 (*text*)
Panama: in GA, 164
Paraguay: in GA, 164
Parthasarathi, Gopalaswami (India): in SC, 80, 88, 201, 234, 239-40, 241, 249, 255, 260, 261-62; quoted in SC, 53, 55, 201, 241, 261-62; in GA, 179, 182-83; quoted in GA, 179
Pazhwak, Abdul Rahman (Afghanistan): as President of GA, 123, 188-89, 192-93, 204, 207, 209-10, 214, 216, 219

Pearson, Lester, 11-12, 16; quoted, 11, 145-46
Perez Guerrero, Manuel (Venezuela), 168
Peru: in GA, 160-62, 164, 168; statement of position, 160-62
Philippines: in GA, 187
Pirzada, Sharifuddin (Pakistan), 131-32; quoted, 131-32
Poland: in GA, 144
Portugal: in GA, 217
Prisoners of war: SC resolution (237) on, 105, 112, 290 (*text*); GA draft resolution on, 185, 187-88

Rabin, General (Israeli Chief of Staff), 44
Rafael, Gideon (Israel): in SC, 77, 79, 80, 83, 91, 194, 199; quoted in SC, 28, 44, 47, 48, 77-78, 80; in GA, 193, 219
Rafid, 91
Refugees: SC resolution (237) on, 105, 112, 290 (*text*); GA draft resolution on, 185, 187-88
Riad, Mahmoud (UAR), 33; in SC, 240-41, 252-53, 263-64; quoted, 253, 263, 264, 275
Rikhye, General I.J., 19, 46
Ruda, José Maria (Argentina), 245-46; quoted, 52-53, 245
Rumania: in GA, 145, 146-47; statement of position, 146-47
Rusk, Dean, 227

Sasson, Elias: quoted, 84
Saudi Arabia: in SC, 44; in GA, 128, 129, 190, 207-8, 214
Secretary-General: relations with SC as defined in Charter, 3; and UNEF, 13-15; SC draft resolution (Canada and Denmark) *re* support to, 29, 107, 281 (*text*); SC draft resolution (U.S.) *re* compliance with appeal, 40, 282 (*text*); and compliance with SC resolutions (Resolution 235), 73, 76, 77, 82, 85, 86, 89, 90, 91; Special Representative proposed, 76, 86, 113, 237, 238-40, 303-4 (*text*), 305-6 (*text*); request for increase in number of observers and cooperation with

UNTSO, 232-34, 266-67, 268, 311 (*text*); Special Representative approved, 252, 271, 273, 275, 276, 279, 309-10 (*text*); appointment of Special Representative, 271; *see also* Hammarsjköld, Dag; Thant, U

Security Council: inaction in Israeli-Syrian situation, 3-10, 21; powers *re* maintenance of peace and security as defined in Charter, 4-5, 10, 41, 47, 48, 111; functions of Presidents, 5-6, 46, 56; members, May, *1967*, 6, 109, 114; summary of work, 220-25

—— sessions, May *24*-June *14*, 28-115; failure to restrain belligerence, 29-45; meetings, May *24*-June *3*, before outbreak of hostilities, 29-45, 107-9; draft resolution (Canada and Denmark) supporting efforts of SG, 29, 107, 281 (*text*); draft resolution (U.S.) *re* compliance with SG's appeal, 40, 282 (*text*); meetings, June *5-14*, 46-106, 109-15; question of condemnation of Israel, as aggressor, 47, 50, 55, 65-66, 74, 92, 96, 110, 112-13; question of demanding troop withdrawal, 49, 50, 51, 53, 54-55, 56, 65-66, 69, 76, 88-92, 96; discussion on call for cease-fire, 51; first resolution (233) on cease-fire, 52-53 (*text*), 55, 56, 66, 112, 283 (*text*); suggestions for "lasting and just peace," 53-56; second resolution (234) on cease-fire, 58-63, 59-60 (*text*), 112, 284 (*text*); reaction of members to second cease-fire resolution, 60-72; draft resolution (U.S.) *re* withdrawal of forces and peace negotiations, 63, 113, 285 (*text*); draft resolution (Soviet Union) *re* condemnation of Israel and withdrawal of forces, 66-67 (*text*), 74-75, 92, 96, 289 (*text*); resolution (235) on cessation of hostilities, 72-73 (*text*), 112, 286 (*text*); question of compliance with three resolutions, 73-76; Special Representative of SG proposed, 76, 86, 113; actions to firm cease-fire, 77-106; action on compliance with resolutions (235), 77-94; proposals to strengthen UNTSO, 84, 86; draft resolution (U.S.) *re* violations of

cease-fire, 88-89, 287 (*text*); consideration to strengthen cease-fire, 88-93, 95-104; resolution (236) on violations of cease-fire, 93-94, 288 (*text*); resolution (237) on refugees and prisoners of war, 105, 112, 290 (*text*); shifting of problem to GA, 106, 114-15; summary and critique of sessions, 107-15; *see also heading* "in SC" *under names of countries*

—— sessions, July *8-10*, 195-203; UAR call for meeting, 194; President, 194 (*see also* Makonnen, Lij); SG request for implementation of cease-fire by observers, 196, 197-98, 202; demand for enforcement of cease-fire, 200, 203; summary of consensus, 202-3, 299 (*text*)

—— sessions, October *25*-November *22*, 230-70; President, 230 (*see also* Adebo, Chief S. O.); draft resolution (Soviet Union) *re* condemnation of Israel and observation of cease-fire, 232, 300 (*text*); draft resolution (U.S.) on violations of cease-fire, 232, 301 (*text*); resolution (240) on cease-fire and cooperation with UNTSO, 232-34, 302 (*text*); draft resolution (India, Mali, Nigeria) *re* Special Representative of SG, 237, 238-40, 241, 245, 261, 262, 303-4 (*text*); draft resolution (U.S.) *re* appointment of Spccial Representative of SG, 237, 238-40, 245, 262, 305-6 (*text*); resolution (242) on designation of Special Representative of SG, 252, 254, 260-66, 271, 273, 275, 276, 279, 309-10 (*text*); draft resolution (Soviet Union) *re* withdrawal of forces and recognition of individual states, 255-59, 262, 307-8 (*text*); summary of work, 269-70

Senegal: in GA, 296

Seydoux, Roger (France): in SC, 89; quoted in SC, 41, 42, 54, 102; in GA, 177-78, 216; quoted in GA, 177-78

Sharm el Sheikh, 15, 26, 49, 69

Sheikh Meskine, 92

Shipping: belligerent rights, 25, 26, 27, 166, 184, 295; passage through Suez Canal, 25-26, 27, 37; blockade

Shipping (*Continued*)
of Gulf of Aqaba, 26, 31, 32, 33-34, 35, 37, 39
Sinai, 7, 17, 19, 48, 49, 51, 236
Singapore: in GA, 187
Solomon, P. V. J. (Trinidad and Tobago), 164-65; quoted, 182
Somalia: in GA, 186, 192, 296
South Africa: in GA, 187, 192, 217
Soviet Union: in SC, 4, 6, 29, 30, 31, 38, 41, 43, 50, 53, 54-55, 56-57, 58, 59, 62, 64-66, 68, 71, 72, 74-76, 78, 80, 82, 85, 87, 89-90, 93, 95-97, 99, 103, 105, 107, 110, 111, 112, 126, 195, 196, 197, 199-201, 231, 232, 233, 234, 236, 240, 245, 251-52, 255-59, 262, 265-66, 266-67, 269, 270 (*see also* Fedorenko, Nikolai; Kuznetsov, V. V.); and Egypt, 8, 17, 51; and creation of UNEF, 17-18; and UAR, 30-31; statement on interests in Middle East, 31-32; demand for condemnation of Israel, 50, 55, 112-13; demand for troop withdrawal, 54-55, 57-58, 65-66, 76, 88, 112-13; and second cease-fire resolution, 59-60; SC draft resolution *re* condemnation of Israel and withdrawal of forces, 66-67 (*text*), 74-75, 92, 96, 110, 289 (*text*); demand for condemnation of Israel's refusal to comply with SC resolutions, 78, 82, 88, 89, 103-4; proposal for transfer of problem to "another body of UN," 106, 114-15; request to SG to call GA emergency session, 116, 118-22; in GA, 5th Emergency Special Session, 123-28, 142, 185, 186, 205, 218-19 (*see also* Fedorenko, Nikolai; Gromyko, Andrei; Kosygin, Alexei); statement of position, 123-28; GA draft resolution *re* condemnation, withdrawal, and restitution, 126, 169, 176-77, 185-86, 291-92 (*text*); statement on sanctions against Israel, 197; demand for enforcement of cease-fire, 200; and Arab states, 205, 214-15; tentative draft resolution (with U.S.) *re* withdrawal of forces and recognition of individual rights of states, 211-13, 222-23, 312 (*text*); in GA, 22d session, 225 (*see also* Kuz-

netsov, V. V.); SC draft resolution *re* condemnation of Israel and observation of cease-fire, 232, 300 (*text*); SC draft resolution *re* withdrawal of forces and recognition of individual states, 255-59, 262, 307-8 (*text*)
Spain: in GA, 186
Spiljak, Mika (Yugoslavia), 132-33; quoted, 133
Sudan: in GA, 129-31, 189-90
Suez Canal, 12, 194-95, 236; crisis (1956) in GA, 17, 171; exclusion of ships destined for Israeli ports, 25-26, 27, 37, 107
Sweden: in GA, 145, 187, 191-92, 214; draft resolution (with Austria and Finland) *re* referral of problem to SC and adjournment of GA, 214-17; resolution transferring problem to 22d session of GA, 217
Syria: Israeli-Syrian General Armistice Agreement (1949), 2, 3; acceptance of cease-fire, 72, 73, 88; acceptance of cessation of hostilities resolution, 73; in SC, 77, 79, 80, 91, 99, 110, 199, 249-50, 261, 264; complaints on renewed Israeli attacks, 77, 82, 84, 91-92; in GA, 128-29, 187, 190-91, 204
Syrian-Israeli relations: border incidents, prewar, 1-10, 27-28

Tabor, Hans (Denmark), 39; quoted, 29; as SC President, 46, 49-50, 51, 56, 58-59, 69, 72, 81, 93-94, 110, 112; quoted, 109
Tanzania, *see* United Republic of Tanzania
Tarabanov, Milko (Bulgaria), 42, 61-62, 254-55, 259; quoted, 44, 60, 62, 88, 90, 106
Thailand: in GA, 181, 187
Thant, U: quoted, 1, 2, 3, 18, 20-21; and prewar outbreaks in Demilitarized Zone, 2-4, 9-10, 12; and withdrawal of UNEF, 18, 20-21; mission to Cairo, 28, 30, 32, 58; appeal for restraint and forgoing of belligerence, 28-29, 32, 38, 39, 40; and compliance with SC resolution (235), 73, 76, 77, 82, 85, 86, 89, 90,

91; report on violations of cease-fire, 87-88; request to SC *re* implementation of cease-fire by increasing number of observers, 196, 199; *see also* Secretary-General

Tiran, Strait of: blockade, 25-26, 32, 33, 34, 36, 37, 48, 49

Tomeh, Georges (Syria), 79; quoted, 80

Trinidad and Tobago: in GA, 164-65, 182, 204, 216

Tsuruoka, Senjin (Japan): quoted, 234

Tunisia: in GA, 180-81, 185, 186, 219

Turbay Ayala, Caesar (Colombia), 156-58; quoted, 157

Turkey: in GA, 144, 186

Union of Soviet Socialist Republics, *see* Soviet Union

United Arab Republic: threat of military action *vs.* Israel, 19; and withdrawal of UNEF, 20-21; and shipping in Suez Canal, 25-26, 37; blockade of Israeli ships and ships destined to Israel, 26, 31, 32, 33-34, 35, 37, 39; in SC, 30, 35-36, 40, 47, 49, 58, 60-61, 77, 99, 196-97, 236, 237, 240-41, 253, 263-64, 275 (*see also* El-Kony, Mohamed A.; Riad, Mahmoud); complaint against Israel, 38; demand for condemnation of Israel, 47; accusation of U.S. and U.K. assistance to Israel, 60-61; rejection of cease-fire resolution, 61; acceptance of cease-fire, 65, 67; in GA, 191, 216 (*see also* Fawzi, Mahmud); complaints *vs.* Israel and call for SC meeting, 194-95; *see also* Egypt; Syria

United Kingdom: in SC, 6, 43, 52, 53, 56, 68-71, 72, 80-81, 84, 85-86, 87, 92, 99-101, 106, 111, 114, 115, 197, 231, 243, 250-51, 252, 262, 269; UAR accusation of assistance to Israel, 60-61; in GA, 135-36, 143, 175, 177, 179; statement of position, 135-36; in GA, 22d session, 226-27; SC draft resolution *re* appointment of Special Representative of SG (Resolution 242), 252, 254, 260-66, 309-10 (*text*); *see also* Caradon, Lord

United Nations Emergency Force (UNEF): demand by Arab states for withdrawal, 7, 8, 18, 19, 20, 30; creation and purposes of, 11-18; Advisory Committee on, 13-14, 15, 19-20, 21; and SG, 13-15; withdrawal, 18-21, 107

United Nations Truce Supervision Organization (UNTSO), 3, 8, 66, 72; reactivation of, 2, 80, 87, 89, 94, 115; Chief of Staff, 9, 10, 46 (*see also* Bull, General Odd); observers, 72, 80, 83-85, 88, 90, 91, 93, 267-68; SG request to SC for increase in number of observers, 196, 197-98, 199, 202; strengthening of, 196, 199, 200; number of observers increased, 203; SG recommendation for increase in number of observers, 232-34, 266-67, 268, 311 (*text*); SC resolution (240) on cooperation, 232-34, 302 (*text*)

United Republic of Tanzania: in GA, 133, 204, 214, 296

United States: in SC, 4, 29, 32-35, 39, 41, 43, 52, 53-54, 55, 56, 58-59, 62-64, 66, 68, 71, 73-74, 79-80, 82-83, 87, 88-89, 97-99, 102-3, 104, 107, 110, 111, 112, 195, 197-98, 231, 232, 233, 234, 240, 242, 246, 251, 259, 262, 265, 269; SC draft resolution *re* compliance with SG appeal, 40, 282 (*text*); UAR accusation of assistance to Israel, 60-61; SC draft resolution *re* withdrawal of forces and peace negotiations, 63, 113, 285 (*text*); SC draft resolution on violations of cease-fire, 88-89, 287 (*text*); objection to calling GA emergency session, 121-22; in GA, 127, 137-39, 176, 179, 186, 187, 205, 206-7, 216, 219; statement of position, 137-39; GA draft resolution *re* stable and durable peace, 138-39, 169, 185, 293 (*text*); tentative draft resolution (with Soviet Union) *re* withdrawal of forces and recognition of individual rights of states, 211-13, 222-23, 312 (*text*); in GA, 22d session, 223; SC draft resolution *re* violations of cease-fire, 232, 301 (*text*); SC draft resolution *re* appointment of Special Representative of SG,

United States (*Continued*)
237, 238-40, 245, 262, 305-6 (*text*);
see also Goldberg, Arthur; Johnson, Lyndon B.
Uruguay: in GA, 163, 164; statement of position, 163
USSR, *see* Soviet Union

Venezuela: in GA, 164, 168, 206; statement of position, 168
Vinci, Piero (Italy): quoted, 181-82, 192

Waldheim, Kurt (Austria), 192

Yarmuk River, 91, 92
Yemen, 7; in GA, 147
Yugoslavia: in GA, 132-33, 160, 173, 185, 186, 204, 296; statement of position, 132-33; GA draft resolution *re* removal of Israeli armed forces, 160, 162, 173, 182, 296-97 (*text*)

Zahedi, Ardeshir (Iran), 131
Zambia: in GA, 186, 187, 296